DISCOVERING
RELIGIOUS HISTORY
IN THE
MODERN AGE

SOAS LIBRARY
WITHDRAWN

SO.

D0303123

18 0804606 7

DISCOVERING RELIGIOUS HISTORY IN THE MODERN AGE

Hans G. Kippenberg

Translated from German by Barbara Harshav

PRINCETON UNIVERSITY PRESS

PRINCETON AND OXFORD

COPYRIGHT © 2002 BY PRINCETON UNIVERSITY PRESS
PUBLISHED BY PRINCETON UNIVERSITY PRESS, 41 WILLIAM STREET, PRINCETON,
NEW JERSEY 08540
IN THE UNITED KINGDOM: PRINCETON UNIVERSITY PRESS, 3 MARKET PLACE,
WOODSTOCK, OXFORDSHIRE OX20 1SY
ALL RIGHTS RESERVED

LIBRARY OF CONGRESS CATALOGING-IN-PUBLICATION DATA

KIPPENBERG, HANS, G. (HANS GERHARD)

[ENTDECKUNG DER RELIGIONSGESCHICHTE. ENGLISH]

DISCOVERING RELIGIOUS HISTORY IN THE MODERN AGE / HANS G. KIPPENBERG;

TRANSLATED FROM GERMAN BY BARBARA HARSHAV.

P. CM.

INCLUDES BIBLIOGRAPHICAL REFERENCES AND INDEX.

ISBN 0-691-00908-2 (ALK. PAPER) — ISBN 0-691-00909-0 (PBK. : ALK. PAPER)

1. RELIGION—HISTORY. I. TITLE.

BL48 .K5213 2002

200'.7'22–DC21   2001038750

BRITISH LIBRARY CATALOGING-IN-PUBLICATION DATA IS AVAILABLE

THE TRANSLATION OF THIS BOOK WAS SUBSIDIZED BY A
GENEROUS GRANT FROM INTER NATIONES

TRANSLATED FROM GERMAN BY BARBARA HARSHAV

THIS BOOK HAS BEEN COMPOSED IN PALATINO

PRINTED ON ACID-FREE PAPER. ∞

WWW.PUP.PRINCETON.EDU

PRINTED IN THE UNITED STATES OF AMERICA

10 9 8 7 6 5 4 3 2 1

10 9 8 7 6 5 4 3 2 1

(PBK.)

SOAS LIBRARY

CONTENTS

CHAPTER TEN
Religion and the Social Bond   136

CHAPTER ELEVEN
The Great Process of Disenchantment   155

CHAPTER TWELVE
Religion as Experience of the Self   175

CHAPTER THIRTEEN
How Descriptions of the History of Religion
Reflect Modernization   187

INTRODUCTION TO THE
AMERICAN EDITION

THE HISTORY of comparative religion has become a subject of increased inquiry. In contrast to previous periods and authors,[1] the idea of a balance between achievements and failures (since its academic beginnings in the second half of the 19th century) has receded into the background, but still remains fundamental. Today the subjective element in scholarship is at stake. Indicative of a new retrospective was a provocative sentence by Jonathan Z. Smith, in his 1982 book *Imagining Religion*: "*There is no data for religion*. Religion is solely the creation of the scholar's study."[2] Sixteen years later in *Critical Terms for Religious Studies*, Smith traced, step by step, how the use and understanding of the Western term "religion" has been expanding since the sixteenth century, and how it has become a universal category, imposed from the outside on native cultures.[3]

Smith's polemical remark did not come from nowhere. It is in line with an issue in cultural studies that bothers historians: the break between sources/data and their scholarly representation.[4] When a historian refers to "facts" or "evidence," he or she does not refer to something natural. "Facts" or "evidence" have to be conceived too. Hayden White regarded the basic historical material as an outcome of narration. Telling a story turns unstructured occurrences into "evidence" or "facts." Both are constituted according to elementary literary forms.[5] Rhetorical devices (called "tropes" by White) as metaphor, metonymy, synecdoche, and irony are involved in establishing them. No wonder White launched a fierce debate. Paul Ricoeur opposed his privileging the narrative form.[6] According to Ricoeur, the academic historian just breaks with the spell of narration, instead of succumbing to it. Hence, Ricoeur discerned three elements: selecting and studying documents as past evidence, explaining actions that generated events, and constructing a text. In this study I assume a model like Ricoeur's, though in respect to rhetoric, White remains more than valuable.

No wonder that historians of religions did not escape that issue. I think there are even good reasons not to avoid it, as became clear in the debate about the work of Mircea Eliade (1907–86). One of the main targets was Eliade's insistence that religion may not be reduced to something else: ". . . a religious phenomenon will only be recognized as such if it is grasped at its own level, that is to say, if it is studied *as* something religious. To try to grasp the essence of such a phenomenon by means of physiology, psychology, sociology, economics, art or any other study is false; it misses the one unique and irreducible element in it—the element of the sacred."[7] In a 1983 essay "In Defense of Reductionism," Robert Segal launched a debate that clarified some crucial issues.[8] First: In natural sciences reductionism means that the central concepts of one science can be completely understood by the principles of another. The subject matter itself is not affected by it. And second: Eliade's insistence on the autonomy of religion makes sense mainly as a rhetoric means.[9]

If Eliade is constructing "history of religions" as 'sui generis,' what kind of construction is it? Ivan Strenski addressed that issue in 1987. In his book *Four Theories of Myth in the Twentieth-Century History*[10] Strenski unpacked Eliade's concept of myth by comparing it with those of other scholars. According to Eliade myths reinstate what happened in the beginning of all time (*in illo tempore*) and disrupt the homogeneity of time. Those involved by performing myths do participate in that "rupture de niveau"—for Eliade, fundamental to sacred. From this analysis it becomes clear that his construction of sacred/profane has a hidden reference: history. That is corroborated by Eliade himself, who, in a preface to the American paperback edition of 1959, advised those interested in his work to start with his *Cosmos and History. The Myth of Eternal Return.*[11] Eliade presented archaic communities as opposing concrete time and showing contempt for history, as he told in the preface to the original French edition. In a final chapter, "The Terror of History," Eliade openly expressed his sympathy with that contempt. When we turn to Eliade's literary oeuvre, his sympathy becomes clear. In the novel *The Forbidden Forest* (1955), his "hero" Stefan learned the lesson in World War II that only contemplation allowed surviving the course of events and preserving identity. If we replace contemplation with mysticism Eliade's idea is similar to Weber's assumption that, in modern rational culture, mysticism remains an alternative option of escaping the tyranny of rationality. Eliade's concept of the sacred opposed to the profane turns out to be closely interwoven with the experience of history in the twentieth century.[12] A similar reflexivity entered the works of Ernst Cassirer, Claude Lévi-Strauss and Bronislaw Malinowski. In their theories, too, a diagnosis of the history of the 20th century is implied. According to Strenski the study of theory should move from a pure textual "approach" to the search for "context." "As an alternative to the study of theory through texts alone, I am thus proposing a style of intellectual history radically informed by the study of context and recovery of intention."[13] This conclusion comes close to the point of departure of the present book. Yet only close, since Strenski phrased his conclusions *not* in terms of a general theory of history, but in terms of an exceptional historical situation in the 20th century. "The catastrophic political upheavals in Europe has a dramatic personal impact [on] all four theorists."[14] In less catastrophic times like today we may not see such theorists again.[15] In contrast to this conclusion, I assume for all theories of religions an element of subjective construction and rhetoric. In fact Eliade's oeuvre can serve as an example of how the meaning of religious data is shaped in the context of experiencing history. When Strenski writes: Scholars did "hide their 'prescriptions' within apparent "descriptions,'"[16] he refers to means, making sense of history. The present study deals with this issue more principally. It asks: What are the rhetorical means historians of religions use when indicating the present status of past religions?

In *Manufacturing Religion*[17] Russell T. McCutcheon has continued the inquiry along Strenski's line, but with a different definition of the key problem: the production of the discourse on sui generis religion, in particular the modes of that production and its sites.[18] By broadening the issue and taking social, political, and institutional contexts in account, McCutcheon explains the career of that discourse. He points out why the hermeneutical approach of Eliade has gained power to the detriment of an approach explaining religious facts in terms of their function. One of the reasons for Eliade's success was a new kind of religious studies at U.S. colleges: teaching about religions in classes with believers from various religious traditions. But McCutcheon is more ambitious. He is convinced that his analysis that contextualizes the *sui generis* discourse will be able to "simultaneously deauthorize" it.[19] Again and again he emphasizes that hermeneutics are a bad legacy and deserve decline. But in contrast to Strenski, he does not give or pretend to give an explanation of the rise of the *sui generis* discourse itself. More important: he does not relate to its existence in other disciplines beyond religious studies. The concept of an autonomy of religion is part and parcel of a tradition in social studies, conceiving of the modern world as an outcome of a process of differentiation. Émile Durkheim and Max Weber conceived of the rise of the modern world as increased independence of social orders as politics, economics, art, and science from religious traditions. While the preceding historians of religions stuck to the metaphor of "survival," these scholars emphasized the lasting power of religions in the modern world. The issue of autonomy of religion cannot be isolated from the issue of modern society.

In *Critical Terms for Religious Studies* Gustavo Benavides conceives of modernity as a self-conscious distancing from the past—a break different in the domain of knowledge than in morality, aesthetics, and religion. While in the realm of knowledge there is progress, in the other domains the past is not superseded by the present in every respect. The modern world is characterized by that split. For that reason, modern reflexivity is always self-referential. The break between past and present has stimulated a "reflexive ordering and reordering" of past and foreign religions (G. Benavides).[20] These ideas are fundamental for our issue of religious history. The writings of scholars of religions reveal that their constructions of religious history were affected by the rise of the modern world. Narrating religious history, they disclosed in past and foreign data actual meanings. While spokesmen of the ascendant scientific-industrial society propagated a renunciation of all traditions, historians of religions described selected parts of an extinct and remote world of religions as a remaining index of human existence. Thus they granted apparently outdated religions a place in their own society and deepened the split in modern culture.

Bruce Lincoln, himself a student of Eliade, in his *Theorizing Myth. Narrative, Ideology, and Scholarship*,[21] again addressed the issue of myth. In contrast to Strenski he found the element of violence not in the external context of the scholar, but in the myth itself. The myth Bruce Lincoln focuses on is a modern one: the origin of the Aryans. Lincoln traced it to a fusion of Herder's concept of "nation"—constituted by a common mind, rooted in language and history—with the common origin of various Indo-European languages. When in the 19th century the Aryan "mind" was compared with the Semitic one, a powerful racial ideology arose that fueled anti-Semitism. Lincoln solves the issue of the subjectivity of the scholar by emphasizing the power of the myth over the mind of his students. His analysis rests on a conception of discourse developed by the French philosopher Michel Foucault: a public talk permeated by power and not by a critique of power, as Jürgen Habermas has argued. The story Bruce Lincoln tells is part of the present book too. But in contrast to Lincoln it follows Habermas more and recognizes other meanings attributed likewise to the very same "myth." Friedrich Max Müller, Matthew Arnold, Cornelis Petrus Tiele, and Max Weber used it to reconstruct two different types of attitudes to the world: a rational one, at home in "Semitic" religions, and a mystical one at home in "Indo-European" religions. Both attitudes are constitutive for modern Western culture, which originated from both roots. That Lincoln is right, focusing attention on internal biases of established historical hypotheses, should not be doubted.

Recently Steven M. Wasserstrom in his *Religion after Religion. Gershom Scholem, Mircea Eliade and Henry Corbin at Eranos*[22] made a fresh attempt to explain the tremendous impact of these scholars beyond their academic reputation. Like Strenski he related their scholarly concerns to an external issue: not catastrophic times, but a hegemony of rationality, suppressing non-rational discourses on the human existence. Like Lincoln he found the solution in a tradition of the academy: the conception of history of religion itself. According to Wasserstrom, the three scholars expected a knowledge from religious history that humankind in the modern age urgently needs. The Eranos-meetings in Ascona were a powerful sounding board for their attempts to rescue a world from the threat of rationality. Wasserstrom reconstructed the genealogy of the concept of history of religion shared by the scholars and their audience. At the end of his analysis he presented a new explanation of the "autonomy" of religion. The alleged contradiction between the sacred and the profane has to do with living in a world torn by rival claims of truth. The concept "history of religion" itself refers to that experience. Wasserstrom's conclusion is bold: 'History of Religions' has its roots in Christian Kabbala, in turn dependent on Jewish Kabbala, which articulated the experience of a dual identity of the Jew in the world. Christian Kabbala responded to the same experience. It was "a notable, original effort at the outset of modernity to address the emerging question of religious plurality."[23]

The way Wasserstrom identifies the main issue, is to the point, though I'm not yet convinced by his answer. He is right: History of religions deserves attention as a concept. In the first chapter of the present study, a survey of philosophical views on historical religions from Hobbes to Schopenhauer reveals a surprising reversal of positions. At the beginning there was a rigorous critique of historical religions in the name of a religion of reason. At the end in the 19th century, the history of religions served as a source of ethics and world views neither overcome nor represented by rational thought. Not by chance do all scholars of religious history have their place in the philosophy of religions, where they got their stimulus for imagining religious history. From the angle of philosophy, the main problem of modernity was the split between increasing rationality and lasting human options.

The present book presents an analysis of the rise of comparative religion between 1850 and 1930. Not by chance did this period coincide in Europe with a period of modernization. Scholars and their audience were confronted with the passing away of religious traditions. In their writings we encounter a special understanding of the modern world. They did not assume a disappearance of the power of religions, judged by some as a liberating development, by others as a severe threat. They had a different understanding. By studying historical and ethnographical evidence, the historian of religions discovers dimensions and options, operating in modern culture too. Religious history helps recognize elements of human existence beyond the realm of progress and rationality. The book aims at reintroducing the category of "history" into religious studies. This seems necessary. Recently two volumes appeared identifying crucial notions on religious studies.[24] Examining the concepts in the two volumes, I was struck by the absence of both "history" and "tradition" from each; ironically, only "modernity" has survived. This seems to be a good starting point for the present study.

INTRODUCTION

*What the faculty of reason is to the individual, history is to the
human race.* By virtue of this faculty, man is not, like the
animal, restricted to the narrow present of perception, but
knows also the incomparably more extended past with which
it is connected, and out of which it has emerged. But only in
this way does he have a proper understanding of the present
itself, and can he also draw conclusions as to the future.
—Schopenhauer, *The World as Will and Representation*

MAX WEBER ends his study of the emergence of modern
capitalism with a comment on the fact that few people consider religion as a historical force in the modern age: "The
modern man is in general, even with the best will, unable to give
religious ideas a significance for culture and national character which
they deserve."[1] Despite many studies that have emphasized this deficiency, the situation today, almost a century later, is still the same. It is
difficult for anyone who talks of religion to avoid being considered a
theologian. Religion is ignored by historical scholarship and exposed
as ideology by the social sciences. It lacks a recognized place in the
academy. This unfortunate situation is expressed in the representations of religious studies. No one wants to deal with the approaches
and projects of scholarly research in religion as part of a history of a
general problem. They have limited themselves to exhibiting the theories and methods available in the field as if in a display window.

By studying religion between 1850 and 1920, this book attempts to
demonstrate that more is possible. Scholars of religion in the nineteenth and early twentieth centuries were stimulated by discoveries
that opened the gates to unknown stages and territories of human
culture. Sensational decipherings of foreign writings of old high cultures, prehistoric finds, information about tribal religions—all were
considered evidence that, alongside and beneath the present civilization, was a past culture that had become foreign. Geological metaphors such as strata, fossils, and survivals were often used, and these
gave the new finds a place in the present. But unlike geology, the
special nuance here often resonated, these were seeds for a new beginning. Even if these metaphors later gave way to psychological and
sociological terms, the conception remained the same. The findings
allowed, even demanded, a diagnosis of modern society. If we recall

Dilthey's famous saying that "only history tells man what he is," perhaps we can easily understand the motives for writing the history of religions. Modern society has a religious history, just as it has a political, social, and economic history.

The result of this approach is that I deal with scholars of religion differently than most. I am less interested in exposing their errors and limitations. Instead, I try to salvage what is to be salvaged. By defending what is useful, omitting what is wrong, toning down exaggerations, reinforcing connections, and placing important statements in a correct relationship, I want to make the early scholars of religion into something they too seldom are: classical theorists of a modern age in which past religion still has a future.

While working on this book, I have received a great deal of support and help. I was able to collect the basic material as a fellow of the Wissenschaftskolleg zu Berlin, and I would like to thank the rector, Dr. Wolf Lepenies, and all the staff for the gift of this year of research. In the spring of 1995, I was given the opportunity to work on the material within the framework of a team directed by Prof. Dr. Jörn Rüsen, *Historische Sinnbildung*, at the Zentrum für Interdisziplinäre Forschung at the University of Bielefeld. I discussed the first drafts with friends and colleagues. For many important comments and criticism, I thank Burkhard Gladigow of Tübingen, Karl-Heinz Kohl of Frankfurt, Lourens van den Bosch of Groningen, Martin Riesebrodt of Chicago, and Friedrich Wilhelm Graf of Augsburg. Mrs. Janna Hassouna helped polish the text. A special word of thanks is due to the publisher. Ernst-Peter Wieckenberg watched over the book in a way that is unfortunately threatening to become a thing of the past.

Bremen, April 25, 1997

DISCOVERING
RELIGIOUS HISTORY
IN THE
MODERN AGE

CHAPTER ONE

FROM THE PHILOSOPHY OF RELIGION
TO THE HISTORY OF RELIGIONS

CHOLARS of religion have devoted little attention to the connections between their views of religious history and the philosophy of religion. Hayden White's comment that "there can be no 'proper history' which is not at the same time 'philosophy of history'"[1] can also be applied to religious history, but that is seldom considered today. On the contrary! Religious studies has taken pains to keep the philosophy of religion far away from its field. Nevertheless, there is a great deal of evidence for the assertion that the historiography of religion was also in fact an implicit philosophy of religion. A search for such qualifications soon yields results, coming up with metahistorical assumptions originating in the philosophy of religion. These sorts of connections have been conscientiously noted by Edward E. Evans-Pritchard, Eric J. Sharpe, Jan de Vries, Jan van Baal, Brian Morris, J. Samuel Preus, and Jacques Waardenburg in their histories of the field. Yet, to date, no one has made a serious attempt to apply Hayden White's comment systematically to research in the field of religious history. But there is every reason to do so. Evidence points to more than simply coincidental and peripheral connections between religious studies as a historical discipline and the philosophy of religion. Perhaps the idea of a history of religions with all its implications can be developed correctly only if we observe it from a broader and longer-term perspective of the philosophy of religion.

The Priority of the Public Good over Private Belief

Thomas Hobbes (1588–1679) directly experienced the English revolution that combined two strands: one was a middle-class revolution that demanded private property, the abolition of feudal despotism, and the sovereignty of Parliament; the second was a radical revolution supported by millenarianism and called for both common property and democracy.[2] During the sixteenth and seventeenth centuries, religious wars raged not only in England but also in other parts of Europe. Hobbes did not perceive them as some unique excess, but simply as a return of the state of nature that had prevailed before the formation of governments. In the state of nature, war prevailed—all-out war. Everyone had to fight for his survival. This disastrous condition was ended when men—purely out of fear for their own death—transferred their sovereignty to one single person, or one single assembly, and authorized that agency to act as their representative and end the state of war. This transfer was also rational in itself, even though they were compelled by the fear of violent death. The sole purpose and reason for the state was to force internal peace.

Hobbes saw the religious wars raging all over Europe in his time as the result of a dangerous error on the part of the clergy. It consisted of the assumption that the Church was identical with the Empire of God and that one man or one assembly could represent this empire. The state had to form a counterweight to that. Hobbes's analysis clearly reveals a royalist position. While serving as a tutor to the noble Cavendish family, he wrote the essay *Elements of Law Natural and Politic* (1640), in which he supported the unlimited sovereignty of the English king over the revolutionary Parliament.[3] Eleven years later in his masterpiece *Leviathan, or the Matter, Forme, -&- Power of a Common-Wealth Ecclesiastical and Civill* (1651), he essentially expanded and deepened his thoughts considerably. The remarkable title contained his basic idea that the state must be a mortal God in order to be able to hold anarchy and civil war in check.[4] Ecclesiastical belief had become a source of horrible and excessive violence. Incidentally, recent historical studies agree with Hobbes's position on this issue. It would be too simple to see·religion only as an ideology concealing class struggle, as Friedrich Engels maintained. The absolute nature of belief generates its own dynamic.[5] Because the opponents are religious groups and so metaphysical values are involved, the state itself must become God in order to defend the internal peace of the community. Jacob Taubes posited this link between political experience and philosophical reflection: "The seventeenth century is the first period of modern history where we see land. In the constellation of this century, we recognize ourselves and our own problems. Hobbes was aware of this period and experienced it as a thinker."[6]

Latent and open civil war can be abolished only if the community has an absolute ruler to whom every citizen owes unquestioned obedience. The boldness of his observation was not lost on Hobbes. Promising unconditional obedience to men is illegitimate. If God's law conflicts with human law, the believer is commanded to obey God rather than man. Hobbes wanted to dispel this objection with a rigorous interpretation of Scripture. Paul's Epistle to the Romans

(13:1–6) and other Scriptures considered it unlawful not to obey the authorities. There is only one single fundamental and absolutely necessary article of faith in Christianity: "Jesus is the Christ." All other dogmas are irrelevant for salvation and hence can be stipulated by the state authority as obligatory in accordance with their goal and function of establishing internal peace.

Hobbes devoted a separate chapter to religion in *Leviathan*. The idea of God as a "Prime Mover" was a thoroughly reasonable assumption.[7] Unlike animals, men observed events around them and tried to understand their causes. The acknowledgment of a single omnipotent God originates in the wish to know the causes of all unpredictable events and possibly to influence them. Religion derived from a natural seed: belief in spirits, ignorance of causes, adoration of what is feared, and belief in omens. Over time, this natural seed was developed in different ways by pagan statesmen and Jewish prophets—to produce a peaceful society. For the Jews, the civil regime was part of the Empire of God; for the heathen the cult of the gods was part of the state regime. In both cases, religion served the public welfare of the citizens. Both solutions managed to gain control over the latent conflict between religion and politics and thus successfully put an end to the state of nature. With this explanation, Hobbes moved completely into the context of ancient historiography, or rather ethnography, which considered religion a part of the political *nomos* of a people. The ancient Jewish historian Josephus had also described the particular nature of Judaism in light of Herodotus's model.[8]

Early Christianity's fundamental distinction between the Kingdom of God and state legislation contained another solution to the ever-lurking conflict between belief in the Kingdom of God and the need for social peace. Jesus Christ taught that His Kingdom was not of this world and required His followers to obey only the laws of the state.[9] Thus, He made a fundamental distinction between the Kingdom of God of the next world and the kingdom of state law of this world. Unfortunately, in the course of history, this initial condition did not endure, because of the "unpleasing priests; and those not only amongst Catholiques, but even in that Church that hath presumed most of Reformation."[10] Misinterpretations of Scripture were the main cause of error.

According to Scripture, the Church had no right to demand obedience from citizens. "I have shewn already (in the last Chapter) that the kingdome of Christ is not of this world: therefore neither can his Ministers (unless they be Kings,) require obedience in his name."[11] Hobbes's argumentation amounts to a rigorous separation of public religion from private religion:

There is a *Publique*, and a *Private* Worship. Publique, is the Worship that a Common-wealth performeth, as one Person. Private, is that which a Private person exhibiteth. Publique, in respect of the whole Commonwealth, is Free; but in respect of Particular men it is not. Private, is in secret Free; but in the sight of the Multitude, it is never without some Restraint, either from the Lawes, or from the Opinion of men; which is contrary to the nature of Liberty.[12]

Hobbes's private religion lacks all independence. As leader of the public religion, the political sovereign decides all questions disputed in the religious wars: what books are canonic, which prophets proclaim the word of God, what is heresy, and so on.[13] Only what has been sanctioned publicly by him can claim to be holy and thus binding on all citizens. Hence, the citizen is to practice his private religion only in seclusion. Even conscience did not give him the duty to make a conviction public or to oppose the demands of the ruler.[14] Even when a believer is unfairly persecuted by a godless ruler, he is obligated to pay lip service and to dissimulate instead of mounting an open opposition.[15] Death for only one article of faith, "Jesus is the Christ," can qualify as martyrdom.[16] Thus Hobbes reached a hypothesis he considered established in the Bible, but which is really in an old heretical tradition:[17] only a strictly internal esoteric piety, which values disguise and concealment higher than courageous resistance, is genuinely Christian. The experience of the horrible religious wars had led him to the radical conclusion that making private belief public endangers the political public good.

Hobbes supported this argument with more categorical distinctions between an internal belief, *fides*, and an external one, *confessio*, between *veritas* and *auctoritas*, between morality and politics. It was important to him to depoliticize religion, which made him the progenitor of a corresponding philosophical tradition.[18] For him, "Private worship" is not an authority a citizen can appeal to. Rather it is to make belief politically neutral, and has no independent authority in moral judgments. The historian Reinhart Koselleck has gone into the political context of these observations. In the social and political milieu of absolutism, acts of state and moral sensibilities were separated: *auctoritas, non veritas facit legem*. The laws governing acts of state could and should be independent from morality. Paradoxically, this separation enabled the development of a civil morality independent from practical political constraints. Among other things, this happened in civil organizations, which had multiplied rapidly in the eighteenth century.[19] Yet during the eighteenth century, the cultivation of civil morality in a state run by "Realpolitik" gained public influence. In the debate with absolutism, citizens began to appeal publicly to their conscience and to their own religion of the heart. They even required acts of state to conform to private civil morality. We shall see in Jean-Jacques Rousseau how the private thus became an independent realm of religious sensibilities and moral judgments. But first we must discuss David Hume. Hobbes knew from his own experience that an irrational religion had firm control of men and their history. Hume went further: the history of mankind is a natural history of religion.

The Pendulum of Religious History

Like Hobbes, David Hume (1711–76) knew a proof of God's existence. Yet this belief based on reason seemed to imply little for the history of religions. To understand that history, the place of religion in human nature had to be determined. In this context, he wanted to rely solely on experience and observation. "As the teaching of man is the only solid basis for other sciences, so the only certain basis we can give this science is inherent in experience and observation."[20] Nevertheless, these are not final authorities either, but are dependent on the laws of cognition; and here, Hume distinguished two categories: impressions that come from objects to the subject ("impressions;" "matters of fact") and are processed into simple ideas; and secondly, "relations of ideas," including laws of geometry, algebra, and arithmetic. They are based on assumptions that precede all experience and can be seen as correct only on the basis of intuition. Compared with them, the facts of experience are more precarious. When people link cause and effect, they are really connecting two different impressions. For example, Hume used the connection of heating water with steam to explain that the assumption of a *necessary* connection between the two does not result from observation itself, but ensues from it: "Necessity is something that exists in the mind, not in the objects."[21]

The title of Hume's *The Natural History of Religion* (1757) adopts a key concept of his time. Natural history was a program to catch the diversities of facts within chronological parameters.[22] In the very first sentence, Hume presents a distinction that was to give the philosophy of religion a special direction and thus marks a watershed: "As every enquiry, which regards religion, is of the utmost importance, there are two questions in particular, which challenge our attention, to wit, that concerning its foundation in reason, and that concerning its origin in human nature."[23] Separating the truth of religion, on the one hand,

and its origin in human nature, on the other, posed the problem in a brand new form.[24]

In *A Treatise of Human Nature* (1739–40), Hume had previously answered the first question concerning the rationality of religion: "The entire structure of the world reveals an intelligent Author." Hume considered a proof of God's existence quite possible: the order of the universe proves the existence of an omnipotent Spirit. In the later *Dialogues Concerning Natural Religion* (1779) he revealed the same view: the functionalism of the world, analogous to a crafted product—proves the existence of a Deity. His *Natural History* also alluded to this teleological proof of the existence of God.[25]

The second question was the subject of the *Natural History*. The history of religion follows from a law other than that of reason. Actual belief in God could hardly derive from knowledge of the order of the universe, as Deism thought. One of the spokesman of Deism, Herbert of Cherbury (1581–1648), maintained that people came to the view shared by everyone on the basis of rational knowledge: that God exists, that He deserves adoration, that virtuous behavior was a duty, sins were to be avoided, and man was an object of reward and punishment.[26] For Hume, on the other hand, "the first ideas of religion arose not from a contemplation of the works of nature, but from a concern with regard to the events of life, and from the incessant hopes and fears, which actuate the human mind."[27] The disturbances of nature, but not her amazing regularity, filled men with the strongest religious feelings. Hence, the resemblance between a belief of reason and historical theism was only external. In fact, they had absolutely nothing in common and had different roots. An earlier letter by Hume, in 1743, indicates why he ruled out the idea that the Deity could be an object of human feelings. Invisible and intangible, the Deity excludes passions and feelings as adequate means for knowing God. All "enthusiasts" are wrong. Even the idea that a prayer could be effective in any way seemed blasphemous to him.[28] The actual history of religion is not advanced by rational thoughts, but by irrational fears.

From this vantage point, Hume interpreted what was then known of the ancient history of religions. Fear of the unpredictability of life led people to assume personal powers behind the forces of nature, and they hoped to influence these powers through cults. In fact, the gods are only representations of *unknown causes*. The initial polytheism soon gave way to a theism that used the fear of believers to concentrate their worship increasingly on a single omnipotent Deity. The resulting theism of the masses shows only "'an accidental correspondence'" with the philosophical theism of the educated. In truth, it was constructed on irrational principles and was merely superstition. That also explains why theism soon lapsed back to polytheism. That is, the *one* God of the people had become too remote, and so they worshipped intervening intermediaries. Thus, in the natural history of religions, polytheism and theism alternate in an ebb and flow. Hume's metaphors of "tides," "pendulum," or "oscillation" indicate the conformity to psychological laws that have historically propelled an anxiety-obsessed belief in God.[29] The history of belief in God inevitably oscillates back and forth between polytheism and monotheism.

In the second part of his *Natural History* (Sections 9–14), Hume compared polytheism and theism, particularly examining their moral regulations. Both forms of religion clearly differed regarding persecution or tolerance, courage or obsequiousness, reason or absurdity, doubt or conviction. And here theism came off badly. If believers directed all efforts at gaining the pleasure of their god, they would start persecuting the followers of other gods. Thus, theism entailed intolerance, while polytheism brought tolerance.[30] Tolerance among the Dutch and the English was not to be attributed to their beliefs, but to the determination of their governments. Once again, we recognize Hobbes's old problem. But it finds another solution. Only as an alternative does Hume allow the state to play a role in forcing internal peace. The major argument is historical. The dynamic of the history of religion produces divergent political norms. The internal peace of a community is dependent on the pendulum stroke of religious history. Reason was no longer to be found only in the rational proof of God's existence. It was also available in a weakened form in the religious history.

The Civilizing of Religion

In France at the same time, Jean-Jacques Rousseau (1712–1778) was working on a purely moral definition of rational religion. He saw religion not as the expression of fear, but as an intuitive recognition of human obligations. Proud of being from Geneva, the stronghold of Calvinism and a citizen (*citoyen*) of that community, Rousseau was still imbued with Protestantism even after he converted to Catholicism at the age of sixteen. In 1742, he went to Paris, where he hoped to make his fortune with a musical notation he had invented. An opera made him famous and gave him entry to the circle of the Baron d'Holbach. One day in 1749, on his way to visit Diderot, who was held prisoner in Vincennes, he read in the newspaper a contest question announced by the academy of Dijon: "Has the revival of arts and sciences contributed to the improvement of customs?"[31] Even as he read the contest question, he was overcome by a vision that he captured in words twelve years later in a letter:

> If ever anything was like a sudden inspiration, it was the emotion that began in me with this reading: suddenly I see my mind blinded by a thousand insights, a plenitude of thoughts surfaced, with such strength and at the same time, in such a muddle that I was thrown into indescribable confusion. . . . O my lord, if I could only write a quarter of what I felt and saw under that tree, with what clarity I revealed all the contradictions of our social system, with what force I demonstrated the abuse of our institutions, with what simplicity did I prove that man is good by nature and it is only the institutions that make men evil.[32]

In 1750 Rousseau submitted to the Academy the work that emerged from this vision, entitled *Discours sur les sciences et les arts*. Science and courtesy, the jury members read, are ruling men and producing a despicable uniformity: "One incessantly follows customs, never one's own genius."[33] There was a connection between the revival of the arts and sciences on the one hand and morality on the other, but it worked in reverse: advances in the arts and sciences led to a loss of morality. Yet Rousseau combined this critical answer to the contest question with a hopeful perspective. Man was still thoroughly capable of liberating himself from his institutional deformities. He only had to learn to distinguish his innate abilities from those acquired later. This criticism of culture affected Rousseau's concept of religion. He consistently distinguished two kinds of religion: one of man and one of the citizen. The religion of man knows no temple, no altar, no rituals, and is limited to the purely internal cult of the Highest God and to the eternal obligations of morality. The religion of the citizen, on the other hand, applies only to one country and prescribes its special gods to him. It has its own dogmas, rituals, and cults.

La profession de foi du Vicaire Savoyard is a magnificent plea for the religion of man. Rousseau included this text, which had already been written in 1758, in *Émile*. Here he argued against both the "natural religion" of the philosophers and the "revealed religion" of the theologians. With his well-known candor, he denounced the nonsense that true religion could be represented by anyone. Imagine that God really revealed Himself through prophets and had His revelation recorded in books. "Who wrote these books?" asked Rousseau. And answered: "'Men.' And who saw these miracles? 'Men who attest to them.' What! Always human testimony? Always men who report to me what other men have reported! So many men between God and me!"[34] Such a religion was a matter of geography. The force of the arguments depends on the country in which they are presented.

"In order to judge a religion well, it is necessary not to study it in the books of its sectarians."[35] If you want to make the right choice among the three major religions of Europe (Judaism, Christianity, Islam), you should simply close the Holy Scriptures. History cannot establish any eternal truths. "I regard all the particular religions as so many salutary institutions which prescribe in each country a uniform manner of honoring God by public worship." But the obligation to obey them did not apply to the dogma of intolerance. "The essential worship is that of the heart."[36] To recognize the true religion, a person needs neither philosophy nor theology. The best teacher is not the judgments of his intellect, but the sensibilities of his heart. "The true duties of religion are independent of the institutions of men."[37] Rousseau saw religion as the strongest social bond connecting people. If Hobbes had political reasons for his great doubt about conscience, for Rousseau, it became an infallible authority that reliably and definitely prescribes the rules of social behavior. "I have only to consult myself about what I want to do. Everything I sense to be good is good; everything I sense to be bad is bad. The best of all casuists is the conscience."[38] There can be no debate about the demands of conscience, for it is an innate principle of justice and virtue, and expresses not judgments but sensibilities. "The forgetting of all religion leads to the forgetting of the duties of man," says the *Profession de Foi*.[39] Atheists cannot conceivably be good citizens.[40]

From this concept of a religion of men, in the well-known Chapter Eight of the *Contrat Social*, "Civil Religion,"[41] Rousseau drew the logical conclusion that all political communities must have been legitimated by religion right from the start. Every state had its own gods. The wars it waged were fought on behalf of its gods. This situation changed with Christianity, which put an end to wars between nations and toppled polytheism. But since it separated political from religious loyalties and Church and State posed competing claims for the loyalties of the citizens, the result was an endless chain of civil wars, as Hobbes had correctly seen. In Rousseau's view, European religious history exists in a permanent dilemma. National religions triggered wars between nations; the universal religion of Christianity incited wars between citizens.

He saw the solution to this problem in a social contract the citizens had to make if they wanted to form a reasonable political community. This contract could be based neither on the religion of men nor on the religion of citizens. The former separates the citizen's heart from the state; the latter demands war with other nations. The task of the necessary civil religion was to reconcile two different things: to see all men as brothers, and at the same time, to love the fatherland. The sovereign must stipulate a civil religion for the citizens and thus make "sentiments of sociability" obligatory for everyone. The positive propositions of this religion were to be the existence of a Deity; a future life; reward for the righteous; punishment for evildoers; the sanctity of the social contract and the laws. "Its negative dogmas I confine to one, intolerance, which is a part of the cults we have rejected."[42]

Hobbes's trust in the powerful state as a safeguard of the internal peace of a society was no longer available in Rousseau. On the contrary: this price seemed too high for him. The wars waged by the states of Europe against one another indicated that religion urgently needed revision. Only if the political religion was balanced with the universal religion that every man is given in his conscience could it provide the foundation of a genuine civil society.

Rousseau's argumentation was to give an important impetus to the philosophy of religion because it shaped a discourse of religion that enabled the public acknowledgment of a religion that was identical neither with that of men nor of the state. Civil society had taken a place in the philosophy of religion, as civil religion.

The Public Examination of Private Historic Belief

The thought of Immanuel Kant (1724–1804) continued the approaches of Hume and Rousseau.[43] His epistemology worked on the problems Hume posed, and his moral philosophy on those raised by Rousseau. As shown by *The Critique of Pure Reason* (1781), Kant combined the two. The concept of God epistemologically is a transcendental idea that exceeds every possible experience, and therefore on principle cannot be proved. But that does not lead Kant to conclude that metaphysical ideas are superfluous and dispensable as illusions. That is, what he had expelled from the kingdom of certain knowledge, he allowed to come back in as postulates of ethics in *Critique of Practical Reason* (1778) and in *Religion Within the Limits of Reason Alone* (1793). Practical reason could also demand acknowledgment from unprovable assertions. Kant listed three such postulates: that God exists, that the soul is immortal, and that we have free will. Even if these assumptions could not be proved, there are convincing reasons for them. In this reasoning, Kant used an important distinction in his *Critique of Pure Reason*: between terms that constitute objects and those that have only a regulating function.[44] For this purpose, Kant put religion completely within the realm of the Should, which is fundamentally different from Being: "Religion is (subjectively regarded) the recognition of all duties as divine commands."[45]

An institutionalized religion is only partly required for attaining moral knowledge. It is reason that decides what is timeless in the historical religion, what is universal in the particular belief, what is common in established teaching, what is unchanging in the ephemeral. Despite all limitations, Kant recognized that a particular religion can achieve a certain preliminary work for the religion of reason. Their relationship is like two concentric circles.[46] The historical revelation can include the religion of reason, but the religion of reason cannot include the historical revelation. Although a historical belief has only a particular validity, that does not make it any less useful. It can be a means to the end of the belief of reason. In this respect, Kant talked of "vanguard, "vehicle," or "organum." The layman must only be liberated from all ecclesiastical dictates and obey his own reason. The apron strings of the holy tradition then become increasingly unnecessary.[47] Where that happens, the particular belief can become the source of a publicly binding morality. Looking at the practical effects of Kant's postulates, it is clearly no accident that they replicate Christian dogmas. Kant acknowledged Christianity as a sensual vehicle of pure religious belief. However, the vehicle needed the canons of reason to be generally obligatory.[48] Ascribing such obligation to it meant succumbing to superstition.

Kant described the procedure of this transformation as a process in the university that was also described as *The Conflict of the Faculties*. Three departments of the university—theology, law, and medicine— draw their theories from texts prescribed by the government: theology from the Holy Scriptures, jurisprudence from statutory laws, medicine from the medical system. It is up to the philosophy department to examine the particular writings in terms of the basic reason of their truth. It was important to Kant to locate this examination in the university because that was the only way to assure that it took place in public. The quarrel with theology accompanying this examination was inevitable since it was the only means to turn ecclesiastical belief into a reasonable belief and to shape the foundations of a civil morality.

Kant's argumentation reversed the usual pattern of establishing ethics through religion. Particular religions had to justify themselves in the court of practical reason occupied by philosophers. Since Kant entrusted the examination to philosophy, he gave it competence in public acknowledgment of religion. The examination was to be free of government interests as well. Kant provided nineteenth-century religious discourse with a crucial model, not only with the reversal of religion and ethics. The concept of a philosophical examination of religion was equally effective. It is not surprising that not only Christianity but other religions, too, were also soon subjected to this procedure.

Historical Religions as Educational Powers

Kant had taken the tension between the history and reason of religion so far that it is no accident that an opposite view was developed, whose leading exponent was Johann Gottfried Herder (1744–1803). Herder marks the start of a reevaluation of historical religions, which had received extremely bad grades from Hobbes, Hume, Rousseau, and Kant. Herder was the first of a series of thinkers who displayed good, even brilliant evidence for them. Herder was born in the East Prussian town of Mohrungen and was sent to study medicine in Königsberg in 1762. There, however, he changed his major, enrolled in theology, and attended Kant's lectures. Kant took a liking to the eighteen-year-old student and allowed him to attend his lectures free of charge. At this time, Herder also became friendly with Johann Georg Hamann (1730–88), the "Magus of the North." After graduation, he was first a preacher in Riga, then went to France. In 1770, he traveled to Strassburg, where he met Goethe.

Like Rousseau, it was a contest question that led him to organize and write his ideas. In 1769, the Berlin Academy of Science announced the contest question: "Could human beings invent language for themselves, left to their natural abilities?" Anyone with a hypothesis on this could submit it by January 1, 1771. Herder did and won first prize with *Essay on the Origin of Languages*.[49] Ever since the mid-eighteenth century, feelings had run high about the question of where language comes from, whether it was a human invention or a gift of God.[50] Christian theologians, led by Johann Peter Süssmilch, opposed the view that language originated in nature (from a humanlike animal).[51] According to Süssmilch, the logical perfection of grammar argues unambiguously in favor of its divine origin. Moreover, in human language, there are several symbols that could not have been invented by the human mind. God gave man language to stir and develop his reason.

Like Süssmilch, Herder rejected a rational theory of language, in which words were regarded only as signs of objects and thoughts. Herder noted that the emotional dimension was missing. "The older and the more original languages are, the more the feelings intertwine in the roots of the words."[52] Human speech and thought would not indicate things without also giving them meanings at the same time. But how is "the interweaving of the roots of the words with ideas" to be explained? Unlike Süssmilch, Herder thought that the spirit of metaphor appeared not only in the so-called divine language, Hebrew, but was available in all languages and must therefore come from human inner life. Metaphors originated in the nature of human speech and hearing: not of individuals, but of "the nation" and the "peculiarity of its way of thinking." With these considerations, Herder granted the sense of hearing a privileged position. In comparison with the cold sense of sight, the perceptions of the ear were distinguished by a special intimacy: words resounded inside the soul.[53] However, such words could also degenerate completely and become a mere instrument of signs, thus forfeiting their spirit of metaphor. Only history teaches the full meaning. "The more original a language, the fewer its abstractions and the more numerous its feelings."[54]

This suggests conclusions that refute current views of reason. Genuine education cannot be an internal, timeless, universal matter. It was necessarily external, temporary, particular. Herder took on this subject in his *Philosophy on the History of Mankind* (1774). Languages inscribed a spirit in human views. This appreciation of languages, which led ten years later to a forthright plea for the philosophical comparison of languages,[55] followed the rehabilitation of particular religions. That is, they have preserved something that has gotten lost in the cold culture of Europe. From this point of view, Herder devoted himself to the differences between East and West. Didn't they show something of the impoverishment of European education? "The human mind received the first forms of wisdom and virtue with a simplicity, strength, and majesty that—put bluntly—is absolutely unparalleled in our cold philosophical, European world. And just because we are so incapable of understanding it, feeling it, not to mention enjoying it anymore—we mock, deny and misinterpret! . . . No doubt religion is also part of this, or rather, religion was 'the element in which all of that lives' and wove."[56]

In *Outlines of a Philosophy of the History of Man* (1784–85), Herder attacked the current assumption that man had become all that he was by himself. This was a delusion. "Not one of us became a man all by himself." Reason is not a pure power, independent of senses and organs. Even in terms of his spiritual capacities, man was not autonomous.[57] While Rousseau heaped scorn on "tradition," Herder made it the prerequisite of true education. If an idea is to be conveyed to someone else, it must have the word as a visible sign. This is the only way the invisible can be made visible and past history remain preserved for posterity. This is the true mission of philosophy. "The philosophy of history . . . which follows the chain of tradition is, to speak properly, the true history of mankind, without which all the outward occurrences of this world are but clouds or revolting deformities. . . . The chain of improvement alone forms a whole of these ruins, in which human figures indeed vanish, but the spirit of mankind lives and acts immortally."[58]

In this "chain of improvement" religion occupies a place of honor, even the religion of savages at the edge of the earth. "Whence is the religion of these people derived? Can these poor creatures have invented their religious worship as a sort of natural theology? Certainly not; for absorbed in labor, they invent nothing, but in all things follow the traditions of their forefathers. . . . Here, therefore, tradition has been the propagator of their religion and sacred rites, as of their language and slight degree of civilization.[59]

Herder had a critical intention in bringing tradition and religion into it. He considered religion as something other than an intellectual exercise, but as an exercise of the human heart and a development of the soul. Since past and foreign religions had preserved human sensibilities intense, Herder ascribed a high status to them. While Herder regarded the history of religion in terms of the education of the subject, he adopted Kant's idea of a public examination of religion, but gave it a different twist. He saw the contempt for tradition in his time as a result of a seizure of power by the intellect, which was to blame for the mechanization of life and for spiritual impoverishment.[60] Awareness of the history of religions could contribute fundamentally to a human culture.

Speeches of Religion as an Individual View of the Universal

Friedrich Schleiermacher's avowed goal was a reevaluation of positive religion. He was born in Breslau in 1768 and died in Berlin in 1834. Pietism and romanticism, the intensity of emotion and natural experience, clashed and combined in him. Schleiermacher was educated by the Moravian Brethren, but left them and went to Halle to study theology (and philosophy). From 1796 to 1802, he served as the Reformed pastor of the Charité hospital in Berlin. He formed a warm friendship with Henriette Herz, and in her salon he was thrilled and inspired by the intellectual debates that were going on in Berlin at that time. The prevailing thought in those salons was not influenced very much by political hierarchies and social conventions,[61] but the transition from the Enlightenment to Romanticism was discussed intensely. Schleiermacher's work on his book, *On Religion: Speeches to its Cultured Despisers*, was accompanied by an animated exchange of ideas with Henriette Herz. The following year, he published the *Speeches* anonymously; it was an enormous success. Although Schleiermacher later rewrote it several times,[62] its first version remained the freshest.

Schleiermacher left Berlin in 1802 but returned in 1807, married in 1809, and accepted a professorship at the new university in 1810. When he died in 1834, nearly 30,000 people attended his funeral, which gives some indication of his outstanding importance for his fellow citizens.

Schleiermacher began writing at a time when positive religions were scorned and hated by many. The horrible persecutions and bloody wars that had taken place in its name were still fresh in people's memory. Schleiermacher blamed that on those who, as he put it, had "pulled" religion from deep in the heart into the civic world.[63] He himself belonged to a generation that had welcomed criticism of absolutism and clericalism, but that had also experienced the outcome of the political transformation of the new civic morality in the disaster of the French Revolution.[64] One who thinks that religions should be taken seriously philosophically, contrary to prevailing opinion, must first correct prejudices about religion. Schleiermacher had also developed a theory of understanding that regarded misunderstanding, and not understanding, as normal. In his hermeneutics, he distinguished two different practices of interpretation: "There is a less rigorous practice of this art which is based on the assumption that understanding occurs as a matter of course. The aim of this practice may be expressed in negative form as: 'Misunderstanding should be avoided.' . . . There is a more rigorous practice of the art of interpretation that is based on the assumption that misunderstanding occurs as a matter of course, and so understanding must be willed and sought at every point."[65] Hans-Georg Gadamer considered Schleiermacher's distinction a unique achievement. For only hermeneutics as the art of avoiding misunderstanding can rise above a pedagogical exercise and turn into a separate method. "Hermeneutics is the art of dealing with the power of misunderstanding."[66]

Something of this hermeneutics can also be seen in Schleiermacher's *Speeches*. The nature of religion is not given in a naïve way, but must be found behind misunderstood rationalizations. The opinion that religion had its place in metaphysics (transcendental philosophy) and morality was predominant. Schleiermacher demanded from his audience to begin with the clear-cut distinction between our piety and what you call morality.[67] Religion, correctly understood, stands beside the realms of thought and behavior as a separate third field. Thus it is also independent of theories and stipulations. Even when God and immortality are doubted, religion does not disappear.[68] It must only be sought.

The *Speeches* present a religion whose center is "the sense and taste for the infinite." Their source is not God, but the universe. Anyone who wants to have the infinite outside of the finite is deceiving himself, for it is the universe that reveals itself to the person who is completely passive and receptive to it. The universe forms its own beholder and admirer. This revelation happens constantly, and hence there is no hope of pinning it down in myths or theories. Schleiermacher was consistent in recognizing no obligatory representation of religion, which gives his view of "history" its specific meaning. Since there can be no final and obligatory revelation of the infinite, it necessarily manifests itself only in individual variations. This multiplicity of religions is quite different from the multiplicity of churches, for, in principle, experienced religion is remote from and opposed to organized and systematic religion. History documents this endless multiplicity of revelations of the universe and is therefore the highest subject of religion.

Anyone who sets out to study the history of religion experiences a wonderful transformation in himself. "From these wanderings through the whole territory of humanity, pious feeling returns, quickened and educated, into its own Ego, and there finds all the influences that had streamed upon it from the most distant regions. . . . You are a compendium of humanity. In a certain sense your single nature embraces all human nature. Your Ego, being multiplied and more clearly outlined, is in all its smallest and swiftest changes immortalized in the manifestations of human nature."[69]

The *Speeches* not only present such a religion, they also represent it. If anything can still represent "religion" today, it is the *Speeches*. In the last part, Schleiermacher gets into the "Social in religion." Here he has to explain how a religion can be represented and conveyed, if it cannot be fixed in myth or doctrine, and is present only in strictly individual views of the universe. His own *Speeches* tacitly had to assume something of that sort.[70] Thus Schleiermacher was consistent in developing a theory of the literary form of the "speech," using a comparison with the competing forms of "book" and "conversation." In the form of the book, religious communication is robbed of its original life. And a conversation does not suit such a serious subject. Only in the form of the "speech" can religion be communicated. And it wants to be communicated. Because everyone who has experienced the effect of the universe does not want to keep this experience to himself but wants to be a witness for others. To communicate it, he uses the arts: "Hence a person whose heart is full of religion only opens his mouth before an assembly where speech so richly equipped might have manifold working."[71]

If we consider Schleiermacher's concluding reflection on the social aspect of religion, we recognize that he shared the view of his predecessors, Rousseau, Kant, and Herder, that religions are objects of public discussion and examination. Speech will create a common bond of all those who feel moved by the universe. Religion remains both subject and object of public discourse when the individual is considered the implacable final authority of religion.

Different Religions, Different Subjectivities

Schleiermacher's definition of religion encountered the sharp opposition of Georg Wilhelm Friedrich Hegel (1770–1831), who allowed himself the following nasty comment: If religion were based only on the feeling of dependence, the dog would be the best believer.[72] The immediacy of a relation was merely a naturalness that still lacked an awareness. From here, Hegel aimed his darts against all Romantics. The unity of nature and mind they glorified was really only the primitive starting point of human history; it was somewhat bestial. Naturally, religion should and must be a matter of feeling. Yet feelings first had to prove their legitimacy. Hegel included this objection in 1822 in a foreword to Hinrich's *Philosophy of Religion*:

> Religion, like duty and law, shall become and even should become a matter of feeling, and lodge in the heart, as freedom also generally lowers itself into feeling and becomes in man a feeling of freedom. But it is entirely something else whether such content, created out of feeling, as God, truth, and freedom, whether such objects should have feeling for their justification; or whether, conversely, such objective content, valid in and for itself, comes to lodge in the heart and in feeling, and feelings, rather, come to receive their content as well as their determination, rectification, and justification from this objective content.[73]

Hegel's rejection of feeling as the basis of religion had serious consequences for his philosophical examination of religions. In natural religions, the spiritual and the natural coincide. But this does not apply to all religions. Thus, Hegel could see positive religions as a potential object of rational cognition, as he showed in his *Lectures on the Philosophy of Religion*, which are based on the assumption that immediacy is natural, but awareness is exaltation above nature. Such an exaltation is characteristic of religions—aside from natural religions. Religions documented a discord of awareness, since they themselves distinguished the true from the natural, and spirit from nature—even if, as Hegel rigorously noted, they were not always consistent. Thus Hegel made the exaltation of the spirit over the natural into a point of view that can produce rational cognition from the study of the history of religion.[74]

Hegel combined awareness with mediation. Thus he both continued Kant's thought and turned against him at the same time. Kant had determined that the pure categories of thought were independent of the things in themselves. Hegel found this claim weak and barren. Doesn't the external always bear the stamp of the internal, and vice-versa? The way of mediating reality by notions is itself historically determined. Thus he was especially interested in the question: Where and how in human history does consciousness of a difference between subject and object, between spirit and nature emerge? In natural religions, it is not yet available. But what about the religions of Asia?

Hegel's picture of India was initially determined by his rejection of Romanticism. The unity of spirit and nature that Schlegel saw as the highest stage of development as exemplified in India, Hegel considered the lowest rung. In 1824, when Hegel acquired more precise knowledge about Indian philosophy, he revised and refined his judgment.[75] In 1823, Henry Thomas Colebrooke had delivered lectures entitled *On the Philosophy of the Hindus* to the Royal Asiatic Society of London, which were published a year later. After reading them, Hegel promptly expanded his *Lectures on the History of Philosophy* with a chapter on "Oriental Philosophy,"[76] correcting the opinion that the Orientals lived in unity with nature, as a superficial and distorted impression. For, as Hegel substantiated his charge, this genuine unity essentially contains the element of the negation of nature, as it is immediate. The spiritual is one with nature only when being in itself, and at the same time posing the natural as negative.[77] Indian philosophy was very familiar with the difference between spirit and nature, since only on this assumption could the spiritual negate the natural. According to the Indian view, the individual gains his freedom from the natural only by losing himself in contemplation in the general substance, from which the universe emerged. The highest thing in religion as in philosophy is that man as consciousness makes himself identical with substance: through devotion, sacrifice, strict atonement— and through philosophy, through occupation with pure thought.[78] Because of Colebrooke's lectures, Hegel realized that Indian thought knew the difference between subject and object, spirit and nature, and consequently deserved its own chapter in the history of philosophy. But this difference had other practical results than in the Greek-Christian religion: the individual obtained his value not by confronting nature as subject, but by vanishing into substance. That was its defect.[79]

As soon as Hegel had carried out this revision, another opportunity appeared for refining his philosophical reconstruction of Indian religion. In 1825 and 1826, Wilhelm von Humboldt had delivered two lectures on the much admired *Bhagavad Gita* at the Royal Academy of Science in Berlin. In 1827, Hegel published a comprehensive review, focusing on a contradiction. The *Bhagavad Gita* inculcates something that was ruled out: that is, it calls for both the performance of dutiful works and the renunciation of works. The demand for action appears repeatedly in Krishna's words on Ardshuna alongside the opposite demand for contemplation without action. Hegel's interpretation fixed on this contradiction. It could not be solved in Indian thinking, he judged. "The solution is impossible because the most sublime in Indian mentality, the absolute Being, Brahman, is as such without qualities. . . . In this separation of the universal and the concrete both are spiritless—that as empty Oneness, this as unfree manifold; man as bound to this is only subject to life's law of nature; elevating himself to that extreme, he is on the escape and in a state of negating all concrete, spiritual activity."[80]

As a philosopher, Hegel indicated one essential feature of Indian religion with special emphasis: the divine substance knows no internal differentiation. Accordingly, the released individual loses himself in contemplation and becomes one with the metaphysical substance. This substance does not emerge as a denial of the world and does not constitute a new autonomous subject—as in Christian religion. Thus, the possibility of a tension with the world is not realized. Renunciation only affects acts conditioned by desire, and not obligatory acts. Nor does this encroach on the existing caste system. The individual released from the world is outside the world, not in it, as in Christianity.

Developing two countermodels of denial of the world by comparing Indian religion with Christianity, Hegel created an unprecedented description of religions. For Hegel, God, ethics, and salvation remained immutable ideas. A glance at the Romantics shows clearly what was new in his view. While they found Indian "worship" a confirmation that man is in unity with nature, Hegel regarded "worship" as a "conception" that creates a form of awareness in which man knows himself as one with the divine substance. The facts of the case are the same. But Hegel perceived "idea" where the Romantics saw only "feeling." Therefore, he viewed religion as the area of development of the subject and the epitome of his experience.

Such a philosophical consideration also required the kind of elements that were remote from Kant's examination of the regulative function of religions. Hegel reconstructed philosophical religion from the history of religions: from the ideas of God, the conception of the soul, religious practice, and so on. These are the independent conceptions of truth Hegel observed. For from these concepts, the position of the individual in the division between spirit and nature can be perceived. Philosophy can think religion, but not replace it.[81] The history of religion documents the process of developing consciousness of the subject.

The Option of Renouncing the World

With Arthur Schopenhauer (1788–1860), philosophy turned even more decisively to the history of religions than Hegel had done. Schopenhauer was an outsider, who received no recognition for quite some time. He was not appointed to a university professorship, even though he received his doctorate in 1813 in Jena and qualified as a university professor in Berlin in 1820. In Dresden, he wrote his major work, *The World As Will and Representation* in 1818, which he expanded to a second volume in 1844. Since no one wanted to read his books, they were pulped. Only at the age of sixty-six did he achieve recognition.[82]

From the start, Schopenhauer placed an extraordinary emphasis on the sources of the history of religion. In the preface to the first volume of his magnum opus, in 1818, he acknowledged: "Kant's philosophy . . . is the only one with which a thorough acquaintance is positively assumed in what is to be here discussed. But if in addition to this the reader has dwelt for a while in the school of the divine Plato, he will be the better prepared to hear me, and the more susceptible to what I say. But if he has shared in the benefits of the *Vedas* . . . if, I say, the reader has also already received and assimilated the divine inspiration of ancient Indian wisdom, then he is best of all prepared to hear what I have to say to him." The new century had a special advantage: the Upanishads gave access to the Vedas. Schopenhauer expected "that the influence of Sanskrit literature will penetrate no less deeply than did the revival of Greek literature in the fifteenth century."[83]

In a debate with Kant, Schopenhauer delineated his basic position. Kant's "logical I," which gives our views and thoughts unity and is the permanent bearer of all our ideas, cannot itself be conditioned by awareness. Something else must assume it. "This, I say, is the *will*."[84] Thereupon, Schopenhauer took a first step: from thinking to willing. The will to live as a practical relationship to the world presupposes the subject-object differentiation. The possibility of knowing the world is formed and conditioned by the will to live. This origin does not ennoble the world; it owes its existence ultimately to a blind, insatiable urge of will. Thus, it is wrong to call it the best of all possible worlds, as Leibniz did. It is "the *worst* of all possible worlds."[85] Yet, there is an escape from this world: the renunciation of will. The pivot and crux of this operation is the process of individuation. The *principum individuationis* is the source of all hatred and grief. When the person sees through these, he can lift the veil of Maya, the hocus-pocus of illusion, all by himself. Thus the egotistical difference between one's own self and the Other fades. Then, discovery of the whole, of the nature of the Things-in-Itself becomes the *Quietiv*.[86] Schopenhauer calls this possibility "asceticism." It is to be found not only in reports of Indian religiosity, but also in German mysticism. Ultimately, it is also encountered in acts. Thus, the lives of saints can be more instructive for philosophers than philosophical treatises. But the ethics of religions can also contribute to closer knowledge. Christianity knows asceticism when it demands self-denial, although this demand is obscured by the Jewish part of Christianity. If that is eliminated, the same thing that is portrayed more fully and vividly in the ancient Sanskrit works is found. The Hindu ethic shows a willingness for voluntary death which is quite foreign to us, as for example when Hindus throw themselves under the wheels of the juggernaut. What has survived as a practice for so long among so many millions of peoples, while imposing the most difficult sacrifice, cannot be an arbitrary whim, but rather must have its basis in the nature of mankind.[87] Moreover, there is also the experience of horror that is triggered by conversion. The story of the conversion of Raimund Lullius is relevant here. He expected the fulfillment of all his wishes when a beautiful woman he had been courting for a long time summoned him to her room, at which time she opened her blouse and showed him her horrible bosom eaten by cancer. From this moment on, as if he had seen hell, he converted.[88] But that was only the second best way.

In the complementary second volume of 1844, Schopenhauer raised the status of the history of religion even more with regard to the denial of the will to live. In accordance with the origin of cognition from the will, which was demonstrated in the first volume, all religions at the peak of mysticism and mystery end in darkness and veils. If the Jewish Bible is taken out of Christianity and the true Christianity of the Gnostics is followed, then Christianity belongs to the ancient, true, and sublime faith of mankind. This faith stands in contrast to the false, shallow, and pernicious optimism that manifests itself in Greek paganism, Judaism, and Islam.[89] There is Indian blood in the body of Christianity that supports its constant tendency to get rid of Judaism. Even Protestantism knows the ascetic spirit of genuine Christianity. For Schopenhauer, the concurrence of this renunciation of the world despite extreme differences in times, countries, and religions was no coincidence. If contemporaries saw it as a stumbling block, he, on the other hand, saw it as a proof of its sole accuracy and truth.[90]

The proximity to and distance from Hegel cannot be ignored. Schopenhauer condemned the miserable Hegelism, that school of dullness, that center of stupidity and ignorance, that mind-destroying, spurious wisdom.[91] Honesty, however, prompted him to say that he interpreted the Indian sources from the same point of view as his opponent Hegel. But what Hegel considered their defect, Schopenhauer saw as their superiority. Thus he turned a principle of subjectivity, which was correct for Hegel only in terms of universal history, into a relevant option: the denial of individuation. But in the process, the history of religions obtained a declarative value that was more existential than in the thought of previous philosophers. *"What the faculty of reason is to the individual, history is to the human race.* By virtue of this faculty, man is not like the animal, restricted to the narrow present of perception, but knows also the incomparably more extended past with which it is connected, and out of which it has emerged. But only in this way does he have a proper understanding of the present itself, and can he draw conclusions as to the future."[92]

From the History of Religion to Rational Religion and Back

A survey of the positions on the history of religions adopted in philosophy from Hobbes to Schopenhauer allows us to talk of a reversal of the starting position. At first there was a rigorous separation of historical religions from rational religion. At the end, the history of religion serves as a source of a reason superior to enlightened thought. Hobbes's own experience was clear proof to him that the more private and apolitical religions were, the more rational they were. Making private beliefs public endangered the social welfare of everyone. Thus, his measure of its rationality was whether it vanquished civil war, especially the horrible wars of religion. For Hume, on the other hand, private religion per se was no longer suspicious, and the state-prescribed religion per se was not rational. The history of religions was subject to a psychological law that made men vacillate back and forth in their history between polytheism and monotheism, tolerance and intolerance. Different types of religions generated divergent public norms. The internal peace of a community depended on whether the pendulum of the history of religion went toward polytheism. Hume assigned the state only the role of a stand-in to compel internal peace.

Separating a rational religion from historical religions posed new difficulties. How could the menacing political function of the church be compatible with the equally obvious social and moral function of a "religion of the heart"? How could the middle class throw off their subordination to historical dogmas and institutions without destroying the morality of the community? Rousseau and Kant worked on this problem and developed a model of behavior of rational religion that was different from that of existing religion. Both thinkers saw the possibility of reforming private religious convictions by means of a public examination and government regulation, thus making them the basis of public morality. Private belief must become public; public requirement of reason must become private. Georg Simmel's phrase is well suited to Kant's and Rousseau's philosophy of religion.

Even before the collapse of the political enlightenment in the French Revolution, there was opposition to such a primarily social and moral view of religion. Religions were much more comprehensive worldviews that molded the thought, behavior, and emotions of human beings. They were a compendium of human culture, either of nations (Herder) or individuals (Schleiermacher). But there was a price for this reevaluation of religions: the Romantic idealization of a unity of spirit and nature. For Hegel, that price was too high. Besides, closer study of Indian religiosity revealed that India had been incorrectly cited as a model for such a unity. Hegel saw the process of a split between spirit and nature, subject and object at work in the great religions. Hence philosophy can identify different structures of subjectivity in the history of religion. While India wanted to overcome the tension between spirit and nature through contemplation, the West cultivated it. What Hegel described as historically universal, Schopenhauer made into individual options, and turned it upside down. India is a good example of how we too can rid ourselves of the false claim to subjectivity.

CHAPTER TWO

DECIPHERING UNKNOWN CULTURES

FOR YEARS, a manuscript of the Avesta, the holy book of the Parsis, was on display in the Bodleian Library of Oxford. Although no one could read it, it was a famous sight and hung on a gold chain. In 1754, a young French scholar, Abraham Hyacinthe Anquetil-Duperron, saw a copy of it in Paris and did what his predecessors had not: he set off for India.[1] As a soldier for the French East-Indian Society, he had time to win the trust of Parsi priests, who helped him penetrate the secrets of the Avesta. In 1762, he returned to Paris with no fewer than 180 Avestan, middle-Persian, and Sanskrit manuscripts. In 1771, he published a first translation of the Avesta. The original was still incomprehensible and he had to rely on a translation of the Parsi priests into modern Persian. Decades later, he did a first translation of the Indian Upanishads in the same way.

Anquetil-Duperron could endure these enormous efforts because they were accompanied by a special joy of discovery. The history and culture of the Jews, Greeks, and Romans were known by humanists, he wrote in his foreword to the translation of the Avesta. "America, Africa, and Asia still remain to be deciphered, I dare say."[2] Deciphering meant more to him than simply breaking an incomprehensible code. It was a metaphor that extended to the scholarly reconnaissance of unknown cultures. Raymond Schwab placed Anquetil-Duperron's vision in the history of the European study of foreign cultures. The first Renaissance, which sent European culture back to Greek and Roman antiquity, was followed by a second Renaissance that tore down the walls the first had erected around Europe. If, in the reign of Louis XIV, "Hellenism" was the fashion, Anquetil-Duperron presented "Orientalism" as a new option. In his biography of Anquetil, Schwab provides a remarkable description of this volte-face:

In 1759, in Surat [the Indian center of Parsis], Anquetil finished translating the Avesta; in Paris in 1786, with his translation of the Upanishads, he dug an isthmus between the hemispheres of the human spirit and liberated the old humanism from the Mediterranean Basin. Just fifteen years earlier, when he taught his fellow countrymen to compare the monuments of the Persians with those of the Greeks, they asked how one could be a Persian. Before him, Latin, Greek, Jewish, and Arab writers were the sole sources of knowledge about the distant past of the planet. The Bible appeared as an isolated rock, a meteorite. People believed that text contained the whole universe; hardly anyone seemed to imagine the immensity of the uncharted territories. His translation of the Avesta marks the opening of the discovery that then spiraled with the excavations of Central Asia, with languages that arose after Babylon. He cast a vision of countless and ancient civilizations, an enormous mass of literatures into our schools, which to this day arrogantly keep the door shut behind the narrow legacy of the Greek-Latin Renaissance; from now on, a few European provinces are no longer the only ones that engrave their names in history.[3]

The force of the upheaval represented by Anquetil-Duperron can hardly be described any better. The cultural walls around Europe tumbled.

A Series of Decipherings of Foreign Languages and Texts

After 1770, Europe must have learned more emphatically than ever before that there were unknown cultures completely independent of the Old World, some of which even predated it. The West, which had based what it considered its unique position on the Jewish-Christian Bible and Greek and Roman antiquity, thus acquired competition. As long as Europeans had still believed that all foreign cultures were pagan or barbaric and thus inferior, they had been immune to such challenge. This changed in the eighteenth century. The authority of ecclesiastical Christianity was undermined by a ruthless criticism. The Renaissance of antiquity, which quickly became attractive among intellectuals, prepared the ground for an intellectual and emotional sensibility to discoveries beyond the West as well. The written legacies of foreign cultures, which had long been a sealed book, were deciphered one after another by Europeans and began to yield their contents. (1771: A. H. Anquetil-Duperron, *Translation of the Zoroastrian Avesta*; 1793: Silvestre de Sacy, *Translation of the Persian Sassanid Texts*; 1801: A. H. Anquetil-Duperron, *Translation of the Indian Upanishads*; 1822: J. F. Champollion, *Report on the Deciphering of Egyptian Hieroglyphs*; 1833: F. Bopp, *Comparative Grammar of Sanskrit, Zend, Greek, Latin, Lithuanian, Gothic, and German*; 1847 and 1850, 51: H. C. Rawlinson, *Translation of Old Persian and Old Babylonian Cuneiform Texts from Behistun*.)

When Friedrich Max Müller propagated the new discipline of religious studies in 1867, he understood clearly how dependent it was on the new discoveries.

During the last fifty years the authentic documents of the most important religions of the world have been recovered in a most unexpected and almost miraculous manner. We have now before us the canonical books of Buddhism; the Zend-Avesta of Zoroaster is no longer a sealed book; and the hymns of the Rig-Veda have revealed a state of religion anterior to the first beginnings of that mythology which in Homer and Hesiod stands before us as a mouldering ruin. The soil of Mesopotamia has give back the very images once worshipped by the most powerful of the Semitic tribes, and the cuneiform inscriptions of Babylon and Nineveh have disclosed the very prayers addressed to Baal or Nisroch.[4]

Although knowledge was meager, there had been information on some of the newly accessible cultures, like the Chinese, the Hindus, the Parsis, for quite some time, because missionaries had been reporting on them ever since the sixteenth century. But Europeans had not immediately accepted even this scanty data about the history and literature of these cultures into the canon of valuable information. This situation did not change until the end of the eighteenth century, with the contribution of Anquetil-Duperron and other linguists.

In a memorable lecture to the Asiatic Society in Calcutta on February 2, 1786, mentioned by E. B. Tylor, William Jones tentatively presented his first assumptions about the affinity of the Indian and Iranian languages with Greek and Latin. This later proved to be the hour when comparative philology was born.

The *Sanscrit* language, whatever be its antiquity, is of a wonderful structure; more perfect than the *Greek*, more copious than the *Latin*, and more exquisitely refined than either, yet bearing to both of them a stronger affinity, both in the roots of verbs and in the forms of grammar, than could possibly have been produced by accident; so strong indeed, that no philologer could examine them all three, without believing them to have sprung from some common source, which, perhaps, no longer exists: there is a similar reason, though not quite so forcible, for supposing that both the *Gothick* and the *Celtick*, though blended with a very different idiom, had the same origin with the *Sanscrit*; and the old *Persian* might be added to the same family.[5]

In 1816, the first comparative grammar of Sanskrit, Greek, Latin, Persian, and German appeared. And in 1833, Franz Bopp collected all findings about the affinity of these languages in his *Vergleichende Grammatik*.

Flagrant political interests also played a role in the deciphering enterprise, since, particularly in India, it was hoped that the new sources would provide knowledge useful for the colonial administration. But the enthusiasm for deciphering was not focused only on this kind of knowledge. One case that revealed the nature and force of the growing interest was the great feat of decoding the hieroglyphs. In this instance, no indigenous priest could come to the aid of the scholars with oral traditions or traditional translations. All the acumen of ingenious decoders was demanded, along with the accident of the right discovery. In 1799, soldiers in Napoleon's army in a military entrenchment in the Nile Delta, where the enemy English fleet was already cruising, found a stone with an inscription in three different languages. According to the Greek inscription, the Rosetta Stone contained a decree of an Egyptian priest dating from 196 B.C. Next to it was the same text in hieroglyphs and another in demotic writing. Thus, there was access to the same text in two languages (Egyptian and Greek) and three scripts (hieroglyphs, demotic, and Greek). The scholars in Napoleon's entourage immediately realized that this inscription gave them the key to decipher the holy tongue of the ancient Egyptians. But when the French army had to surrender to the victorious English forces, the scholars had to yield to the demand of the English conquerors to turn over the stone. The French were left with only a copy, while the original was taken to England and later wound up in the British Museum.

Nevertheless, the overwhelming breakthrough in the deciphering was the work of a Frenchman. Although Thomas Young of England did take a few considerable steps toward deciphering, it was the Frenchman Jean François Champollion who officially informed the Académie Française in a letter of 1822 that he had succeeded in deciphering the hieroglyphs. Ever since Hellenistic antiquity, hieroglyphs had been incomprehensible, and the principle had been misunderstood as a kind of pictographic writing. Champollion was the first to realize that the hieroglyphs were not pictographic writing, but phonetic signs like the alphabet. English scholars had difficulty acknowledging his achievement, as indicated by a report on the Rosetta Stone in an official journal of the British Museum of 1836, arguing that Champollion was indebted to the decisive comment of the English Dr. Young. Otherwise, the Frenchman might have remained all his life in the mistaken view that hieroglyphs indicated words but not phonetics. "M. Champollion has no claim of any kind as a *discoverer* of the phonetic value of Egyptian hieroglyphics."[6] In fact, the deciphering relied on the advance work of several scholars in various European nations. How absurd to use the discoveries of foreign cultures to legitimate national superiority![7] In any case, this absurdity documented the intensity of the competition between the great European scientific nations to pioneer in deciphering.

Unknown cultures of the Nile Valley, later of the Tigris and Euphrates and the Iranian plateau, emerged from oblivion. If any of those involved had believed at first that the new discoveries would support the authority of the Bible, it soon became clear that the opposite was the case. Above all, those discoveries undermined biblical chronology, which calculated the entire timespan of the world as six thousand years. The value of these discoveries was controversial in other respects, too. When the Avesta was published, many scholars were disappointed at the rather unedifying contents. Zarathustra could not have written such simple-minded things! "L'Europe éclairée n'avait pas besoin de votre Zende-Vesta (sic!)" ["Enlightened Europe did not need your Zende-Vesta (sic!)"], shouted the English scholar William Jones to Anquetil-Duperron.[8]

Many big and small steps had to be taken to overcome all resistance and grant the familiar cultures an unbiased hearing. At first, the personal motives and predilections of the scholars involved had played a role in the decipherings. Georg Friedrich Grotefend, who worked on deciphering cuneiform writing in the early nineteenth century in Göttingen, had developed a penchant for picture puzzles even as a child. Champollion had also had a boyhood dream of deciphering the hieroglyphs. But powerful scientific institutions immediately took over from individual fighters. England launched the Asiatic Society of Bengal in Calcutta in 1784 and the Société Asiatique was founded in Paris in 1821. Thanks to the efforts of these institutions, the most important books of the Orient stood on the shelves of interested scholars at the end of the century. On International Orientalist Day in London in 1874, F. M. Müller proposed the publication of known texts in a series, *Sacred Books of the East*. By 1898, fifty volumes had appeared.

An Oriental Renaissance

Couldn't the Orient—like Antiquity in the past—become the source of a renaissance in the modern age? In *La Renaissance orientale* (1950), Raymond Schwab showed how attractive that idea once was.[9] The metaphor of the orientalist renaissance comes from the 1842 book by Edgar Quinet, *Génie des religions*. Quinet celebrated the discovery of the Orient as a historical moment that ended the neoclassical period of the Renaissance, while the metaphor of the renaissance itself was not shaped until the nineteenth century.[10] Expectations in Germany were similar. During the Age of Enlightenment, the religion of India, considered congealed in superstition and ritual, had served as a warning. It went untapped simply because India was no match for enlightened reason. And this was to change only when reason was called into question. It was no accident that Johann Gottfried Herder praised the youthful spirit, devotion, and wisdom of the East in 1774, and held it up to the affected, cold European world as an example. Europe was incapable of understanding or feeling, let alone enjoying this spirit.[11]

The revision of this judgment can be observed especially well in attitudes toward India. As the Enlightenment gave way to Romanticism, India attracted the interest of the intellectuals,[12] as exemplified by the Schlegel brothers. August Wilhelm Schlegel had been the first holder of a chair of Indology in Germany since 1818. In his lectures *Über Literatur, Kunst und Geist des Zeitalters*, he lamented that, because of the Enlightenment, people thought only in categories of quantity and utility, and had lost the sense for the miraculous, for the unity and wholeness of life, which could be found in India. Schlegel had to admit, however, that this sense was not preserved pure in India either. It first had to be recovered from the literature. A theory of decline had to come to the aid of the Romantic reevaluation of India, as was later the case with F. Max Müller. The title of a book by Friedrich Schlegel of 1808 concisely expressed the interpretation of the Romantics in diametrical opposition to the Enlightenment: *Über die Sprache und Weisheit der Indier* (On the Language and Wisdom of the Indians). What F. Schlegel expected from a study of India was nothing less than a new humanism. Through the study of Greek, scholars in Italy and Germany had revived knowledge of Antiquity, and so "the shape of all the sciences, we can even say of the world, changes and regenerates. . . . And we dare claim that the effect of the study of India would be just as great and general, if it is grasped forcefully and introduced into the circle of European knowledge."[13]

Unlike England, German interest in India was more cultural than political. Its awakening indicates a change in cultural consciousness. Awareness of the characteristics of India (and other newly discovered cultures) was accompanied by an awareness that Western culture could not claim absolute value. The more uncertainty about the scope of reason spread among intellectuals within Europe, the more important it became to devote serious study to newly opened sources outside of Europe. Since the Enlightenment had criticized religion, it was no accident that an examination of these documents focused on religion.

The Discovery of Prehistory

Along with the discoveries of foreign cultures, the discovery of prehistory also stimulated curiosity about one's own history and origin.

Virtually nothing was known about humans. Anquetil-Duperron clearly realized this deficiency:

> The stars have been measured, the sea has been fathomed, the whole surface of the earth has been explored and its shape determined; the secret of nature in its products and the laws that regulate its course has been admired: all this for man. But man himself has remained unknown. We can take two paths to the knowledge of this very interesting entity: observation of his nature: what he can do, what he must be; and contemplation of his acts: what he is.

Metaphysics (Anquetil's term) took the first path and described man as an object subject to the law of nature; *History* followed the second path and showed him in action: his thoughts, his spirit, his events.[14] The new decipherings and discoveries of the nineteenth century thoroughly changed this situation. Apparently the time had come to fill in the missing chapters of the history book of mankind.

As long as biblical chronology was the measure, there was not enough time to contain all the new data on the various peoples on the earth allegedly coming from a single set of parents. This dilemma granted a certain plausibility to the assumption that the various races of humanity had different origins. The nations of Europe had nothing to do with the tribal nations overseas.[15] The attraction of this so-called polygenesis waned only when a different solution to the dilemma of the inadequate time frame appeared and the idea of a creation was replaced by the concept of a gradual development.

Until the mid-nineteenth century—in line with the Bible—man was considered a newcomer in the realm of nature, as geology seemed to confirm. Although belief in Noah's flood had been abandoned, geologists still calculated a sequence of natural disasters to account for the stratification of the earth and the fossils contained in those layers. The layers of earth gave information about periods of past life. And since the first indications of man came from the highest strata, there was at least a grain of truth in the biblical narrative that man had first appeared in a late stage of Creation.

Yet, ever since the 1820s, discoveries had surfaced that did not tally with the assumption that man was the final product of Creation. In the caves of England and France, amateur archaeologists found stone tools of humans next to extinct animal species. Since this anomaly could not be explained, it was dismissed with the claim that the original contents of the caves had later been disturbed by humans. And since the excavations were not carried out patiently, strata by strata, but were done to achieve a quick archaeological success, this explanation was thoroughly plausible. Only a few lone individuals harbored doubts. In France, Jacques Boucher de Perthes in the three-volume *Antiquités Celtiques et Diluviennes* (1847, 1857, 1864) persisted in claiming that human instruments appeared in connection with extinct animals. (Thus, the biblical dating was not yet directly refuted, for humans really did appear late in the natural realm.)

The breakthrough came in 1858 from a cave in England. An English amateur archaeologist had learned from the newspaper that a cave near Torquay in Devonshire contained a great many prehistoric remains that were obviously untouched. The owner was quite aware of the value of his possession and wanted money before he would allow an excavation. And so the amateur archaeologist induced the Geological Society in London to purchase the so-called Brixham Cave from its owner. That same year, a committee was formed that grasped the opportunity and did the right thing. It decided that the cave had to be excavated so that the sequence of the strata as well as the location and provenance of the organic remains could be clearly determined.[16] After only a few weeks of digging, those involved realized that the human stone tools were indeed connected with extinct animals. In September of that year, one of the excavators, the teacher William Pengelly, addressed a packed assembly of the society: "Several well marked specimens of the objects called 'Flint Knives,' and generally accepted at the present day as the early product of Keltic or pre-Keltic industry, have been exhumed from different parts of the cavern, mixed in the ocherous earth with remains of *Rhinocerous, Hyena,* and other extinct forms."[17]

The official reversal of science was completed by the recognized geologist Charles Lyell. In 1863, he formulated the way an overdue truth is dealt with: "Whenever a new and startling fact is brought to light in science, people first say, 'it is not true,' then that 'it is contrary to religion,' and lastly, 'that everybody knew it before.'"[18] Thus it was in this case too. In *The Geological Evidences of the Antiquity of Man,* Lyell compiled all discoveries that confirmed the simultaneity of human artifacts and extinct species of animals, and attempted to explain them. Gradual changes of environmental conditions must have been to blame for the extinction of the animal species.[19] Lyell began with the model of a slow transformation and reckoned with what was then the inconceivable period of ten thousand years. Even if he did not come even close to the real dimensions, it was clear in any case that the biblical chronology with its six thousand years of human history had become untenable. New empirical findings kept cropping up that discredited adherence to the short period of Old Testament chronology.[20]

By the end of the seventeenth century, the biblical model of world history was so altered that its weaknesses no longer directly impeded historical work. The point of departure was the contradiction between the Hebrew Bible and the Greek translation of the Old Testament, the Septuagint, that had been canonized by the Old Church. The Septuagint had made prehistory, prior to Abraham, about a thousand years longer than the Hebrew Bible. Ancient extrabiblical sources on the history of Babylon and Egypt (Berossos and Manetho) calculated much longer periods than even the Septuagint. Hence, by the late seventeenth century, more historians decided to calculate the pre-Christian calendar differently, counting all events before the beginning of the Christian era backward from that moment.[21] However, this method circumvented the problem of biblical chronology rather than solving it. A new discovery about the real age of the world and human beings was not achieved. That was left for the mid-nineteenth century, when prehistoric finds and Darwin's book a year later revealed a view of the incredible depths of human prehistory.

Prehistoric archaeology inspired the new human science with its metaphors. Just as geology isolated distinct strata of earth, so prehistoric archaeology did the same with the legacies of human life. In the works of those who undertook to reconstruct the history of human culture, geological metaphors of strata and fossils played a decisive role, fostering the notion that human prehistory had occurred in a separate habitat and period. In any case, the remains revealed painfully little about the way of life and thought of early man. All those involved at that time seemed to want to solve the riddle of those remains and reconstruct the forms of life and thought of early humans.

The discoveries had another, equally revolutionary consequence. If it had once been assumed as self-evident that the old Oriental high cultures were closest to the beginning of human history, this assumption was now dubious. Prehistoric archaeologists were the first to reach this conclusion:

> Nevertheless, geologically speaking, and in reference to the date of the first age of stone, these records of the valley of the Nile may be called extremely modern. Wherever excavations have been made into the Nile mud underlying the foundations of Egyptian cities, as, for example, sixty feet below the peristyle of the obelisk of Heliopolis, and generally in the alluvial plains of the Nile, the bones met with belong to living species of quadrupeds, such as the camel, dromedary, dog, ox, and pig, without, as yet, the association in any single instance of the teeth or bone of a lost species.[22]

The caves of Europe held the earliest evidence of mankind, so advances in the early times had to be sought here. Müller and Tylor both began their investigations in Europe. The oldest languages of

Europe and the traces of past cultural stages in contemporary Europe were their most important guideposts to the early history of man.

Darwin's Evolution

Charles Darwin's contribution in this respect can hardly be overestimated. Miraculously, it came at the same moment as the prehistoric finds. *The Origin of Species*, which appeared in 1859, confirmed the assumption that mankind was immensely old. The work contains both metaphors and models of interpretation that made this fact intelligible. Neither creation nor catastrophes, rather extremely slow and imperceptible changes, were responsible for the variety of species. Darwin boldly asserted that "the amount of organic change in the fossils of consecutive formations probably serves as a fair measure of the lapse of actual time."[23] Previously, there had been talk of God and Creation; Darwin spoke of a nature seething with fertility. Darwin's travel valise helps us understand this metaphor. John Milton's poetry and Lyell's *Principles of Geology* accompanied him on his world tour. Milton's *Paradise Lost* combined the image of the Creation with the act of sensual love and fertilization.*

It led Darwin to the old idea of a *natura naturans*. The all-out struggle and the "survival of the fittest" were not decisive for Darwin's *Origin of Species*, as was assumed under the impression of H. Spencer's ideas. Darwin started with a surplus of descendants which increased the chance that some of them were better suited to natural conditions than others. His model was selective breeding, which he knew from English cattle breeding. The whole living world is like a tree that keeps branching and recognizes both living and dead twigs and branches. Darwin did not formulate any abstract law of evolution, but rather presented his observations as a drama starring *natura*

---

*John Milton, *Paradise Lost*, 7:449–58:

> The Sixt, and of Creation last arose
> With Evening Harps and Mattin, when God said,
> Let th' Earth bring forth Soule living in her kinde,
> Cattle and Creeping things, and Beast of the Earth,
> Each in their kinde. The Earth obeyd, and strait
> Op'ning her fertil Woomb teemed at a Birth
> Innumerous living Creatures, perfect formes,
> Limbd and full grown: out of the ground up rose
> As from his Laire the wilde Beast where he wonns
> In Forrest wilde, in Thicket, Brake, or Den.

Beer 1983, 34–36.

naturans. The plot was the history of nature. Dissatisfaction with Darwin's interpretation of natural history soon followed. The emergence of the species as a chain of accidents displeased many, who substituted another model that made progress a natural law instead of an accident, which is why Spencer's interpretation could so quickly supersede Darwin's metaphors.

An approach focusing on the development of the individual organism supplemented the theory of evolution. The theory of recapitulation assumed a parallel between the emergence of the individual organism and the genus as a whole. The idea was that the sequence of life as a whole could be observed in the embryo. In their individual development, organisms would recapitulate natural history as a whole. This "biogenetic formula" also established evolution as a paradigm of regular progress. For Darwin, the variations of the species had accidental reasons with their roots in the cooperation of natural selection and the pressure of food. For Ernst Haeckel, who promulgated the "biogenetic formula," there was less accident involved. If orthogenesis is needed for information on phylogenesis—he thought—a constant development can be discovered in nature, where a hierarchy of forms can be seen.[24] "The sequence of forms which the individual organism goes through during its development from the ovum to its definitive state is a brief, concise recapitulation of the long sequence of forms, which the animal forefathers of the same organism or the original form of his species went through from the oldest times of the so-called organic creation to the present," wrote Haeckel.[25]

The discovery of the prehistory of mankind was impelled by both doubt and caution. On the one hand, the chambers of human prehistoric times could surely be opened. But on the other hand, all sorts of irrational things might be lying under the top stratum of human rationality. It was philosophy that had prepared the ground. In Kant's thought, *soul* was merely the epistemological function of the ego. While this philosophy established the rules of a rational cognition, it had unintentionally turned the irrational into a realm of its own. The more determined the claim to rational cognition and the stricter the criteria of reason, the more powerful was the realm beyond reason. Whatever was not exact or moral in reality was ascribed to that realm. The evident weakness of transcendental reason prepared the ground for a philosophy empowering nature.[26]

By the mid-eighteenth century, a dimension of man that Sigmund Freud was to call the unconscious a hundred years later was repeatedly claimed by poets and thinkers. That a person knows more than he himself is aware of; that he makes assumptions in his sensual perceptions which he himself does not comprehend; that his behavior is steeped in motives that are hidden from him—J. W. von Goethe had already come up with these notions:

> That which heedless man ne'er knew,
> Or ne'er thought aright,
> Roams the bosom's labyrinth through,
> Boldly into night.

The sum of our existence, divided by reason, never works out whole, but always remains a wondrous fraction, thought Goethe. German Romantics exploited this wisdom and called the "wondrous fraction" the *soul*. "And my soul stretches / Its wings out wide, / Flies through the quiet lands, / As if to home, inside." The Romantic soul roams the world, unrestrained and homeless. The Romantic is not even sure if the soul is *his*. Instead, it expresses the eccentricity of man. The soul lodges elsewhere than in awareness: in the vitality of man. And there it can be the gateway to powers the philosophers' reason could not dream of.[27] Soul is an organ of experience, which is not controlled by the mind. *Soul* is the possibility to escape from conformity.

Wherever such notions gained the upper hand, the subject lost his safe hold and became eccentric. Hence the step to the soul as psyche. The soul is not at home in an indivisible ego. It is the gateway to the awful or beautiful other. This affects the concept of understanding. The act of understanding cannot be external and disinterested, but is always internal and intuitive: soul dives into soul. From this empowerment of the irrational, the ego itself is grasped. The emptiness left behind in the ego by Kant's critical philosophy was discerned and filled by the Romantics. The Romantic soul is different from the aware, knowing ego. If men refer to themselves, this self-reference is always tuned in one way or another. Romantic natural philosophy concluded from this that the soul is indissolubly woven into the processes of life.[28] There was also a parallel change in the idea of life. The organic was separated from the inorganic by the discovery of the cell. Life was neither simple nor available. It was a process.[29]

CHAPTER THREE

WHAT LANGUAGES TELL OF THE EARLY HISTORY

OF THE RELIGIONS OF EUROPE

Friedrich Max Müller:
A Philologist Becomes a Scholar of Religion

IN THE nineteenth century, a growing audience followed the disclosure and study of mysterious texts of past and foreign cultures. The deciphering and translation of new sources was only the beginning. The discoveries still had to be described, classified, and explained. For the moment, they were like foundlings whose origin and history posed riddles. When the enthusiastic Egyptologist Baron Christian Karl Josias von Bunsen, the Prussian ambassador in England, and the Sanskrit scholar Horace Hayman Wilson managed to persuade the East India Company to subsidize a critical edition of the Rig-Veda, he asked the young editor F. Max Müller to publish "chips" from his workshop from time to time. "Your work is not finished when you have brought the ore from the mine; it must be sifted, smelted, refined and coined before it can be of real use, and contribute towards the intellectual food of mankind," Müller later recalled Bunsen saying in 1846.[1]

F. Max Müller (1823–1900) more than fulfilled this wish in his *Chips from a German Workshop* and many other publications. He received a doctorate in Leipzig, studied in Berlin with Franz Bopp, the author of the first comparative grammar of Indo-European languages, and then went to Eugène Burnouf at the Sorbonne in Paris, who put him to work on the edition of the Rig-Veda.[2] To collate the manuscripts, he had to go to England, and from 1848 until his death in 1900 he made his home in Oxford. It was a fateful encounter with Baron Bunsen that allowed him to remain and work in England, as Müller noted in an evening lecture at the Royal Institution, recorded and later included in a review of Müller's writings by E. B. Tylor. When the young F. Max Müller, who was once again in financial straits, felt obliged to prepare for his departure from England, he applied for a visa at the Prussian embassy in London. By chance, the Prussian ambassador to England, Baron Bunsen, had been told of the young multilingual Orientalist by Alexander von Humboldt and the Oxford Sanskrit scholar H. H. Wilson. Bunsen, who had himself dreamed in his youth of editing the Vedas, invited the young scholar to his office to find out about the state of the work. When he learned of Müller's difficulties, he encouraged him to stay in England until he had completed his collections and promised financial support if necessary.[3] He was as good as his word. He and Wilson managed to get the East India Company to take over the plan and provide financial support. Bunsen's wife saw their meeting as a great event in her husband's life, since the two shared a spiritual affinity and a heartfelt sympathy.[4] In 1854, he was appointed professor for modern European languages at Oxford. He was denied a chair in Indology, which went instead to M. Monier Williams, and was appointed professor of comparative philology in 1868.[5]

It was not only his background as an Indologist that prepared Max Müller to edit the Rig-Veda. His German origin and proximity to the Romantic tradition can be seen in his reevaluation of the sources. Inspired by the Romantics' conception of a genuine prehistory,[6] Müller's interest was aimed completely at the beginnings. Like those who focused on human evolution, he was occupied with the gradual growth of the human spirit. "Language, mythology, religion, nay, even philosophy can now be proved to be the outcome of a natural growth, or development, rather than of intentional efforts, or of individual genius."[7] This was also his conviction. Yet he expected insights into the beginnings of religion from history, and all his interest was focused not on the progress of development, but on its earliest starting point. Although the threads that led from the present to this beginning had become tenuous, that did not keep him from trying to find them. He thought that progress entailed a degeneration of human ability. Study of the beginnings gave hope of a renewal of the original. The overwhelming resonance Müller's public lectures encountered indicates the considerable intellectual interest this plan attracted in England.

Public Lectures

F. Max Müller presented his findings in 1870 in four lectures in London and later published them in German and English as *Introduction to the Science of Religion*—the first work of its kind. A preliminary copy of the lectures appeared in a weekly journal that same year. Since F. Max Müller wanted to treat the subject more completely in a book, the publication dragged out. Publishing the book, which was ready in 1873, was—as he put it—an act of self-defense, since his lectures had been printed in America without his permission. Translations were being prepared in France, Italy, and Germany. This fuss shows not only how much Western scientific nations communicated with each other at that time, but also indicates the broad international interest in a nontheological exploration of religions. E. B. Tylor, Müller's academic colleague in Oxford after 1883 and a keen observer of the English scene, devoted a few clever sentences to the public's growing interest in this subject:

> There is in England at this moment an intellectual interest in religion, a craving for real theological knowledge, such as seldom has been known before, and never has had such opportunity of being satisfied. When an inquirer examines some doctrine with a new light, and declares it to look quite different from what it seemed before, the more educated part of the religious world are becoming less and less satisfied with the simple old plan of drawing their curtains and closing their shutters, and then declaring with an easy conscience that there is no light there.[8]

Müller also used lectures later on to focus publicity on religious studies. Lectures, delivered by prestigious scholars and sponsored by private endowments, were widespread primarily in Anglo-Saxon countries and enjoyed great popularity in England and the United States.[9] The Hibbert Lectures, endowed by the estate of Robert Hibbert, who died in 1849, were famous in this respect. Hibbert had decreed that the interest of his legacy was to be devoted to research on the spread of Christianity in its simplest and most comprehensible form and to the promotion of an independent judgment about religion. Since an unbiased treatment of religion was progressing in Germany and Holland, but had encountered obstacles in England, influential Englishmen (including Müller) proposed to the trustees of the Hibbert estate to use the money for lectures in religious studies by internationally eminent scholars. Thus the findings of independent research would also be known in England. The administrators agreed and prominent scholars of religion were soon delivering the Hibbert Lectures.[10]

The first lectures of this new series were delivered by Müller himself in the spring of 1878: *Lectures on the Origin and Growth of Religion, as Illustrated by the Religions of India*. When they were announced, the audience was too big for the designated hall in Oxford (the chapter house of the abbey). So Müller had to give the lecture twice.[11] A newspaper reported on the event: "No person who had the good fortune to be present at these lectures is likely to forget the extraordinary spectacle."[12] In the edition of her husband's letters, Georgina Müller quoted the closing words of his last lecture. He hoped, Müller said, that someday, the underground field of human religion would become accessible and offer a refuge for those who strove for something better, purer, older, and truer than what they found in the temple, the mosque, the synagogue, and the church. In this quiet crypt, said Müller graphically, believers of all religions were to worship what was most valuable to them. And then he enumerated what that was for a Hindu, a Buddhist, a Moslem, a Jew, and a Christian.[13]

It was only in 1888 that the lectures became milestones in religious studies, when the Gifford Lectures were added. Lord Gifford had left the large sum of £80,000 to finance regular lectures by scholars at the four Scottish universities of Edinburgh, Glasgow, Aberdeen, and St. Andrews.[14] The scholars were to be chosen without any consideration of their personal beliefs. The only criterion was that they were to be outstanding specialists in "natural theology" and were to treat knowledge of God in a strictly scientific way, like astronomy or chemistry. The success of all these attempts to publicize religious studies contributed to the broad resonance of the first world parliament of religions in Chicago in 1893.[15]

Why Languages Create Worldviews

In his first series of lectures in London in 1870, Müller presented the hypothesis that only a linguistic classification of religions guaranteed a reliable basis for scientific inquiry. Müller concentrated on the linguistics of religions to achieve an insight into their early history. In this process, he profited from the turn taken by the investigation of languages since Herder: away from the assumption of a rational theory of language, toward the comparison of languages in order to discover its educational potential. Nothing was left of the old concept of a proto-language except a common human competence to form a picture of the world independent of all external constraints.

Comparative analysis of languages had already proven its value in deciphering texts. It had also shed light on exciting prehistoric connections: that there was an Indo-European family of languages that included such distant members as Greek, Latin, Sanskrit, and English. Müller saw the extremely productive comparative philology as a model for the study of religions, too. The newly discovered texts of the Vedas and the Avesta were the holy texts of current religious communities in India. But his interest focused entirely on the old texts. Not once did Müller travel to India. "My India was not on the surface, but many centuries below it," he explained.[16] Like other religions, in the course of its history, the Indian religion had also moved away from its pure origin and had degenerated.[17] This is why it seemed so urgent for Müller to find a connection with the beginning.

Even before Müller, J. G. Herder and W. von Humboldt had philosophized about languages and had assigned them an active role in the structuring of human relations to reality. In 1824–26, W. von Humboldt advanced the hypothesis that "an authentic worldview [is inherent] in every language."[18] He considered language the organ of thought and thus came close to the views of his contemporary, Hegel. Vis-à-vis the speaker, words were objective; vis-à-vis the objects, they were subjective. Von Humboldt distinguished three aspects in his analysis of language: the sensual impression produced in the observer by an object; the way it was received by the subject; and the effect realized on the hearer by the speech sound. W. von Humboldt had an interactive connection of these three aspects in mind. Speech is principally dialogic. When words are communicated, they make something subjective objective and thus establish a worldview in thought. While weaving a worldview through their use of language, men weave themselves into a web at the same time.[19] This view continued to exercise an effect in nineteenth-century Germany for some time.[20]

Müller's view took on a special intensity in the debate with Darwinism. While Darwin saw no insurmountable boundary between the animal and the human realms, Müller considered language a fortress on the border between the two. Language is the fundamental and definitive barrier that divides the world of animals from the world of humans. "Language is our Rubicon and no animal will dare cross it," he would say.[21] Language ennobles man, lifts him out of the realm of nature, separates him unambiguously from all animals. Thus Müller defied all the encroachments of evolutionism. He countered attempts to derive language from signals as they are known even in the animal kingdom by insisting that language fundamentally and originally expresses conceptions about things and does not simply indicate them.[22] Keep in mind that he translated Kant's *Critique of Pure Reason* into English and deduced from it the right to apply words to experiences.[23] This text had shaped his view of the nature of words. Precisely because language is the vehicle of conceptions of things, he saw it as the most promising path to the early history of the human picture of the world. If we want to know ourselves, we have to decipher our own history. It is a holy book for us, as is nature.[24] To learn this history, we must study languages. For they are an unbroken chain from the beginning of history to the present. They move the immensely remote early human history into an attainable distance and can link contemporary man with his beginnings. "Language is the autobiography of the human mind," remarked Müller.[25]

Mythology or the Power of Language over Thought

In 1856, Müller explained how such an autobiography could look in an essay titled "Comparative Mythology."[26] He compared words of the Indo-European family of languages with one another and thus reconstructed the common social and natural world of all Aryans before they were divided into separate nations. The names of the gods were also part of this earliest phase of language development and Müller devoted special attention to Greek mythology. England at that time identified itself with ancient Greece, which is difficult for us to imagine, especially since many Greek myths were felt to be offensive, telling of gods who lied, stole, or committed adultery.[27] As Greece was advanced as an ideal, Greek mythology needed explanation. Müller shared this feeling. Only a few scholars had dared to think that the same facts could yield the opposite conclusion, that the Greek view of human nature was different from that of Victorian England and possibly for good reason. For example, J. A. Symonds wrote: "The deities are male and female, not because their names have genders, but because the thinking being, for whom sex is all-important, thinks its own conditions into the world outside it."[28] Such daring interpretations were not Müller's forte. It was important for him to reveal a pure early age of human religiosity that complied with the romantic middle-class intellectual ideal.

In his view, mythical thought had a place between the emergence of languages and the formation of the state.[29] The names of the Indo-European gods came from this stage, and had originally been signs for natural phenomena like sun, dawn, sky, and so on. For Müller, etymology was the way to the genuine origin of human thought, corresponding to the Greek meaning of *etymon* as truth. "There was a time when the etymological meaning of a word represented what really was to the early framers of language the most striking feature of an object, or the most important characteristic of a new conception."[30] In the beginning, words were still a kind of unconscious poetry on the processes of nature, as Herder had thought too.[31] Yet, in the course of their history, men had forgotten the origin of words and abandoned their relationship to sensual reality. Max Müller advanced the thesis that, when we use a word that was first used metaphorically, without a clear understanding of the steps that led from the original to the metaphorical meaning, we are in danger of mythology; when the steps are forgotten and artificial steps are substituted, we get mythology or what he calls a "disease of language."[32] In this respect, Müller followed Friedrich Schleiermacher, who had also dissociated myth from religion. Led astray by language, men began to imagine natural processes as persons with a gender and started telling stories about these persons. This thinking established a prosaic relationship between the observer and nature, destroying poetry at the same time.

The myth of the young Daphne can serve as a prime example. She flees from Apollo who is in love with her. When she is embraced by his shining beams, she dies and turns into a laurel tree. Müller wanted to solve the riddle of this tale by a comparison with the Indian Vedas. The Greek *Daphne* turns out to be a symbol of the dawn that must retreat before the rising sun. That Daphne turns into a laurel tree is no longer puzzling when we know that the word also means fire and the laurel tree burns especially easily. A homonym, a second meaning of the same word, is responsible for the change in the tale.[33] By carving the myth into strata, Müller could expose an older, original stratum under the newer ones. The key to an insight into the early stages of human thought was not the mythical narratives, but rather the root meanings of names. Müller took word comparison and etymology as scientific tools of excavation to expose the pure beginnings of human religion. It was not by accident that he picked up metaphors of archaeology. Imprints of the earliest human view of the world remained preserved in language, even if they were buried under later myths.[34] They remained like fossils in the stream of the creation of myths.[35] The authenticity of these earliest expressions can be seen because they are expressive and poetic, and not yet instrumental and prosaic like the later ones. In early human times, an event like a sunrise was a revelation that produced in the human mind both the feeling of dependence as well as joy.[36] Thus a comparative philology can help tell the oldest histories of religion.

But what yielded the glance under the mythology? Müller saw a universal human ability standing independent next to sensual perception and rational cognition.[37] This ability, which Schleiermacher had already dealt with, allows man to perceive infinity in the finite world. The history of language, which leads us back to the oldest time of man, gives the elements of an "authentic religion." It consists of an intuitive cognition of God, a feeling of dependence, a belief in God's rule of the world, a distinction of good and bad, as well as the hope for a better life.[38] The philologian Müller became a preacher and theologian when he described the authentic religion.

In this context, Müller spoke of mysticism not as exclusively internal, but as something to do with the external sensual world.[39] In this respect, he was a child of "German mysticism." German mystics believed in the revelation of God not only within man, but also outside in nature, in the Holy Scripture, as well as in history. In the nineteenth century, when German intellectuals were surfeited with the rationalism of the Enlightenment, quite a few of them turned to this tradition. Müller's thesis of the infinite in the finite was part of this as were the words of Novalis: "What is outer is what is inner, raised to the condition of a secret—(Perhaps also vice versa)."[40] In the same vein as these intellectuals, Müller placed comparative philology in the service of a philosophy of religion, which was to take over the defense of fantasy and sensibility in an age of prosaic thought, even of increasing atheism.[41] It soon became apparent that, with these philosophical, even theological views, he discredited his work in religious studies and contributed to the decline of his theory of myth.[42]

A Philological Find of the Century

In his very first lecture in 1870, Müller asserted that religions had to be studied in the framework of comparative philology. He divided religions by language family into Aryan and Semitic religions. Both comparisons between these language families as well as their structures would allow insights into early human history. For us, this division is unfortunate. Thus, it is important and helpful that Maurice Olender has studied the prehistory of this pair of terms more closely. For a long time, the term "Aryan" was used predominantly in linguistic philosophy as the equivalent of current terms like "Indo-Germanic" or "Indo-European." The term "Semitic" came from biblical exegesis. The languages of biblical peoples were first called "Aramaic" or "Oriental," until in 1781 A. L. von Schlözer (followed a year later by J. G. Herder) called it "Semitic" following the mention of Shem in Genesis 5:32.[43] Initially, the contrasting pair was not yet loaded with assertions of an alleged superiority of the "Aryans" over the "Semites."

When Müller reached the sources of the two linguistic streams with the help of philology, he began working on the pure origins in a Romantic vein. At the end of the Indo-European stream, he found what he considered "the most important discovery which has been made during the nineteenth century with respect to the ancient history of mankind. . . : Sanskrit DYAUSH-PITAR = Greek ZEUS PATHP = Latin JUPITER = Old Norse TYR. Think what this equation implies! It implies not only that our own ancestors and the ancestors of Homer and Cicero spoke the same language as the people of India . . . but it implies and proves that they all had the same faith, and worshipped for a time the same supreme deity under exactly the same name—a name that meant Heaven-Father."[44] All names referred to one common older form, *dyau pitar*, which translates literally as: "Oh, Father in Heaven." In the Hibbert Lectures on the origin and development of religion, Müller explained that those names are not just names, but are a magic language which the fathers of the Aryan race bring so close to us as if we see them face to face, as they called an invisible essence with the very same name thousands of years before Homer and the poets of the Vedas, the most spiritual and lofty name their dictionary could supply, the name for heaven and light. And "in these words resides the oldest human prayer, the oldest poetry," he added in the German edition.[45] (Keep in mind that Müller's father was the poet who wrote "Winterreise" and the "Die Schöne Müllerin.") Müller's interpretation confirmed that one of the roots of scientific Indology was in the "Romantic critique of the present."[46] The great admiration for the original went hand in hand with an unconcealed rejection of the prosaic and calculating thought of the present.

What did a comparison of the oldest documents of both language families yield? The striking feature of the Aryan religion, "if it had to be characterized by one word, I should venture to call it a worship of *God in Nature*, of God as appearing behind the gorgeous veil of Nature, rather than as hidden behind the veil of the sanctuary of the human heart." "A worship of *God in history*," he called the striking feature of all Semitic religions, on the other hand, "of God as affecting the destinies of individuals and races and nations rather than of God as wielding the powers of nature."[47] Thus from the earliest names of God, Müller ascertained an original stage of religions, in which the divine was "revealed" pure to the human mind. Etymology led to the pure beginning of our worldview as well as our mind.

With these observations, Müller continued the century-old discussion that had involved Herder about whether the Hebrew language was a revelation of God. What is lost, asked Müller, if it is not a revelation of God, but rather of the human mind? "Does language excite admiration less because we know that . . . the invention of words for naming each object was left to man, and was achieved through the working of the human mind?"[48] Müller could hardly repress his satisfaction that language promises information about the human mind. With the discovery of Sanskrit, Europeans became aware of a period of their own existence, which had shaped them but which they could not preserve in their memory. To make this clear, he constructed the hypothetical case: what if the Americans lost their awareness of the origin of their language and literature and had to rediscover the English origin in order to understand their own culture fully?[49] The same was true today of the Europeans with India.

When Müller often spoke emphatically of the Aryans as "our own ancestors," we think we hear a racist tone.[50] Therefore, a precise interpretation of his judgment of the Aryan is essential because racism was rife in his day. One exponent was Joseph Artur de Gobineau. After he recognized—as he wrote in the preface to the four volumes of *L'essai sur l'inégalité des races humaines*—that there were strong and weak races, he observed the strong races to grasp their aptitudes and explore their genealogy. Ultimately, it turned out that all human creativity and greatness originated in one source only: the Aryans. Their name meant "honorable": men who warranted attention and respect and who had simply taken what came to them even if it was not given voluntarily.[51]

A comparison of de Gobineau's observation with Müller's shows the difference clearly. In de Gobineau, the Semitic god, El, is responsible for a corruption of the Aryan god.[52] Müller, on the other hand, never asserted that Semitic views were inferior to Aryan ones and had to be removed from European culture. On the contrary—he maintained that the Semitic conception of god was superior to the Aryan, as seen in his argument with Ernest Renan. Renan wanted to explain the emergence of monotheism among the Jews and Arabs as an instinct of the Semitic race. Müller vigorously contradicted that. The difference was not because of instinct, but rather because of language. The Semitic names of god could protect the original revelation of the infinite more effectively against mythological corruption than the Aryan names of god.[53] Only when the Aryan names were compared with the Semitic was it possible to discover that the Aryans did not deify the natural sky either at first, but had understood it as a place of the revelation of infinity. The Aryan religion could not preserve this beginning. It was only because of the discovery of India that the earliest Indo-European religion was professed again. There is no evidence that Müller called for the expulsion of the Semitic. Rather, *pace* George Steiner, we could posit a thesis of the two roots of European culture. This one wanted to expand the awareness of European culture, but not to Aryanize it. Müller's special emphasis on the Aryans as "our own ancestors" served this purpose.[54]

English Protest Against an Indian Genealogy

According to his own statements, Müller's enthusiasm for India encountered considerably less favor in England than on the continent. "In France, Germany and Italy, even in Denmark, Sweden and Russia, there is a vague charm connected with the name of India.... A scholar who studies Sanskrit in Germany is supposed to be initiated in the deep and dark mysteries of ancient wisdom.... In England a student of Sanskrit is generally considered a bore, and an old Indian

Civil Servant, if he begins to describe the marvels of Elephanta or the Towers of Silence, runs the risk of producing a count-out."[55] It is not surprising that the relations of the Germans and the British to India were very different. German interest in India—if at all—was cultural; while British interests, on the other hand, were blatantly economic and political. In 1875, the jurist Henry Sumner Maine asserted this difference in attitude: "No one can observe the course of modern thought and enquiry on the Continent, and especially Germany, without seeing that India, so far from being regarded as the least attractive of subjects, is rather looked upon as the most exciting, as the freshest, as the fullest of new problems and of the promise of new discoveries."[56]

The objections presented against Müller in England were aimed particularly at his term of "our own ancestors." Müller's claim of a close relationship between Indians, Greeks, and English encountered a stark rejection. John Crawfurd, a former chairman of the Ethnological Society, was outraged that the common language of such different peoples should allow talk of a common race:

> I can by no means, then, agree with a very learned professor of Oxford [Max Müller], that the same blood ran in the veins of the soldiers of Alexander and of Clive [Robert Clive, Baron Clive of Plassey, commander of the British troops in India] as in those of the Hindus whom, at the interval of two-and-twenty ages, they both scattered with the same facility. I am not prepared, like him, to believe that an English jury, unless it were a packed one of learned Orientalists, with the ingenious professor himself for its foreman, would "after examining the hoary documents of language," admit "the claim of a common descent between Hindu, Greek and Teuton," for that would amount to allowing that there was no difference in the faculties of the people that produced Homer and Shakespeare, and those that have produced nothing better than the authors of the Mahabarat and Ramayana; no difference between the home-keeping Hindus, who never made a foreign conquest of any kind, and the nations who discovered, conquered, and peopled a new world.[57]

The image of the process concerning the genuine descent shows how much Müller strained English feelings of superiority and awareness of nobility.

Hellenism versus Hebraism in Cultural Discourse

If we want to know why Müller attached so much importance to the discovery of the Aryan religion, we can get some help from one of his contemporaries, Matthew Arnold, who also lived in Oxford and was friendly with Müller for a while.[58] Arnold had written poetry before he became the most famous critic of English society. He was a sensitive and thoughtful observer of England's meteoric industrialization, lamenting that the English middle class, who advanced modernization, had nothing in mind but gainful employment.[59] As an authority on continental literature, he realized how unsophisticated criticism was in England, while it was the accepted thing in France and Germany. He explained this as the English mania of giving all reasonable ideas a direct practical application. To overcome this provinciality, he tried to publish continental intellectuals like Heinrich Heine in England. And from Heine, who had also drawn a bead on "genuine British narrow-mindedness,"[60] Arnold was only too glad to borrow the term *philistine* to apply it to the English middle class.[61]

In *Culture and Anarchy: An Essay in Political and Social Criticism*, whose modern title is in striking contrast to its publication date of 1869, he judged the provincialism of the puritanical English middle class harshly. That class had failed to add critical reflection to its practical commitment. In this respect, Arnold adopted the pair of terms, *Hebraism and Hellenism*,[62] which Heinrich Heine had also had a hand in shaping and changing.[63] Hebraism and Hellenism stood for two distinct human capacities: to act conscientiously and to think impartially. Only when both are balanced and keep one another in check can one speak of a functioning culture. The culture of the English middle class had lost this balance and sacrificed Hellenism to Hebraism. Interests dominated discernment. Anarchy was the result.

Arnold sought the reasons for preferring the practical over the intellectual in England's religious history. The imbalance of the English middle class was a delayed result of the Puritan rejection of the Renaissance. While the Renaissance helped revive Greek thought, the Puritans preferred their stubborn religious obedience. Puritanism had unilaterally motivated economic success, but this was perverted, because work, which Puritanism itself initially regarded as a curse and only a necessary means to survive, had become a goal in itself through this link. Religion had become a soulless engine. If anyone thought that the children of God proved themselves through works, Arnold recommended a glance at London, an unspeakably disgusting city.[64] Arnold was not content with just diagnosing the situation; but he also demanded favoring a new *Hellenism*, a return to a spontaneous, impartial existence, over *Hebraism*. That was the only way both halves of human life—spontaneous perception and practical behavior—could be reunited. Arnold's thought was an important attempt to make experiences of modernism comprehensible from the history of religion. *Hellenism* and *Hebraism* were historical phenomena that extended into the present and determined the English ethos of modernization. The close link between Puritanism and capitalism that Max Weber revealed fifty years later in his famous essay *The Protestant Ethic and the "Spirit" of Capitalism* had already been denounced as an evil of English culture by Matthew Arnold. The crisis of modern industrial society is also a crisis of religion.

This diagnosis of modern culture also sheds light on Müller's writings on the history of religion. That is, an implicit reason for Müller's description of the Aryan religion as our forgotten origin was a negative interpretation of modern economic culture. But it was no longer Hellenism that should and could give human life its meaning independent of superficial economic interests, but rather an even earlier stage that was preserved pure only by India. It teaches us that there is more to see in nature than raw material for market products: that is, the revelation of an incomprehensible divinity.

A Result Remaining after the Decline of Müller's Mythology: Two Different Directions of the History of Religions

Müller's religious studies had attracted enormous attention, and Müller completely dominated the debate about myth. This argument was not purely scholarly. "All England" followed it, wrote R. M. Dorson.[65] Yet Müller was not concerned with analyzing the newly discovered finds as systematically as E. B. Tylor did with primitive peoples. His continuing aims for the philosophy of religion were too ambitious. From the 1880s, his work became the object of violent criticism. As Müller became more and more famous, the attacks grew harsher. His explanation of countless myths of the course of the sun became a favorite target of mockery. That it was always the sun was a complaint Müller heard early on and to which he reacted gruffly. "'Always the Sun, and always the Sun,' people exclaim, and yet it is not our fault if the Sun has inspired so many legends and received so many names. And what else do you expect at the bottom of mythology if not the reflection of heaven and earth in the mind and language of man?"[66] In 1870, an ironic interpretation of Müller as a sun hero was circulated. It said that Max Müller was a symbolic name, whose real meaning had been eclipsed by mythological tales. Max was *maximus*, identical with the Sanskrit *maha*; Müller in late High German meant one who crushes grain. Thus, the name meant "The ringleader of the crushers." This meant the sun, especially sunrise.[67] This is an endearing, ironic document of the quarrel over solar mythology. The eclipse of solar mythology, as Dorson called the battle between sun mythologists and the explorers of primitive folklore,[68] corresponded, on the other hand, to the rise of Tylor and his adherents. Müller was to live several more years. But his scientific work had become outdated even in his own lifetime.[69]

One of those responsible for the eclipse of solar mythology was Andrew Lang. In an important critical article, "Mythology," in the *Encyclopedia Britannica* of 1884, he examined Müller's mythology. Lang's discussion conveyed an almost physical sense of the airy and shaky foundations of Müller's big structure. Lang made it clear that Müller had not succeeded in really explaining the irrational and scandalous elements of Greek mythology.[70] This observation was especially devastating. The more Müller eked an authentic religion out of mythology, the more incomprehensible were the mythological embellishments. Lang's remarks led inevitably to the conclusion that the details of the construction Müller presented so eloquently were not well thought out.

Only the find of the century remained unaffected by this criticism. And as the high esteem of Müller's mythology declined, this thesis did not. Rather, it was rescued by a Dutch scholar of religion, Cornelis Petrus Tiele (1830–1902), an expert in ancient pre-Asian religions.[71] In view of his significance for religious studies in the late nineteenth century, Tiele is currently underestimated. On the other hand, in an obituary, Pierre Daniel Chantepie de la Saussaye counted him, along with Müller, as one of the founders of the scientific study of religion (1909). His *Histoire comparée des anciennes religions de l'Egypte et des peuples sémitiques* (Comparative History of the Ancient Religions of Egypt and the Semitic Peoples, 1882) was one of the books of Nietzsche's "ideal library" and one of the most important reference works in religious studies of its time.[72]

Tiele argued with Müller in an article in the same *Encyclopedia Britannica* that included Andrew Lang's damning review. What he wrote under the rubric of *Religions* (1886) led to a completely different judgment. Tiele thought there was a development of religions, and he linked this assumption with the claim that the more independent religions were of language and nationality, the more advanced was their development.[73] What Müller had described as two authentic initial conditions of religion, Tiele saw as the results of two distinct directions of the development of religions. He worked out this view in detail later in his Gifford lectures of 1896.[74] Tiele separated "stages" and "directions" in the history of religions. Natural religions were followed by the stage of ethical religions. From then on, religions took different directions. Indo-Europeans and Semites had formed different conceptions of the relationship between gods and man. Tiele called the former "theanthropic" and the latter "theocratic." In the first case, the differences between gods and man were small; both could even be considered as related. It did not even matter if the gods really did control fate or were subject to it, like the Greek gods. In the second case, the Semitic religions had elevated the deity to absolute ruler and creator of the world. Man could relate to Him only as His creature and slave. In the first case, the shrines of the gods are open to all seekers, and in the second case an unconsecrated person cannot enter on pain of death. From this perspective, Tiele compared the various religions. While the later phenomenology of religion was constrained to allow the differences between religions to be absorbed in a common psychological denominator, quite a different interest was operating in Tiele. He saw equal and competing conceptions ("religious root-ideas or principles") at work in the history of religion of the two major language families. Even where one of the two conceptions is unilaterally preferred and cultivated, the other is never completely absent. In this sense, Müller's "find of the century" outlasted the decline of his interpretation of myths. Recent studies of comparative linguistics and comparative religion indicate that even today his find is still granted a certain value, even though its significance has long since ceased to be as sensational as it was in his own time.[75]

Thanks to Tiele, Müller's find of the century escaped the eclipse of solar mythology. When Tiele embedded the different relations to the world in religious studies, he enriched its evolution with the components of different directions of development. This had a considerable impact on the broader history of research in religion, and it is no accident that we shall often encounter Müller's find of the century when we examine other thinkers, including Max Weber.

CHAPTER FOUR

THE PRESENCE OF THE ORIGINAL RELIGION

IN MODERN CIVILIZATION

The Quarrel over the Alleged Degeneration of Primitive Peoples

IN OXFORD, during the 1860s, when Edward Burnett Tylor (1832–1917) began to study the religions of tribal societies, most of his contemporaries considered such an activity futile. These societies were seen as the late products of a degeneration, not representing an initial situation of history, but rather the remnants of a declined high culture. This had been viewed differently in the eighteenth century, when, influenced by Rousseau and the Romantics, the picture of the "noble savage" had determined the European perception of foreign peoples, whose natural religion corresponded by and large to the requirements set by philosophers for the religion of reason: that it make do with belief in God and in the moral obligations of man.[1] Nevertheless, this positive judgment had subsequently changed. Sailors and merchants from Portugal and France observed that the inhabitants of the West African coast worshiped carved wooden idols they used for magical purposes, and talked of *feitiço* (literally, what has been made) or *fétiche*. In 1760, Charles de Brosses made this into *fetishism*, a form of religion at the inception of all religions.[2] This was one of many signs that the religions of primitive peoples did not fulfill the hopes pinned on them. Thus, in the first half of the nineteenth century, the judgments of the religions of "natural peoples" turned into the opposite. This was not an original, natural religion, but a late dilapidated product, an assumption supported by other observations. The sight of the nomads among the ruins of the ancient Persian empire or the peasants next to the Egyptian pyramids, for example, constituted proof that current tribal cultures were the remains of declined cultures. A theory of degeneration thus arose that denied the religions of non-European tribal societies a paradigmatic value for the initial condition of human culture.

This negative judgment had substantial reasons to buttress it. Christian missionaries too often failed miserably in their efforts to replace tribal religions with Christianity, leading them to conclude with impeccable logic that natives in their natural state were fixed in their views. Statesmen used a similar reason to legitimate the rule of European powers over colonized peoples, arguing that only support from outside could bring improvement to the natives. According to Bishop R. Whately, who later committed this widespread view to paper, "All experience proves that men left (to themselves) in the lowest . . . degree of barbarism never did, and never can, raise themselves, unaided, in a higher civilization."[3] The present-day primitive was the result of a process of change, which was the exact opposite of progress, namely, degeneration. Infuriating experiences in the colonies, superficial observations, and substantial interests hardened into a firm opinion and formed a suggestive whole.[4] An entire phalanx of authorities in government, church, and scholarship was certain that primitives were incapable of developing without help from outside.

While it is difficult for us to comprehend this controversy, it is closer to us than would seem at first glance, since current theories of dependent development are quite similar to the degeneration thesis. They also tend to see the "ostensible" archaic societies of the Third World as the result of a degeneration, albeit under the pressure of the world market. Instead of developing, these societies reverted to a subsistence economy. In nineteenth-century terminology, the archaic societies outside Europe degenerated. Even if a comparison is not altogether appropriate, since the explanation at any one time is quite different, it can help us understand the debates on tribal societies that have recurred since the mid-nineteenth century. Anyone who shakes his head in amazement today that scholars could have been so naïve as to regard non-European peoples as examples of a prehistoric European way of life and thought should remember that this claim had to be asserted and argued strenuously against the view that the culture of non-European peoples was the product of a degeneration. E. B. Tylor regarded that view as profoundly reactionary.

Primacy of Primitive Cultures over High Cultures

When E. B. Tylor began studying religion in tribal societies, a lively debate about the thesis of degeneration was already in progress, conducted both in book reviews and in learned societies like the Ethnology Section of the British Association for the Advancement of Science. Ever since 1867, John Lubbock had repeatedly raised the subject at their meetings and had delivered a distinguished lecture that argued against assuming degeneration and advocated the development of primitive societies.[5] Tylor took his side, asserting in *Primitive Culture* that the arguments for degeneration were based on theology rather than ethnology. The facts were against degeneration: "So far as history is to be our criterion, progression is primary and degradation secondary."[6] Tylor saw tribal societies as the initial situation of human history. Others also joined in the controversy, and in 1871, those included even Charles Darwin. In his famous book *The Descent of Man*, he discussed critically the evidence that all civilised nations are the descendants of barbarians, and stood unreservedly with Lubbock, Tylor, and MacLennan: "To believe that man was aboriginally civilised and then suffered utter degradation in so many regions, is to take a pitiably low view of human nature."[7] A new consensus soon caught on that non-European societies represented the beginning of human history, not some remnant of high culture.

This classification of primitive societies in human history had profound results, but turned the previous hierarchy of cultures on its head. Instead of the old high cultures, primitive societies like those of non-European peoples moved to the beginning of history and provided the measure for the condition of the beginning. Since their own society had become too complex to show its basic structure directly, this skeleton could be perceived by comparing it with less developed societies, as expressed by the term *primitive*.[8] The word was not considered pejorative at that time as it might be today, but expressed the originality of the lifestyle of these peoples against the claim of degeneration. Unlike the previous terms, *wild* or *barbaric*, which indicated deficiencies in comparison with developed civilization, *primitive* granted the peoples thus designated a place at the very beginning of the sequence of structures of human lifestyles, without arguing for any inferiority.

Independent of Tylor, archaeologists had already pointed out that prehistoric finds fundamentally changed the position of old Oriental high cultures in human history. Tylor's view was similar:

> Do these savage views represent *remnant* or *rudiment*? If they represent a remnant of broken down high culture, they are of comparatively little consequence. But . . . if they represent human thought at a comparatively rudimentary stage, they become of immense practical interest. To understand the rude animism of the lower races and to trace it onward as modified from century to century to fit with more advanced intelligence, is indispensable to the full comprehension of not only the historical but the actual position of philosophy and theology.[9]

For Tylor, the cognitive value of all ethnological information depended on whether primitive societies represented the beginnings of human culture. What Indian high culture was for F. M. Müller, tribal societies were for him.

E. B. Tylor's Road to Oxford

When Tylor was appointed to Oxford in 1883, he happened to be teaching in the same city as Müller. Although both had pursued similar scholarly goals, there was hardly any personal contact between them. Even before he came to Oxford, Tylor had read works by Müller, as indicated by his reviews of Müller's *Chips from a German Workshop* and *Lectures on the Science of Language*. In *Primitive Culture*, he argued repeatedly with Müller's interpretation of myths[10] and adopted his thesis of the Indo-European god of heaven.[11] Tylor's hopes for the discovery that primitive cultures represented the pure initial situation were just as high as Müller's. And religion and philosophy were high on his list, too. Two-thirds of *Primitive Culture* deals with religion. Many of his contemporaries must have disliked his notion that the religions of the colonized peoples they were striving to convert to Christianity were valuable evidence of an original natural religion of mankind. Müller had encountered similar resistance, as did Tylor's rejection of high church theology. Like Hume, Tylor thought religion emerged from human thoughts and feelings without the involvement of revelation.[12]

Tylor was self-educated, like the scholars of the caves mentioned earlier. He came from a wealthy Quaker family, but his health prevented him from taking over the family business. He occasionally revealed his religious affiliation, as in his review of Müller's *Chips*. Müller studied the religion of the heathens sympathetically and saw the institutionalization of religion as a decline to be counteracted only by a continuous reformation. The old Quakers, Tylor commented, had known that belief in God's goodness was not limited to a race or sect.[13] In 1855, he had traveled to Mexico, where he chanced to meet the archaeologist H. Christy and accompanied him. His first book was the fruit of this trip: *Anahuac: or Mexico and the Mexicans, Ancient and Modern* (1861). This was followed in 1865 by *Researches into the Early History of Mankind and the Development of Civilization*, which appeared in a German translation a year later. Six years later, in 1871, *Primitive Culture: Researches into the Development of Mythology, Philosophy, Art, and Custom* appeared in London. A German translation was published two years later and was closely studied and analyzed by German scholars like Erwin Rohde. In 1883, Tylor became the keeper of the Pitt-Rivers Museum in Oxford and was appointed reader in anthropology a year later, then waiting twelve years to be promoted to professor. Throughout the years, Tylor was a conscientious teacher, even though few students attended his lectures. Robert R. Marett, one of Tylor's younger colleagues who would later take his place and was to be just as important for religious studies, passed on the malicious gossip that someone once happened to pass by the lecture hall and heard Tylor say: "And so, my dear Anna, we observe. . . ."[14] Anna was Tylor's wife.

The Comparison of Civilized and Primitive Societies

To produce proof that modern culture developed from a primitive one, Tylor used two fields simultaneously that today seem to have little or nothing to do with one another: the culture of primitive tribal societies and superstitions in modern societies. He saw them as closely connected, which becomes comprehensible through a brief look at the comparative method. Following an established pattern, Tylor assumed three progressive stages of social organization: the savage (hunters and gatherers), the barbaric (livestock breeders and farmers), and the civilized.[15] If the European present is taken as the objective of development—as Tylor did—not all nations are equally advanced. Nations outside Europe are at even earlier stages and serve as evidence for the early history of civilized nations. The metaphor of childhood, which Müller had already used, also surfaces in Tylor. Its point was the assumption—which Herder had made—that man is more than he knows about himself. As small children, we thought in ideas we no longer used later on and so they were lost. A concept of the unconscious emerged around these facts in the mid-nineteenth century. "What was formerly conscious has thus become unconscious, but this unconscious is the basis of our present consciousness," claimed Carl Gustav Carus in 1846.[16]

To obtain information about this lost history, Tylor took advantage of the comparative method that had been used so successfully in linguistics, comparative anatomy, and jurisprudence.[17] Its basic premise was formulated concisely by the jurist John F. MacLennan: "In the sciences of law and society, old means not old in chronology, but in the structure: that is most archaic which lies nearest to the beginning of human progress considered as a development, and that is most modern which is farthest removed from the beginning."[18]

To prove that civilized peoples had also once been barbarians, Tylor concentrated his investigations on remnants of previous stages at a time when folklorists were wandering all over Europe, recording customs, tales, and myths. Europe recovered its ancient history. The fundamental nature of survivals for Tylor's cultural reconstruction is indicated by his methodical considerations in *Primitive Culture*. The chapter "The Science of Culture" is followed by "The Development of Culture," and then "Survival in Culture." Here is his definition of survival: "These are processes, customs, opinions, and so forth, which have been carried on by force of habit into a new state of society different from that in which they had their original home."[19]

What explained the permanence of such survivals—aside from the succinct reference to "the force of habit"—remained obscure. The fact is what counts, and contributes per se to the knowledge of our own civilization. But it does show that progress in civilization entails a loss of elementary human culture. This destruction proceeds almost unnoticed, but an investigation of the remains of savage and barbarian behavior and thought in our midst reveals that they are still here. We must only learn to decipher them correctly. "The European may find among the Greenlanders or Maoris many a trait for reconstructing the picture of his own primitive ancestors."[20] Survivals are the milestones that all societies, even ours, have to pass on the way to civilization, and it is only when they are proved that a historical sequence emerges from the types of human organizations. But this proof brings more than just a confirmation of development. It also shows what elements of contemporary culture have archaic origins and are thus valuable evidence of the basic structure of human culture.

This proof of development was so important to Tylor because he did not assume a regular progress. Observation of a survival is necessary to discover whether a society has in fact gone through a sequence of stages. His view is "statistic" rather than "statutory." Only in a large number of cases does progress occur, but not in all cases. Typically, Tylor was in the tradition of induction. Only observed cases could lead to general rules. This peculiarity of his thesis of development shows that, despite a preference for independent developments (especially of inventions), he had no trouble accepting the existence of diffusion or degeneration; rather, he simply relegated the theory of degeneration to second place, but did not exile it.[21] This peculiarity of his thesis of development also has a quite different effect: since progress is not a law, mankind progressing toward civilization might still learn from its past.

When Civilization and Culture Are Separated

Tylor's unpublished works indicate that he initially wanted to call his book *Early Civilisation*, and changed the title to *Primitive Culture* shortly before it went to press.[22] Since Tylor uses civilization and culture almost synonymously from the very first sentence of his book, the importance of this change should not be overestimated. Nevertheless, the definition emphasizes the element of subjective (cognitive, aesthetic, and normative) capacities.[23] Presumably, for Tylor, culture had more to do with the subjective capacities of men than with the distinct stages of social and economic organization. Thus, the difference in meaning between the terms *civilization* and *culture* may have determined a change of title at the last minute. That is, Tylor repeatedly indicated that social organization and culture did not proceed at the same pace.[24] While social progress takes the line of savagery-barbarism-civilization, the tendency of culture needs only to be similar,[25] and can even consist of a step backward. In history, the paths of socially acquired knowledge and individually embedded morality have repeatedly split. For example, Christianity filled human awareness with duty, holiness, and love; yet, in light of the knowledge collected so far, it has fallen behind.[26]

Tylor may have had a "German" notion of culture in mind. And even though he was familiar with W. von Humboldt's works, Tylor was certainly referring to Matthew Arnold, who—as demonstrated above—also insisted on a difference between cognition and practical behavior.[27] Matthew Arnold's essays are an important document to show that, even in England, the terms *culture* and *civilization* did not simply coincide, but were deliberately distinguished. The independence of cognition from the practical requirements of the control of nature made time lags between culture and civilization possible and beneficial. Müller had assumed this view of culture, too. Finding it again in Tylor shows how interested early research in religion was in investigating and representing religion as independent of the level of social and economic organization.

It may be astonishing that a hardboiled advocate of evolution, as Tylor was generally considered, should be interested in such time lags. In this respect, however, we must revise our judgments. In an admirable study, *Evolution and Society: A Study in Victorian Social Theory*, J. W. Burrow tried to explain why evolution was so attractive in the last half of the nineteenth century. The interpretation he proposes also sheds some light on our problem because it contradicts the widespread opinion that nineteenth-century evolution was a conviction of a regular progress. Such a belief was held by eighteenth-century Enlightenment thinkers. But in the second half of the nineteenth century, after the intermezzo of *degeneration* and *polygenesis*, when anthropology had returned to a belief in progress, this was no longer clear. In the meantime, many intellectuals realized that irrationality in its greatest variety was also part of human history. The turn to survivals hints at a doubt about the omnipotence of reason:[28] "The theory of

'Survivals' encouraged men to see parallels between primitive and civilized practices, but it drew the sting and the stimulus from the comparison by regarding the former as relics, aliens from another era."[29]

People were aware of the power of the nonrational, which had already been introduced by theories of degeneration and polygenesis. Those who did not want to follow those theories found Tylor's conception of social evolution interesting, since it offered another solution for the same doubt. On the one hand, it maintained the idea of *one* human nature. (In this context, note that Tylor did not assume any change of human nature in the course of development, as did H. Spencer, who established a link between biological and cultural progress.)[30] On the other hand, Tylor's theory of development offered room for the irrational in its most variegated forms, but maintained distinctions in cognitive, aesthetic, and moral respects between men, times, and peoples, without challenging the principle of human equality.

The Necessary Revision of Bourgeois Judgments about Primitive Religion

Tylor's books analyzed all previous anthropological information comprehensively and critically with information from various sources: ancient historians, Spanish chronicles, reports of missionaries and travelers, and others.[31] In his day, analysis of these sources was still rife with pure fantasy, so Tylor undertook to combine work on the sources with methodical rules. As far as possible, every report was to be checked against a second, independent one, before it was used.[32] According to Robert H. Lowie, "It is impossible to exaggerate Tylor's services in separating the dross from the gold."[33]

In *Primitive Culture*, Tylor reconstructed early societies from numerous reports of human behavior and views. He wanted to do the same as Müller, who had successfully fought prejudice against Indian religions. Compared with Indian religions, the savages came off badly. But that was precisely why he considered it so urgent to understand savage religions.[34] He collected and edited reports that had been ignored and scorned by the smug bourgeois of Europe. Tylor never forgot this circumstance. The importance he attached to this point of view was expressed in an 1866 article in the *Fortnightly Review*, a journal of popular science. There Tylor outlined for the first time the essential features of the religion he had discovered, *The Religion of the Savages*, explaining to the reader how urgent it was to revise his prejudices. He made his point with a frightening story drawn from ped-agogy. A few years earlier, he had read in a pedagogical magazine about how teachers were to educate children to allocate their sympa-thies correctly. They were to be told the tale of the broomstick that had inadvertently been left outside the house on Christmas Eve and had to stand out in the cold watching the celebration inside in the warmth. If the children began empathizing with the poor broomstick, the teacher was to yell at them: "You stupid children, don't you see that this is about a dead stick of wood?" Tylor found this story dis-gustingly typical of the English philistine of his day who had nothing in his head but money, position, and comfort. Everything else was outside his limited horizon.[35] We have already encountered the phi-listine connection with Arnold's cultural criticism. Like Arnold and Müller, Tylor was also convinced that progressive civilization pro-duced a bigoted bourgeois culture.

His description of foreign cultures repeatedly shows this perspec-tive. One example will suffice. Tylor noted that progress out of bar-barism frequently left behind one quality of barbaric life that modern man could only regret: "The Creek Indians, asked concerning their religion, replied that where agreement was not to be had, it was best to 'let every man paddle his canoe his own way': and after long ages of theological strife and persecution, the modern world seems coming to think these savages not far wrong."[36]

Similar phrases often appear in Tylor's description, and reflect the meaning of anthropological facts for progressive civilized European culture. Tylor applies the same point of view here that he took in his criticism of the philistines. Religion in lower races has become the victim of narrow-mindedness in civilized cultures. The primitives who, "like children," ascribe life to dead objects presuppose a concept of a person that does not come initially from the fact of human will, but rather from two other phenomena: breath and the appearance of people in dreams. They used animism to explain natural phenomena. Only when we assumed these explanations among them could we understand their burial rites and sacrifices. Since none of the initial assumptions of these rituals can be recognized anymore in later stages of social development, we can understand them only if we restore them in this mode of thought. This applies also to mythical tales, which Müller had wanted to explain with his "disease of lan-guage." Tylor's rearrangement of the sequence of primitive cultures and high cultures also affected the interpretation of myths. What Mül-ler had considered a late manifestation, Tylor saw as the basic princi-ple of mythology: the anthropomorphic view. "The simple anthro-pomorphic view, as it seems to me, is itself the fundamental principle of mythology . . . language only needs to accompany and express it. It is only in a further advanced stage that the celebrated definition of mythology as a 'disease of language' need be brought into play, when myths come to be built upon mere names."[37]

Tylor proposed a new term for this worldview. He rejected the established term, *fetishism*,[38] which was connected with the judgment of tribal religions as irrational. Fetishes belonged in the realm of witchcraft and were not a genuine part of religion. Tylor introduced the term *animism*, which fit the worldview of primitive cultures better than Müller's theory of myths. Incidentally, forty years later in 1899, Tylor's *animism* encountered a basically similar argument when R. R. Marett indicated that, concerning animism, an experience of power preceded this interpretation both logically and historically. The restless search for the sources of human culture replaced Müller's *comparative mythology* with Tylor's *animism*, until that in turn had to make way for *pre-animism*.

The Concept of the Soul as Ally against Materialism

Tylor characterized animism alternatively as religion, crude philosophy, or savage theology. All three are intertwined in his thought and are three sides of one and the same principle. In Tylor's thought, the concept of the soul is a constant in human culture. It was created by man derived from inductive observations of nature. All primitive explanation is rooted in the concept of *soul*. Ideas of the *soul* must have explained such phenomena as dreams, illness, and death: the "conception of the Human Soul is a crude but reasonable inference by primitive man from obvious phenomena."[39] First, *soul* indicated the invigorating principle in man, and was then extended to animals and objects, and ultimately developed into the idea of spirits and gods. Spirits had taken over the task of explaining phenomena of external nature.[40] The idea of God resulted from that.[41] The idea that religious development proceeded continuously and produced soul, spirit, and god all in a row was soon challenged, and with good reason.[42] Basically, Tylor himself could have known that the idea of God did not develop from the concept of the soul. Yet, considered historiographically, such biases are instructive, for they reveal something about a scientist's vital intellectual interests. It was clearly very important to Tylor to prove the concept of the soul as the basic universal principle of human cognition in all its ramifications, from science to theology.

Tylor's view of the soul was still linked to Enlightenment philosophy, but this observation should not obscure the fact that he too saw the soul as the vehicle of emotion and fantasy. And this is the key to understanding why Tylor combined the process of understanding primitive culture with self-knowledge. In addition, however, the soul was also an organ of scientific cognition. He saw the soul as the intellectual concept of a philosophy of nature that interpreted sensual phenomena as expressions of will of a spiritual essence. As natural phenomena became known gradually and increasingly as effects of laws, one area after another was removed from animism and subordinated to natural law. Nevertheless, animism would never be completely dispensable.

Close as Tylor's animistic explanation of the world and life was to science, it was separate from it—and not at peace. A militant scientific theory had waged war with the theory of animation from time immemorial.[43] From the earliest savage philosophy through contemporary theology, despite all changes in its essence, the concept of the human soul has moved unaltered through human history. It connected savage fetish worshipers with civilized Christians and was the vehicle of individual personal existence. Nevertheless, it had powerful opponents: "The divisions which have separated the great religions of the world into tolerant and hostile sects are for the most part superficial in comparison with the deepest of all schisms, that which divides Animism from Materialism."[44]

Tylor wrote in England at a time when diametrically opposed expectations concerning the achievement of science clashed with one another. Between 1850 and 1900, there were scientists who wanted to explain everything, including the human mind, by natural law. Turner called this trend Victorian scientific naturalism. It was contested often by the Church. But it would be wrong to see this as a struggle between science and the Church. It was rather a struggle between the advocates and the opponents of a total scientific claim.[45] The opponents of such an excessive claim vigorously challenged the assertion that, like everything else, the human mind was also under the control of natural laws.[46] This is what Tylor meant when he spoke of materialism.

Tylor's position in this quarrel was strangely ambivalent. With scrupulous scientific methods, he derived a concept of the soul as a constant element from the history of peoples. In primitive cultures, it was a way to explain natural phenomenon and thus did not require any additional explanation itself.[47] At this early stage of mankind, the concept of the soul and scientific explanations are the same thing. Only in the course of time did a rational theory remove objects from animism and subordinated them to natural laws.[48] Thus, as civilization progresses, the territory claimed by animism gradually became smaller and finally shrank to the principle of human subjectivity. But this could not be reduced any further and remains valid in modern culture.

The discovery of the initial condition of culture shed a brand-new light on the debate about the scope of scientific explanations. If the prehistory of scientific cognition is in the theory of the soul, this is confirmation of the notion that human concepts are formed independent of the external reality they are to explain. This prehistory runs counter to the claim that human intellectual activity can be ascribed to natural law. Tylor's interpretation of the structural nucleus of human culture thus supports his criticism of the narrow-mindedness of the contemporary bourgeoisie.

Irrationality in Civilized Society

In Tylor's view, the study of early societies served to gain self-knowledge of our own modern civilization. As he demonstrated pure remnants of older stages in this civilization, he created a picture of it characterized by internal complexity. In 1869, in a lecture "On the Survival of Savage Thought in Modern Civilization," he presented this new picture. In Europe, in three out of four cases, superstition was an instance of survival.[49] In a contribution to the discussion appended to another lecture on "The Philosophy of Religion among the Lower Races of Mankind," he explained that "religions of savage races afford explanations of otherwise obscure beliefs and rites of the civilized world, and not *vice versa*; so that it is rather in the doctrines of low tribes than among high nations that original theological conditions are to be sought."[50] Tylor's survivals were more like fertile shoots than dead fossils. Later criticism of Tylor generally ignored this function. The modern civilized world bears its beginning in itself twice: in the developed structure of culture and in the customs outdated by development. What to the enlightened thinkers had become incomprehensible in modern society could be classified with ethnological parallels. Tylor did not spare examples here either. If we wanted to know why we toss a coin, we should study the oracle practices of primitive peoples, which teach us that it is supernatural beings who turn coins onto the right side as they fall.[51] If it is bad luck to get out of bed with your left leg first, it is assumed that right and left indicate not only directions, but also represent good and bad.

Tylor generally counted on the possibility that survivals could attain renewed vitality. Animism can win back areas it lost to the opponent "Materialism," as happened in the case of witchcraft in Europe. In this perspective, Tylor was especially interested in spiritualism, which was very popular in the 1870s in England, and then on the continent. Animism survived in the form of survivals in popular beliefs and was resurrected in the great modern movement of spiritualism.[52] Perhaps it was this phenomenon that led Tylor to grant belief in the soul such a paramount place in human history. In any case, Tylor found the spiritualism of his time worthy of closer investigation and studied it for a few months in London in 1872. He collected his observations in a journal published in 1971 by G. W. Stocking: "In November 1872, I went up to London to look into the alleged manifestations. My previous connexion with the subject had been mostly by way of tracing its ethnology, & I had commented somewhat severely on the absurdities shown by examining the published evidence." Tylor did not give up this critical position. But his last entry of November 28 does show a slight wavering of his judgment, indicating a dilemma extremely characteristic of his position:

> What I have seen & heard fails to convince me that there is a genuine residue. It all might have been legerdemain, & was so in great measure, except that legerté is too complimentary for the clumsiness of many of the obvious imposters [sic]. The weight of the argument lies in testimony of other witnesses, such as Sergeant Cox declaring he has seen a table rise in the air. . . . My judgment is in abeyance. I admit a prima facie case on evidence, & will not deny that there may be a psychic force causing raps, movements, levitations, etc. But it has not proved itself by evidence of my senses, and I distinctly think the case weaker than written documents led me to think.[53]

The ethnography of European remnants produced a new interpretation of his own civilized society. Comparison with primitive cultures made it possible to know and describe the internal complexity of this society. Through comparison with primitive cultures, irrational elements in modern society became comprehensible. And in the process, the picture of both changed. Tribal cultures became more philosophic. Animism emerged as a kind of philosophy of nature that explained everyday phenomena like dreams, illness, death, or misfortune. On the other hand, the picture of modern societies became more contradictory and colorful since primitive views and behaviors existed in them.

Animism in Progressive Civilization

The Survival metaphor was a double-edged sword. While Tylor trained his eyes on the irrational elements of modern culture and made them comprehensible through the history of religion, he also contributed to the recognition of irrational beliefs and behaviors as part of modern culture. Seen in this perspective, evolution has preserved something of the Romantic perspective[54] and has borne the seed of the recognition of a cultural pluralism.[55] Since the original context of the nonrational is reproduced in our own society, an outdated culture reemerged in civilized society. Lest this become a dangerous superstition, it must be destroyed—as Tylor explained in the last sentence of *Primitive Culture*. Science has the mission of reforming religion.

Other early scholars of religion in the nineteenth century shared the view that previous forms of life still existed in modern society, but they did not all speak of survivals. Scholars had realized long before, that Johann Jakob Bachofen in his famous "matriarchy" in 1861 had not interpreted the progression from matriarchy to patriarchy dialectically. Matriarchy was not kept and preserved in patriarchy, but had been only superficially subjugated to it. Matriarchy expressed the permanent awareness that legal relations between human beings could not be shaped exclusively in abstract principles remote from nature. In matriarchal culture, "Nature puts the law on her lap." Hence Bachofen could see it as a form of thought that had not yet lost its right to exist.[56] F. M. Müller meant something similar when he claimed that, in the history of languages, we became aware of a period of our own lives that we could not have preserved in our memory, but which nevertheless had shaped us. Europeans could be compared hypothetically with Americans forgetting the origin of their language and literature, and having to rediscover the English origin of their tradition to achieve a new historical dimension of their awareness. Comparison with childhood had been a means for Müller to ascribe to us what is past and what is foreign to us.[57]

These and similar metaphors were used by scholars of religion at that time to determine the place of the newly discovered religions in modern society. I shall abstain from presenting all of them here, but their function should be clear: instead of a harmonious and unbroken progress from primitive to modern civilization, they express the presence of the beginning in modern civilization. If man does not simply submit to civilization, but would like to know pure information about himself, he was to glance in the mirror of tribal culture.

CHAPTER FIVE

ON THE ORIGIN OF ALL SOCIAL OBLIGATIONS:

THE RITUAL OF SACRIFICE

NEITHER F. M. Müller nor E. B. Tylor had paid much attention to the establishment of religions in society. William Robertson Smith was the first to do that, thus marking the start of a new stage in the study of the history of religions. Given Müller's claim that the Semitic religions cultivated obedience to the demanding God the Creator and upheld ethics, it is no accident that this change in the study of religion was carried out by a Semitist and Bible scholar. Robertson Smith exercised considerable acuity to find a way to ascertain information on the assumed formation of society from ancient biblical and pagan sources. Henceforth, the history of religions was to be a source of completely unexpected insights into the emergence and function of elementary social structures.

William Robertson Smith (1846–94) came from Aberdeenshire, Scotland, and was tutored privately at home by his father, a man of broad education. Smith was fifteen years old when he began attending university in Aberdeen, along with his brother George. Since the parents did not think the boys could keep house for themselves, they sent their older sister Mary Jane along. But the shadow of death lay over the lives of the three children in Aberdeen. All were afflicted with tuberculosis. First the sister died, then George fell gravely ill. He took his examinations on his sickbed, and died three weeks later in 1865. W. Robertson Smith died of the same disease twenty years later at the age of forty-eight.

After the horrible time in Aberdeen, from 1866 on, Robertson Smith studied mathematics and Bible in Edinburgh, where another sister kept house for him. In Edinburgh, he met the attorney John F. Mac-Lennan, one of the leaders of the incipient British social anthropology. Both frequented the same club, the Edinburgh Evening Club.[1] But Robertson Smith did not stay in the city for long; he was drawn to travel abroad. Languages were no obstacle—indeed, he became legendary for his linguistic proficiency. He knew fluent Arabic, wrote excellent Latin, knew Dutch, French, German, Greek, and Hebrew. In 1868 he attended the University of Bonn, and in 1869 he went to Göttingen, where he devoted himself to Arabic.

Revolutionary Results of Wellhausen's Bible Criticism:
First the Prophets, then the Law

In Göttingen, the Scotsman, eager for knowledge, met Julius Well-hausen, his senior by only two years. This encounter was to leave a permanent mark on Smith and was decisive for his academic career. Like Robertson Smith, Wellhausen had studied Arabic and the Old Testament. He had just become an outside lecturer and was waiting for his first appointment, which soon took him to Greifswald in 1872. What Wellhausen—and Abraham Kuenen (1828–91)—claimed about the emergence of the Bible fascinated the young Scotsman very much, and he soon combined it with the comparative ethnology he had brought from Edinburgh's intellectual circles.

Julius Wellhausen was the first to realize the subversive effect on understanding the history of ancient Judaism if Karl Heinrich Graf's assumption were correct that the canonic sequence of the Old Testament books did not correspond with their chronological emergence. The pivot and crux of the argument was the fifth book of Moses, Deuteronomy, which was in all probability the same as the book found in 621 B.C.E. in the Temple of Jerusalem, presented to King Josiah (2 Kings 22ff.). King Josiah must have been horrified to read there that Moses had ordered that the God of Israel was to be worshiped ritualistically on Mount Zion in Jerusalem, the chosen place, and nowhere else. If the nation were to neglect this and worship the Canaanite gods of the country, it would have to reckon with God's wrath. Josiah also became aware that the nation of Israel had broken the covenant and ignored some of God's laws to protect their impoverished Jewish brothers from violence and slavery. Understanding that he and the nation had constantly violated the demands God had revealed through His prophet Moses, Josiah immediately centralized the Israelite ritual. He regarded Israel's disobedience a plausible reason for the decline of the Northern Kingdom, and for the collapse that was now threatening his own kingdom. God's rage was aroused against His nation.

Discoveries of books are often documented in the history of ancient religions, and are usually forgeries to advertise beliefs or to reform ritual.[2] This was Wellhausen's interpretation as well. Certain circles in ancient Judaism had been behind the program of Deuteronomy. After the destruction of the southern state, too, which Josiah could no longer stop, and the return of many Jews from exile in Babylon in the fifth and sixth centuries, Deuteronomy, which had renewed and codified the previous older prophetic message, became the basis of Judaism. Only now were Moses' priestly laws recognizing Jerusalem as the sole legitimate shrine inserted and codified in the biblical text. What seemed to be especially old were in fact some of the newest parts of the Old Testament.

From this solid point in the history of biblical sources, Wellhausen made a brand-new reconstruction of the history of ancient Judaism: first came the prophets and then the Law. The historian Wellhausen did not want to remain with a dismantling of the literary works in sources. Criticism, he argued, "must aim further at bringing the different writings when thus arranged into relation with each other, must seek to render them intelligible as phases of a living process, and thus to make it possible to trace a graduated development of the tradition."[3] At the same time, the term *development* should not be misunderstood in the sense of evolution. Wellhausen's work was dominated by German historicism, and he described the historical phases with constant reference to the history of a nation, in this case, the Jewish nation.[4] At first, a type of religion prevailed in Israel that was similar to other ancient pagan religions. Yahweh was not worshiped exclusively. This changed only with the appearance of the prophets. When the Northern Kingdom and then the Southern Kingdom were threatened with military defeat, the prophets became aware of the awful seriousness of Yahweh's justice, and berated the Nation of Israel for ignominiously abandoning the Covenant with God and worshiping other gods. With this message, they destroyed the illusion that God was unconditionally on the side of His nation. Deuteronomy finally canonized this view. Israel's entire history was shaped by a permanent disloyalty to its God and Lord, the cause of the curse that had befallen the nation. Deuteronomy thus justified a concentration of all religious activities in Jerusalem and the ritual there.

With a historical and critical analysis of the biblical sources, Wellhausen derived a religion from preexilic Judaism that was fundamentally different from postexilic Judaism. It was dominated by prophecy and not the law, ethics and not the Temple ritual. A few decades later, when Max Weber gave prophecy a key role in the history of western religion, he assumed Wellhausen's view of history that prophecy was the core of the religion of ancient Israel. In comparison, the priestly Temple ritual was a dead habit.

These concise hints are enough to indicate the revolutionary consequences Bible criticism must have had for understanding the history of ancient Judaism. In his *Geschichte Israels* (History of Ancient Israel) of 1878, J. Wellhausen derived them mercilessly and did not flinch from provocative expressions. Moses was the author of the Mosaic constitution, just as our Lord Jesus Christ was the founder of the

Lower Hessian church regime.[5] Representatives of the church and orthodox thinkers found these and other statements, indeed the whole view, outrageously offensive. The more approval critical biblical scholarship encountered even among Christians, the more violent were the controversies in the religious communities. In the United States a few decades later, they led to the separation of a fundamentalist camp, which vehemently turned against this kind of criticism of the biblical tradition. Wellhausen foresaw the land mine inherent in his discovery, and preferred to give up his professorship in Old Testament at Greifswald. In 1882, he moved to Halle to a chair in Semitic Languages, a process that seems like the harmonic counterpart to the dramatic events his classmate and student Robertson Smith faced in Scotland. Wellhausen could get out of the way of an argument,[6] but Robertson Smith was forced to confront it. Wellhausen's reflection on his discovery, however, shows clearly that his historical discoveries complied with a bourgeois Protestant prejudice against the Jewish Law, and thus not only encountered rejection, but could also count on approval, outside the narrow church walls, in any case.*

The Heresy Trial against William Robertson Smith

In Scotland, a critical theological investigation of biblical texts was even less compatible with an ecclesiastical teaching position than in Germany. In a notorious heresy trial in 1881, William Robertson Smith was dismissed from his position as professor of Hebrew and Old Testament in Aberdeen. The same church that had appointed him eleven years before, at the age of twenty-four, to the Free Church Divinity

---

*"In my early student days I was attracted by the stories of Saul and David, Ahab and Elijah; the discourses of Amos and Isaiah laid strong hold on me, and I read myself well into the prophetic and historical books of the Old Testament. Thanks to such aids as were accessible to me, I even considered that I understood them tolerably, but at the same time was troubled by a bad conscience, as if I were beginning with the roof instead of the foundation; for I had no thorough acquaintance with the Law, of which I was accustomed to be told that it was the basis and postulate of the whole literature. At last I took courage and made my way through Exodus, Leviticus, Numbers. . . . But it was in vain that I looked for the light which was to be shed from this source on the historical and prophetical books. On the contrary, my enjoyment of the latter was marred by the Law; it did not bring them any nearer me, but intruded itself uneasily, like a ghost that makes a noise indeed, but is not visible and really effects nothing. . . . At last, in the course of a casual visit in Göttingen in the summer of 1867, I learned through Ritschl that Karl Heinrich Graf placed the Law later than the Prophets, and, almost without knowing his reasons for the hypothesis, I was prepared to accept it; I readily acknowledged to myself the possibility of understanding Hebrew antiquity without the book of the Torah." Wellhausen 1957, 3–4.

College could no longer tolerate the brilliant young scholar. Tutored at home by his father, Robertson Smith seemed to lack experience of group discussions and the concomitant training in consideration. Instead, he saw merciless controversy as the midwife of truth.[7]

It all began in 1875 with an article by Robertson Smith in the ninth edition of the *Encyclopedia Britannica*. When he was asked to write the article on the Bible, he saw it as a chance to publicize the new discoveries of Bible criticism. An Edinburgh newspaper got hold of a review copy of the brand new volume of the encyclopedia and asked a member of the theology faculty of the University of Edinburgh to review the articles pertaining to theology. When the reviewer read Robertson Smith's article, he was horrified. It said that Deuteronomy was not by Moses! Robertson Smith had written: "Beyond doubt the book is, as already hinted, a prophetic legislative programme; and if the author put his work in the mouth of Moses instead of giving it, with Ezekiel a directly prophetic form, he did so not in pious fraud, but simply because his object was not to give a new law, but to expound and develop Mosaic principles in relation to new needs."[8]

The reviewer was not alone; ecclesiastical leaders were also furious with Robertson Smith and informed him of their disapproval. W. Robertson Smith was thereupon suspended from his position, but only to go on the offensive and elucidate the discoveries of higher biblical criticism. Meanwhile, in 1878 and 1879, he traveled to Egypt, Syria, and Palestine for several months in connection with his ethnological interests, which had never died out ever since he had met J. F. MacLennan in Edinburgh. In June 1880, when he published his article, "Animal Worship and Animal Tribes among the Arabs and in the Old Testament," the break with the ecclesiastical leaders could no longer be healed, since he challenged them with the claim that biblical tribes owned totems like contemporary tribes in Arabia or America. And as with those tribes, totems had regulated membership in clans among biblical tribes, too. Since it was a matrilineal descent, they had practiced exogamy and polyandry: a woman married several men from other tribes! His concluding remarks sound provocative even to our ears, which have become insensitive to religious indecency: "It does not appear that Israel was, by its own wisdom, more fit than any other nation to rise above the lowest level of heathenism."[9]

When the members of the Synod had read the article, they were certain that their professor had to be dismissed. They recorded their motives in a resolution: "First, concerning marriage and the marriage laws in Israel, the views expressed are so gross and so fitted to pollute the moral sentiments of the community that they cannot be considered except within the closed doors of any court of this Church.

Secondly, concerning animal worship in Israel, the views expressed by the Professor are not only contrary to the facts recorded and the statements made in Holy Scripture, but they are gross and sensual— fitted to pollute and debase public sentiment."[10] Robertson Smith responded to this defeat by accepting an invitation to deliver lectures in Glasgow and Edinburgh lucidly summarizing the views of the new biblical criticism.[11] But he had to earn his bread somewhere else. After his sensational dismissal, he became full-time editor of the famous ninth edition of the *Encyclopedia Britannica*. Two years later, in 1883, he was appointed professor of Arabic at Cambridge. Shortly after, at Trinity College, he met the brilliant young student James George Frazer, whom he employed to splendid advantage on the encyclopedia.

Before the Prophets: The Common Sacred Meal

Robertson Smith focused on the Jewish ritual, biblical criticism and seemed to shed a new light on its history. J. Wellhausen had been sure that the centralization of ritual by Josiah raised new questions for the history of ritual in the previous period, and assumed that this ritual was fundamentally different from the Temple ritual established under Josiah. Wellhausen's description conceived of the little bit of information and the few sources relating to it as evidence of an authentic community life:

> In the early days, worship arose out of the midst of ordinary life, and was in most intimate and manifold connection with it. A sacrifice was a meal, a fact showing how remote was the idea of antithesis between spiritual earnestness and secular joyousness.[12] Human life has its root in local environment, and so also had the ancient cultus; in being transplanted from its natural soil it was deprived of its natural nourishment. A separation between it and the daily life was inevitable, and Deuteronomy itself paved the way for this result by permitting profane slaughtering. A man lived in Hebron, but sacrificed in Jerusalem; life and worship fell apart. The consequences which lie dormant in the Deuteronomic law are fully developed in the Priestly Code. . . . The warm pulse of life no longer throbbed to animate it.[13]

With the centralization of the cult under Josiah, the celebration lost its original character: "In the Mosaic theocracy the cult became a pedagogic instrument of discipline. It is estranged from the heart. . . . It no longer has its roots in childlike impulse, it is a dead work, in spite of all the importance attached to it, nay, just because of the anxious conscientiousness with which it was gone about."[14]

Wellhausen not only took the Bible apart critically, he also put the chronologically and factually rearranged sources back together. In the process, a completely different and unprecedented picture of the history of Israel emerged, for which, however, the analysis of sources was only a necessary but not a sufficient condition. It also needed an independent historical idea, which derived its force from the assumption that the ritual had its roots in the life of the local community. When Wellhausen used the word *life* in the quotation cited earlier, he wanted to evoke in his readers the association of original, fresh, spontaneous, and natural. Like Herder and the Romantics, Wellhausen also contrasted the warm pulse of life with ecclesiastical institutions and theological abstractions.[15]

This review of Wellhausen elucidates a great deal about Robertson Smith. Here and there, the Scotsman still used the older geological metaphor of Survival to characterize the chronologically profound dimension of ancient religions. The development of human religious thought was embodied in religious institutions just as the history of the earth's crust is manifested in geological formations, he wrote. Old and new are maintained in layers lying beside and under one another, thus the task of the scholar: "The classification of ritual formations in their proper sequence is the first step towards their explanation, and that explanation itself must take the form, not of a speculative theory, but of a rational life-history."[16] He also followed this method with the Bible. "A just view of the sequence and dates of the several parts of the Pentateuch is essential to the historical study of Hebrew religion."[17] When Robertson Smith spoke of the "process of development," we must not be too quick to think of British evolution. A previous study gives sufficient information about his divergent understanding of development.

> The fundamental principle of the higher criticism lies in the conception of the organic unity of all history. We must not see in history only a medley of petty dramas involving no higher springs of action than the passions and interests of individuals. History is not a stage-play, but the life and life-work of mankind continually unfolding in one great plan. And hence we have no true history where we cannot pierce through the outer shell of tradition into the life of a past age, mirrored in the living record of men who were themselves eyewitnesses and actors in the scenes they describe. Not mere facts, but the inner kernel of true life, is what the critical student delights to find in every genuine monument of antiquity; and the existence of such a kernel is to him the last criterion of historical authenticity.[18]

Like his great Göttingen model, Robertson Smith also saw the organic unity of history in life, and considered historical sources of primary importance as key witnesses to the life of a community. The historian should not be satisfied to dismantle the sources, but should also grasp and describe the life behind the tradition. The older the sources, the greater the probability that he has come upon a new and unadulterated life.

How MacLennan Gave Primitive Religions a Social Basis: Totemism

At the same time that W. Robertson Smith started studying the early stage of Israel, another process was also taking place, which A. Kuper called *The Invention of Primitive Society*. E. B. Tylor's ethnology had indeed determined the layers and developments of culture, but the social and legal principles that gave primitive peoples their internal order still had to be defined. This task was assumed by British jurists who studied the social structure of non-European peoples. John F. MacLennan, whom Robertson Smith had met in Edinburgh, played a substantial part in this pioneering work. Back in 1865, MacLennan had attempted to reconstruct "rude modes of life" on the example of survivals of legal history.[19] And in the days when Robertson Smith occasionally met him at the Club in Edinburgh, MacLennan had published a path-breaking study that forged links between previous analyses of religion and social structures. In this study, "The Worship of Animals and Plants," which appeared in two parts in 1869–70, he introduced a new term: *Totemism*, as a concise indication of the social function of primitive religion. Among the North American Ojibwe Indians, *totem* represented a holy entity assigned to a group of men. MacLennan related this find to the well-known so-called *Fetishism*. This was also a fetish, but with three social functions: The totem was connected with a tribe; it was passed on through the maternal line; and it regulated marriage according to the principle of exogamy.[20] In terms of the social orders pertaining to them, previous discoveries about primitive religions were still more or less in limbo. MacLennan gave primitive religions a place in the social life of primitive peoples, as A. Kuper put it: "Totemism was fetishism but given a sociological anchor in . . . primordial society."[21]

MacLennan's discovery gave primitive religions a social anchor, on the one hand, and opened a whole new perspective for the study of the history of religion, on the other. As for the sources of the history of religion, they could become testimony for the existence and structure of society. Ten years after MacLennan, W. Robertson Smith seized this possibility in his essay "Animal Worship and Animal Tribes among the Arabs and in the Old Testament." In the process of proving totemism among the Arabs and in the Old Testament, Robertson Smith exposed a social practice of Semitic religion that corresponded extensively with other ancient and primitive religions. On the whole, the Semitic religion could become a key witness that religion and social order interact under archaic conditions. Religion was an indispensable source for discovering social structures.

As J. G. Frazer stated in the obituary of his teacher and friend Robertson Smith, MacLennan exercised a profound and long-lasting influence on Robertson Smith.[22] But only after Robertson Smith died did it become clear that that influence was not purely advantageous. MacLennan's hypotheses of totemism and matriarchy are products of an earlier social science that died out under the light of critical scrutiny. A 1910 article by Alexander A. Goldenweiser definitively showed that the totem construct was untenable. Nevertheless, it was MacLennan's totemism that led Robertson Smith to the idea of reconstructing a unique social life of ancient Israel from textual sources. Not all the results achieved declined with totemism.

The Priority of Ritual over Myth

In 1887, the Burnett Fund invited Robertson Smith to deliver a series of three lectures on "The Primitive Religions of the Semitic Peoples in Relation to Other Ancient Religions and to the Spiritual Religion of the Old Testament and Christianity."[23] He was to deliver them in the same city of Aberdeen where he had lost his professorship so spectacularly. He delivered the first series from October 1888 to March 1889. In 1890, Smith became seriously ill. Yet, in 1890 and 1891, he delivered the second and third cycles of lectures, but was prevented from publishing them.[24] Only recently were parts of them found and published by J. Day. Measured by his plans, Robertson Smith's project remained incomplete. All that is completely preserved are *Lectures on the Religion of the Semites* (1889; 2nd ed., 1894) from the first cycle of lectures, which Smith reviewed for a second edition shortly before his death in 1894. Like other classics of religious studies, this one also came from one of the British lectures that contributed so much to spreading the discoveries of the discipline.

The title of the work that emerged from these lectures could identify Robertson Smith as a supporter of the linguistic philosophical tradition in the study of comparative religions. F. Max Müller's comparison of the notion of god in Indo-European and Semitic religions and the concomitant discovery of two diametrically opposed relations between gods and men was well known. In the case of the Semitic peoples, the gods were infinitely remote from men and demanded their unconditional subjection. In the case of the Indo-European peoples, the distances were significantly less: gods and men were even related. Robertson Smith knew the claim "that the conception of a god immanent in nature is Aryan, and that of a transcendental god Semitic." Yet he was not convinced by it: "The former view is quite as characteristic of the Baal worship of the agricultural Semites as of the early faiths of the agricultural Aryans."[25] Unlike the expectations generated by the title of the book, Robertson Smith modified the linguistic philosophical conception. In his view, it had been the prophets who had ensured the sharp schism between God and physical nature. Thus, what Müller had considered a feature of the language, Robertson Smith saw as an achievement of the biblical prophets. He thus rejected Müller's clear distinction between the Aryan and the Semitic religions. While withdrawing the linguistic foundation from Müller's distinction, he opened a different panorama of the early history of religions. The further back one went in their history, the greater was the agreement between the Semitic and the Indo-European religions. Both branches of ancient religions lost their peculiarities when their origin was traced from an even older stage of primitive religion. He concentrated (not limited himself!) on his comparison of the Semitic peoples because he considered the Semites a remarkably homogeneous family of peoples. By comparing the Hebrew religion with the religions of the Arabs and other peoples, he wanted to ascertain the basic inventory of one common religion. Thus, as he stated in the preface, the author began with the institutions of religion, primarily the sacrifice. Once again he was helped by J. Wellhausen, who had published his *Remnants of Arabic Paganism* in 1887, an important preliminary work for him, as Robertson Smith noted gratefully in his preface. But Robertson Smith's concentration on the Semites also corresponded with a certain methodological caution.[26] For at the same time, in the 1890s, the plausibility of evolution was dwindling. In 1896, a theoretical turn of the tide was indicated when a scholar like Franz Boas pointed out that too little attention was paid to the fact that, along with an independent development of culture or religion, there was also dissemination: the monopoly of evolution on the explanation of the history of religion was broken, with diffusion staking its claims.

Let us now consider how Robertson Smith reconstructed the religion of this family of peoples. The Middle Eastern revelation religions—Judaism, Christianity, and Islam—were indeed created by prophets and were thus "positive" religions. Yet they had emerged from an older basis. "No positive religion that has moved men has been able to start with a *tabula rasa*, and express itself as if religion were beginning for the first time; in form, if not in substance, the new system must be in contact all along the line with the older ideas and practices which it finds in possession."[27]

But what was this older basis? Robertson Smith's sharp mind found a methodologically convincing way to determine it. The history of ancient religion showed clearly that religion consisted less of concepts of belief than of institutions and traditions: "So far as myths consist of explanations of ritual their value is altogether secondary, and it may be affirmed with confidence that in almost every case the myth was derived from the ritual, and not the ritual from the myth; for the ritual was fixed and the myth was variable, the ritual was obligatory and faith in the myth was at the discretion of the worshipper."[28]

Semitic Sources for an Archaic Killing Ritual

The priority of rituals above all beliefs dominated Smith's treatment of the sources of the ancient history of religion. In the process he sketched the following picture. Starting with the relationship between gods and their worshipers, Robertson Smith described the link between gods and places as parallel to that of man and these sites. In man's relationship to these sites, the dominant principle was that the sites could not be used for profane purposes, but were holy. The central act that brought gods and man into relationship had been sacrifice, which was originally neither tribute nor gift, but the community of man and god in a meal. Since the slaughtered animal had initially been the totem of the group, it was an unforgivable crime to slaughter it privately. Private slaughter would be tantamount to murder, since the animal was holy and could only be slaughtered and consumed together. Ultimately, the totem was related to all other group members. Sacrifices were thus generally a collective and ritual matter, and the alliance between gods and worshipers was substantiated and renewed in the subsequent ceremonial community meal.

The idea of a system of laws that was absolutely binding on all participants in the ritual must have emerged from the set of norms and concepts Robertson Smith assumed for this holy act. If violations of the system occurred, they had to be punished by expiation, and as happened more often, the originally joyous ceremony became a gloomy means of atoning for wrong and assuaging divine rage. Now only priests, and not laymen, could guarantee the correct implementation. Thus, the sacrifice gradually lost its cheerful character and became a very serious occasion.

Robertson Smith argued especially with Old Testament and Arabic information, inferring from casual indications like 1 Samuel 20:6 and 20:29 that sacrifice had initially been a matter of the clan and had had a cheerful character in Israel, too.[29] To learn more about this, he followed the comparative procedure established by MacLennan that, in the science of law and society, "old" is not to be measured by chronology, but with the yardstick of structure.[30] In such investigations, as Robertson Smith also maintained, one should start with areas where a simpler condition of life and religion prevailed, even if the information came only from a later time. Most reports of the religion of pagan Arabs first came from sources that were much more recent than the Bible. Yet, said Robertson Smith, "In many respects the religion of heathen Arabia, though we have few details concerning it that are not of post-Christian date, exhibits an extremely primitive character, corresponding to the primitive and unchanging character of nomadic life. And with what may be gathered from this source we must compare, above all, the invaluable notices, preserved in the Old Testament, of the religion of the small Palestinians states before their conquest by the great empires of the East."[31] Even though the Arabs lived hundreds of years after the biblical Hebrews, their rituals could shed light on the elementary Semitic religion demanded by the prophets.

In this vein, Robertson Smith used the report of the fourth century A.D. author named Nilus to reconstruct an allegedly much older public rite of a camel sacrifice in which all members of the tribe participated:[32]

Now in the oldest known form of Arabian sacrifice, as described by Nilus, the camel chosen as the victim is bound upon a rude altar of stones piled together, and when the leader of the band has thrice led the worshippers round the altar in a solemn procession accompanied with chants, he inflicts the first wound, while the last words of the hymn are still upon the lips of the congregation, and in all haste drinks of the blood that gushes forth. Forthwith the whole company fall on the victim with their swords, hacking off pieces of the quivering flesh and devouring them raw with such wild haste that, in the short interval between the rise of the day star, which marked the hour for the service to begin, and the disappearance of its rays before the rising sun, the entire camel, body and bones, skin, blood and entrails is wholly devoured.[33]

Robertson Smith found all essential elements of a primeval totem ritual in it. Yet, in the process, he vastly overestimated the credibility of his source, which could not withstand a critical examination. Basically, only the fact of the camel sacrifice among the Bedouin is credible. Everything else goes too far from what else we know about the religion of the Bedouins and hence must be doubted, such as animal sacrifice as a substitute for human sacrifice, offering and consuming the sacrifice before sunrise, the appearance of a prince as the lord of sacrifice, one single priestly class, the singing of hymns, or the hasty dismemberment and raw consumption of the whole animal. All those are novelistic elements with no parallel, as Joseph Henninger discovered in a thorough analysis in 1955.

Robertson Smith found himself on more solid ground with his theory of the sacrifice as a ceremonial common meal.[34] There are also other indications that animals could be slaughtered only ritually. Here, a considerable role is played by the idea that the life of an animal dwells in his blood (Leviticus 17:11) and this requires special ritualistic precaution. Under these conditions, all slaughters were always also a sacrifice, just as every sacrifice entailed a community meal.[35] The attribute of holiness sanctioned this collective usufruct and excluded private acquisition. At that time, holiness and impurity were synonyms and were not yet separated. At a later period, animals who were slaughtered were regarded as private property offered as a proxy sacrifice for their owner. Robertson Smith interpreted the old Semitic view of holiness with ethnological information about *tabu*, from the Polynesian *ta-pu*, which meant *thoroughly marked*. The first to mention it was James Cook, who noted it in his journals on his third journey around the world in 1776–80.[36] In these journals, which were continued after his death by his successor King, the allusion to the biblical *sacred* appeared to be better understood.[37] Robertson Smith used the allusion to make Semitic terminology more comprehensible: "Rules of holiness in the sense just explained, *i.e.* a system of restrictions on man's arbitrary use of natural things, enforced by the dread of supernatural penalties are found among all primitive peoples."[38] "Even in more advanced nations the notions of holiness and uncleanness often touch. Among the Syrians for example swine's flesh was *taboo*, but it was an open question whether this was because the animal was holy or because it was unclean."[39] *Holy* and *forbidden* were combined in ancient Judaism, as indicated by the word *kherem*.[40]

The link Robertson Smith produced between the ascription of holiness and the revelation of a legal title had been established over two hundred years earlier by Thomas Hobbes.[41] Through the common consumption of flesh and blood—of a divinity, as Robertson Smith incorrectly thought, under the handicap of totemism—the participants created an indissoluble social bond of all involved. A political community with its own authority and dignity inevitably grew out of the ritual group. Devotion to this community was ethically exemplary, civil norms like loyalty were ennobled by religion. The gods watched over the civil life of their community and used their power to guarantee that all their laws were followed. These laws were sanctioned by the deity. Breaches of social order are recognized as offenses against the holiness of the deity. When Robertson Smith wrote that every crime punished by death or ostracism in ancient communities can certainly be assumed to have been originally a crime against holiness, it pleased Émile Durkheim a few years later, for he also assumed that the condemnation of certain offenses as crimes originated in a violation against the system of holy laws.

Religion and Magic: Public versus Private Rituals

If religions are public institutions, they should be investigated like political institutions, thought Robertson Smith. Just as these latter existed before there was an explicit political theory, so religious institutions should also be investigated independent of all myths and theologies.[42] Nevertheless, he did not stop at an analogy of the two institutions. He considered religious and political institutions as parts of a larger whole, i.e., the general public of a social community. "To us moderns religion is above all a matter of individual conviction and reasoned belief, but to the ancients it was a part of the citizen's public life."[43] Between the two institutions there were reciprocal dependencies; hence Semitic monotheism was connected with the triumph of monarchy over aristocracy in Asia, and analogously, Greek polytheism was linked with the triumph of aristocracy over monarchy in Greece.

The political experiences of a ritual community could not fail to affect the history of religion. The medium of the public drastically marked the history of religions. Robertson Smith made that clear in ancient Israel, where the political catastrophes experienced by the Jewish people also encompassed and changed their view of ritual. The cheerful communal sacrifice meal gradually became a gloomy expiation. "When a national religion . . . shares the catastrophe of the nation itself, as was the case with the religions of the small western Asiatic states in the period of the Assyrian conquest, the old joyous confidence in the gods gives way to a somber sense of divine wrath, and the acts by which this wrath can be conjured become much more important than the ordinary traditional gifts of homage."[44]

The harsh political blows of fate that struck Israel placed a heavy burden on the relation of the believers to their God, and the prophets established and stabilized this new experience of the remoteness of

God. Instead of the cheerful community sacrifice, the expiatory burnt offering was now typical of the relation the Jewish people maintained with the God who was angry with them. The centralization of ritual under Josiah finally sealed the separation of sacrifice and a cheerful common meal.

In Robertson Smith's reconstruction, the public nature of the ritual played a definite role in this historical development of religion. Thus, he could understand the sequence discovered by Bible criticism of sacrificial meal of clans, prophetic meaning of national catastrophes, and finally expiatory sacrifices in the Temple in Jerusalem—as an internally consistent course. Political threats had destroyed the cheerful harmony of the people with its God and substituted an awareness of loss and sin. Sacrifice was banned from everyday life. The losses of the people demanded another means: the gloomy burnt offering.[45]

If men still wanted to enlist the help of the gods for their private matters or matters that even ran counter to the interests of the community, they had to try to obtain this help in some other way than ritual. Robertson Smith saw this as the place of magic.

> There was therefore a whole region of possible needs and desires for which religion could and would know nothing; and if supernatural help was sought in such things it had to be sought through magical ceremonies, designed to purchase or constrain the favour of demoniac powers with which the public religion had nothing to do. Not only did these magical superstitions lie outside religion, but in all well-ordered states they were regarded as illicit.[46]

With the idea of magic as a religion abused by individuals for selfish purposes and thus illegal, Robertson Smith gave the study of magic an important stimulus, which was adopted by Émile Durkheim as well as his students Henri Hubert and Marcel Mauss, and still reverberates to this day.

The surprisingly great effect of Robertson Smith's studies may be understood better if the presence of the Bible in the bourgeois culture of Protestant countries in the nineteenth century is considered. Even if personal belief had long ceased to be self evident, the everyday ethos of many citizens still had its roots in the Bible. English intellectuals like Matthew Arnold recognized that the work ethic of the contemporary capitalistic world had its roots in the biblical ethic, in Hebraism. Scientific discoveries relating to the Bible could thus still affect major issues of lifestyle even if the citizen's belief in Christian dogma was already shaken. That conformed with Robertson Smith's thesis that the fundamental principle of the history of ancient religion was action and not dogma. Just as the contemporary primitive cultures were made historically exotic and moved to the beginning of history so they could be claimed as models and paradigmatic for one's own culture, so Robertson Smith transferred the Bible to a remote early time. In the process, it did not lose its normative value, but rather—absurdly—even gained. This was also the reverse of another fact that must seem profoundly strange to us today: that the Bible had nothing to do with Jews then living in Europe. In the Protestant thought of Germany and elsewhere, Judaism was considered dead,[47] even though in the second half of the nineteenth century many Jews fled to Germany from pogroms in the East.

By the end of the nineteenth century, when his own society was criticized, there was increasing interest in W. Robertson Smith. James George Frazer, who had met him at Cambridge in the 1880s, praised him in the foreword to the first edition of *The Golden Bough* as the originator of the central idea of his book, "the slain god." In 1912, in *Totem and Taboo*, Sigmund Freud worked on the thesis that killing an animal was one of those acts individuals were allowed only when the whole tribe carried them out and bore collective responsibility for them. Freud explained to his readers that psychoanalysis revealed who the totem animal was: it substituted for the father. And Émile Durkheim, the great French sociologist, acknowledged in 1907 that it was only when he read the lectures of Robertson Smith that he clearly saw the central role of religion in social life. In Cambridge, a few years after Robertson Smith's death, his claim that the ritual act was more solid and more constant than myths and lore was to become the agenda for the "Cambridge Ritualists," a group of scholars that formed in Cambridge under the aegis of Jane Ellen Harrison.

CHAPTER SIX

UNDER CIVILIZATION:
THE MENACING REALM OF MAGIC

Current Harvest Customs as Evidence of Old German Paganism

WALD- UND FELDKULTE (Worship of Forest and Fields) was the unappealing title of a two-volume work that appeared in Germany in 1875 and 1876. The same author, a German self-taught scholar, had published other books with similarly eccentric titles that had not attracted much attention: *Roggenwolf und Roggenhund. Beitrag zur germanischen Sittenkunde* (Rye-Wolf and Rye-Dog: Contribution to the Study of German Customs) (1865–66) and *Die Korndämonen* (The Grain Demons) (1868). In the foreword of his new book, the author, Wilhelm Mannhardt (1831–80), complained bitterly that science had maintained an almost deathly silence about his two previous books: "For one who works alone in the provinces, who never has an opportunity to discuss his studies with those engaged in the same endeavors, it is doubly disheartening if his call encounters no echo, if no rebuking or appreciative voice offers a challenge."[1] The man who wrote that had been treated badly by life in every conceivable way. A curvature of the spine physically disfigured him, and though he obtained his doctorate and was qualified to teach, he was not appointed to any professorship. Disappointed, he withdrew to his parents' house in Danzig, where he earned his living as a librarian.

It was English classicist and anthropologist James George Frazer, a genuine bookworm, who discovered Mannhardt's books and helped the unrecognized man achieve respect and influence. In 1890, in the preface to the first edition of *The Golden Bough*, a classic in religious studies, Frazer acknowledged that the works of the late Wilhelm Mannhardt had been very useful to him in his study of the superstitions of European peasants. Frazer had come upon these works when he was seeking an explanation for the barbaric succession of priests in the ancient shrine of Diana of Aricia. While searching for analogies, he came across the popular superstitions and customs of contemporary European peasants, the most extensive and reliable sources for the primitive religion of the Aryans. "Indeed the primitive Aryan, in all that regards his mental fibre and texture, is not extinct. He is amongst us to this day," Frazer rejoiced.[2] One of his main witnesses for this claim was Mannhardt. With a fine feeling for the extraordinary achievement of this man, Frazer reported that, through investigation, written surveys, and examinations of the literature of folklore, Mannhardt had made a great many exhibits available. Mannhardt's weak health had collapsed before he was able to complete his work, but his working documents had been deposited in the university library in Berlin and deserved to be examined in the interests of science. As we shall see, a thorough examination took place only decades after Frazer's death and produced rather unexpected results. But Mannhardt could not enjoy the recognition he had sought, for in 1880 he died at the age of forty-nine.

Even in his youth, Wilhelm Mannhardt had been drawn to mythology. In traction and "robbed of a sharp grasp of things outside myself by unusual shortsightedness, I was thrown back onto the internal world of fantasy," he wrote in the preface to *Wald- und Feldkulte*.[3] His interest in German mythology had been stirred by a Danish friend who boasted of the powerful Nordic mythology and to whom he wanted to present something of equal value from Germany.[4] With this in mind, he had read the third edition of *Deutsche Mythologie* (Teutonic Mythology) by Grimm, who had composed the image of German paganism from various sources. This result seemed of paramount significance to Mannhardt: "The first thing was . . . to mark out a way for the nations so they would seem to guide their own childhood over a broad *Mare incognitum* to the golden land and add a considerable piece to their life and personality by extending their self-memory backward to a distant period. An image of the old German religion now rose up before the eyes of the amazed contemporaries."[5]

Like F. M. Müller, Mannhardt understood the past that surfaced from oblivion as a childhood we have forgotten. Only when we use extant documents to become aware of it again do we reclaim a lost dimension of ourselves.

Mannhardt was familiar with Müller's comparative mythology but considered it badly constructed. Müller's *Aryans* were chronologically much too distant ancestors, while Mannhardt found them close by among the Germanophone country people of his own time. His *Aryans*, the peasant underclass of Europe untouched by history, had the great advantage of living in Europe today. To know more about "the beliefs of our national pagan prehistory,"[6] you only need to keep your eyes open in the country and study the life and thought of the peasants, where you will find not only sunken remnants of a mythology, but also the seeds of mythology in general. In this respect, Mannhardt

had read and understood E. B. Tylor.[7] While collecting as much information as possible from the German country folk about their customs,
Mannhardt approached his goal of constructing a German or Germanic mythology.[8] But he realized he was not alone: other peoples of
Europe were also being studied. Even those "who lacked any knowledge about the religion of their forefathers" tried to learn "how, in the
time of an unbroken national character before the introduction of
Christianity, the spirit of their people expressed itself in its most ideal
concerns (e.g., Slavs, Magyars)."[9]

> Christianity was not popular. It came from abroad, it aimed at supplant-
> ing the time-honored indigenous gods whom the country revered and
> loved. These gods and their worship were part and parcel of the people's
> traditions, customs, and constitution. Their names had their roots in the
> people's language, and were hallowed by antiquity; kings and princes
> traced their lineage back to individual gods; forests, mountains, lakes had
> received a living consecration from their presence. All this the people
> were now to renounce; and what is elsewhere commended as truth and
> faithfulness was denounced and persecuted by the heralds of the new
> faith as a sin and a crime. The source and seat of all sacred lore was
> shifted away to far-off regions forever, and only a fainter, borrowed glory
> could henceforth be shed on places in one's native land.[10]

The formation of nation-states in Central Europe had lent a political
dynamic to the study of mythology, particularly pre-Christian paganism, as Mannhardt knew. The formation of nations in Christian Europe required pagan private coaching.

Mannhardt profoundly admired Jacob Grimm. Grimm had not perceived mythology as a product of conscious thought, but rather as
comparable to language creation of the unconscious poetizing folk
spirit. *"Thus he laid the ground for the scientific understanding not only of
German, but also of Greek and Roman and all other mythology."*[11] But he
also saw his limits. Grimm had often not distinguished strictly
enough between the metaphors of the poet and the myths of the folk.
Since the folk did not participate in historical changes to the same
extent as the upper classes, the remnants of previous cultural stages
could be found in their traditions. One of the cultures not yet distorted by history was the property "of underdeveloped, lower circles
of the folk."[12] Therefore, Mannhardt focused on the difference between the intellectuals and the folk, using well-known geological
metaphors:

> As the organic remains of various periods of the shaping of the earth are
> deposited on top of one another on a mountain, the memory of the folk

preserves unknown deposits of various epochs of culture, which always went through the same process, with many inclusions; but the position of the strata has shifted and intersected many times; through disintegration, blending, or purely external combination with the products of other strata, the content of each individual layer has been altered. Thus, the history of the prehistoric world could be reproduced from fossils as the activity of the geologists and paleontologists was preceded by the elementary work of descriptive mineralogy, zoology, and botany.[13]

Mannhardt—a student of Tylor in this point as well—moved back and forth between geological and folklore metaphors. And like Tylor, his account raises the scientific status of folk customs. Many of them may look like junk if wrenched out of their original life context. In his account, it was a living practice of peasant religiosity. His metaphor of *psychological fossilization* bridged the two opposing poles, just as Tylor swung back and forth between *survival* and *revival*. The human mind needed "to bring the emotional fossils of the past back to life."[14] They contain the possibility of recreating emotional life. As with Tylor, Mannhardt's research was also used as the acquired knowledge for a reform of religion.[15]

Harvest Customs and the Mannhardt Survey of 1865

Broadly as Mannhardt's program was calculated, its implementation was very concrete and precise, both in its objects and in its method. In about 1860, he planned to collect mythical and magic songs into a sourcebook of German folk tradition, but he soon dropped this plan. Instead, he investigated agricultural customs,[16] expecting that they were most likely to contain the remnants of German paganism he was looking for. Thus, when compared with that of Grimm, his work resolutely shifted the point of view of the study from idea to practice. Mannhardt organized a large-scale empirical survey in Germany and adjacent countries to yield information about the presence of primitive rites in contemporary Central Europe. Just as several old houses in the cities of the Hanseatic League had modern facades, while the faded glory of the Renaissance still remained in the rear and the Gothic still dreamed under the roofs, among the country people there were still individual areas of life, corners of the world of imagination where a several-thousand year old history had passed, leaving almost no trace. That was especially the case with harvest customs.[17] The value Mannhardt ascribed to his discoveries is revealed by his comment that a scientific study of folk culture could react adequately to the challenge of Darwinism and make its own contribution to the prehistory of the human race.[18]

Hence, Mannhardt carried out a large survey in 1865. The brothers Grimm had done something similar in 1815 with circular letters to collect their folklore data. Mannhardt asked the target group for information about the harvest customs of their region. The survey initially contained twenty-five questions, later thirty-five.[19] With the support of the Berlin Academy of Science, Mannhardt sent the questionnaires to the neighboring countries of France, Holland, Denmark, and Russia, headlined BITTE or DEMANDE.[20] Fifty thousand copies altogether went to teachers' colleges, agricultural societies, gymnasium students, inspectors, and so forth.[21] In addition, he conducted interviews with prisoners of war from Denmark and other countries.[22]

The Tragic Fate of the Grain Demons

From his many letters, Mannhardt received 2,100 replies. In *Korndämonen* of 1868, he presented the first results of his analysis, which confirmed his assumption that "the individual fragments of every tradition combine into an interlocking whole."[23] The appearance of the old names of the pagan gods (Odin and Wotan) in the harvest customs proved to him that they were remnants of a Germanic religious ritual.[24] However, the formulation of some of the queries tended to beg the question. Take for example question no. 2.

> Do special ancient customs exist to tie . . . the last sheaf and thresh the last bundle? In many places in southern and northern Germany, the last sheaf is shaped in the form of an animal or trimmed with wooden images of such animals. . . . In other regions, stretching from Scotland and England, all through Germany to the Slavic east, the last sheaf is made into a dummy in a human shape. . . . This dummy is taken to the barn high on the harvest wagon and water is poured on it several times. In threshing, the last bundle is again often made into a dummy that is thrown on the threshing-room floor by the person who made the last flail, a neighbor who has not yet threshed. This person is himself bound into a sheaf and wheeled through the village. A celebratory meal follows at which the dummy in the shape of a cake is put on the table. . . . Are there such customs in your area, even if they are preserved only in remnants?[25]

In any case, the answer he received matched his expectations. The growth of vegetation was caused by a demon who assumed the form of an animal. When the harvest worker mowed the grain, the demon flew from field to field and finally hid in the last sheath. To cut it was dangerous, for it meant death. The harvest workers were willing to do that only if they got a special bonus from the landowner. The grain demon had to die for the numen of the vegetation to reproduce in renewed fertility.[26]

To prove how old this vegetation ritual was, Mannhardt went back to prehistoric times and sought in the Greek cult of Demeter a correspondence with the German folk custom. The farther back in antiquity he went, the more he thought he could discover beneath the top layer of meaning another, barbaric stratum preserved in an ancient tale from Phrygia. During the harvest, Lityerses (the name of the person in question) invited a passing stranger to take part in a meal, but afterward he bound him in a sheaf and then cut off his head. There were analogues in Germany and Sweden of strangers passing by a harvest field being taken for an appearance of the spirit of grain escaping the sickle: "Thus the assumption is justified that the Lityerses song preserved the memory of an ancient barbaric custom that strangers who were proscribed anyway, were beheaded as representatives of a demon dwelling in the grain."[27]

Mannhardt's next book, *Wald- und Feldkulte*, filled in this outline even more. The first part expanded the source material of the tree cult of the Germans, and the second part presented more ancient parallels. Referring to Müller and Tylor, he analyzed the masses of material and composed the picture of an archaic vegetation cult, like a mosaic, out of various scattered sources.

Mannhardt had dreamed of the golden land where the European nations would be led by a study of mythology. At the end of the journey over the *Mare incognitum*, he himself assumed, however, that his contemporaries would be amazed at the image of the old-German religion that would emerge from it.[28] In fact, he had found a barbaric cult devoid of any ethics.

A Reevaluation of Mannhardt's Survey, a Hundred Years Later

Precisely one hundred years after the survey, the material collected by Mannhardt was reevaluated in 1965. The folklorist Ingeborg Weber-Kellermann studied it from the perspective of more recent folklore and concluded that Mannhardt's model of interpretation was one-sided and had overlooked other possibilities aside from the vegetation cult. Mannhardt had asked whether the custom of tying up the lord of the manor or strangers who came to the field to beg for a tip was known.[29] A reexamination of the answers showed that Mannhardt had not paid attention to the regional dissemination of harvest customs. When this was done later, it was discovered that the harvest customs had been especially widespread in regions where agricultural workers gathered the harvest and where peasant village cooperatives had already retreated to the background or had disappeared altogether. It must have been the new social groups of agricultural workers who maintained the custom, for where these groups were lacking, the harvest rituals played a smaller role. This produces a different interpretation. Mannhardt had interpreted the shackling of the farm owner or a stranger as a symbolic shackling and killing of the escaping grain spirit. Now it was more obviously as a playful begging custom used by the agricultural workers to express the fact that during the harvest, they were lords of the fields by virtue of their work. The binding and release of the farm owner supported their demands of him. If this new interpretation is considered more plausible, Mannhardt's explanation collapses. These are not remnants of an old vegetation cult, but rather new demands for social equality. This interesting result of a reexamination of Mannhardt's survey a hundred years later not only sheds a whole new light on the history of rural customs, but also undermines a far-reaching interpretation that Frazer presented on the basis of Mannhardt's account.

James George Frazer's *Golden Bough* and the Journey to the Underworld

James George Frazer (1854–1941), who first publicized Mannhardt's findings, was originally a classical philologist. The facts of his life are quickly told: he was born in Glasgow and enrolled at the University of Glasgow at the age of fifteen. In 1874, when he was twenty, he became a student of classical philology at Trinity College, Cambridge, where he remained to the end of his life. Fortunately, William James wrote a letter about Frazer in Cambridge in 1900, which gives a rare glance at the man who largely disappeared behind his work. At the time, James was in Great Britain for the Gifford Lectures, which produced the famous *Varieties of Religion Experience*. His letter described Frazer, his table companion, as "a sucking babe." After Tylor, he was considered the greatest authority in England on the superstitions of primitive peoples. Yet that was in harsh contrast to Frazer's personal convictions. "He knows nothing of psychical research and thinks that trances, etc., of savage soothsayers, oracles and the like are all feigned! Verily science is amusing."[30]

As a young scholar, Frazer made his first contribution with a translation and commentary of Pausanias's *Description of Greece*. As he was working on that, he noted Tylor's *Primitive Culture*. His fervent interest finally focused on anthropology in 1884 when he met William Robertson Smith in Cambridge, where the latter had been appointed professor of Arabic after his sensational heresy trial. Robertson Smith found Frazer to be an enthusiastic anthropologist who could help him with the ninth edition of the *Encyclopedia Britannica*, which he was then editing, and he offered the young classical philologist the two articles on "Totem" and "Taboo." These articles, which received attention in France where Durkheim discovered them, completed Frazer's transformation from philology to anthropology.

In March 1885, at the conference of the Anthropological Institute in London, the brand-new anthropologist delivered a lecture entitled "On Certain Burial Customs as Illustrative of the Primitive Theory of the Soul." He began with an ancient custom: Why did a man who had been incorrectly declared dead have to enter his house through the roof and not through the door when he returned home? This question had preoccupied Plutarch. Frazer took it up and his lecture poured a flood of evidence of similar notions and customs from all over the world onto the audience. These all amounted to one and the same view: since a dead man is considered a spirit, he had to take the path of all spirits. He ended his lecture with the English idiom, "And down the chimney he came—this is an English answer to a Roman question."

Tylor was in the audience. In the subsequent discussion, Tylor took the floor and praised Frazer's explanation as original and independent. In this discussion, in turn, Frazer divulged something of his relationship to Tylor. It had been Tylor's reading of the texts that had introduced a new epoch in his life. His comment also shows that he had grasped Tylor's concern: "There was a large substratum of savagery underlying all our civilization."[31] Yet the emphasis had shifted. What Tylor tried to prove inductively with *survivals*—that our civilized society also had primitive and raw predecessors—was a given for Frazer. Under our civilization was savagery. It was only important to discover it. The outmoded custom in the middle of civilization (here, Classical Antiquity) allowed a glance into this underworld.

In 1890, the three-page article "Taboo" became a two-volume work, *The Golden Bough: A Study in Comparative Religion*. Frazer could no longer get away from anthropology. In the preface of his book, he frankly expressed his debt both to Tylor and, even more, to Robertson Smith. He had drawn the central idea of his own book from Robertson Smith's *The Religion of the Semites*: "the conception of the slain god."[32] Frazer gave free rein to his extraordinary literary talents in this material, which made his book standard reading for many generations. For example, in his introduction to the later, abridged edition of 1922, he wrote:

> Who does not know Turner's picture of the Golden Bough? The scene, suffused with the golden glow of imagination in which the divine mind of Turner steeped and transfigured even the fairest natural landscape, is a dream-like vision of the little woodland lake of Nemi—"Diana's mirror," as it was called by the ancients. No one who has seen that calm water, lapped in a green hollow of the Alban hills, can ever forget it. . . . Diana herself might still linger by this lonely shore, still haunt those woodlands wild.
>
> In antiquity this sylvan landscape was the scene of a strange and recurring tragedy. On the northern shore of the lake, right under the precipitous cliffs on which the modern village of Nemi is perched, stood the sacred grove and sanctuary of Diana Nemorensis, or Diana of the Wood. . . . In this sacred grove there grew a certain tree round which at any time of the day, and probably far into the night, a grim figure might be seen to prowl. In his hand he carried a drawn sword, and he kept peering warily about him as if at every instant he expected to be set upon by an enemy. He was a priest and a murderer; and the man for whom he looked was sooner or later to murder him and hold the priesthood in his stead. Such was the rule of the sanctuary. A candidate for the priesthood could only succeed to office by slaying the priest, and having slain him, he retained office till he was himself slain by a stronger or craftier.[33]

A critical reader of Frazer's fascinating description, Jonathan Z. Smith, calculated that only 10 percent of his material came from ancient sources, as opposed to 90 percent from his literary imagination.[34] The ancient sources are, in fact, inconceivably meager: a very short note by Strabo ("The temple of the Arician, they say, is a copy of that of the Tauropolos. And in fact a barbaric and Scythian element predominates in the sacred usages, for the people set up as priest merely a run-away slave who has slain with his own hand the man previously consecrated to that office; accordingly the priest is always armed with a sword, looking around for the attacks and ready to defend himself")[35] and the late and hardly credible report of an unknown ancient author who asserted that the holy tree of Aricia was the same one that Virgil mentioned in the *Aeneid* (Servius ad Aeneid VI 136). The *Aeneid* says that only he who has first plucked the golden fruit from this tree can go to the underworld and come back unharmed.

> A bough is hidden in a shady tree;
> Its leaves and pliant stem are golden, set

> Aside as sacred to Proserpine
> . . . Only he
> may pass beneath earth's secret spaces who
> first plucks the golden-leaved fruit of that tree.[36]

With his mysterious title, Frazer struck a captivating chord. Frazer illuminated the dark forest of savage superstition, wrote his Cambridge colleague, Jane Harrison, in her memoirs. And she added: "The happy title of that book—Sir James Frazer has a veritable genius for titles—made it arrest the attention of scholars. . . . At the mere sound of the magical words 'Golden Bough' the scales fell—we heard and understood."[37]

The Tragedy of Magic Rites

Frazer repeatedly claimed that the sole purpose of his book was to explain the barbaric succession in the priesthood of the Diana shrine in Aricia. But the way he did that raised doubt that this was the only intention. In the preface to the second edition, which appeared in 1900 and had grown to three volumes, he complained that even friendly critics had not believed that. Once more he repeated that his book was really not a general treatise on primitive superstitions, but was only the investigation of one special, narrowly defined problem.[38] He stood by his fiction, even if the literary feats tell something different. Not until the preface of the third edition that appeared in 1911–15 and had swollen to no fewer than twelve volumes did he finally let the cat out of the bag: "Should my whole theory of this particular priesthood collapse—and I fully acknowledge the slenderness of the foundations on which it rests—its fall would hardly shake my general conclusions as to the evolution of primitive religion and society, which are founded on large collections of entirely independent and well-authenticated facts."[39] In the thrilling preface to *Balder the Beautiful*, we even learn that the priest of Nemi was basically only something like a puppet used by the author of the tragedy to represent human foolishness and human suffering to the reader. Now they could once again disappear into the closet after their work is done. In reality, the gradual development of human thought from savagery to civilization had been the object of his investigation.[40]

The crux of this assertion is that it remains disconnected like a Maori custom alongside a Saxon one. Frazer's systematically fastidious statements hover over the waters and do not give the material any clear internal order. Scholars who searched in *The Golden Bough* for contradictions and inconsistencies found a rich booty. Considering the author's paramount intelligence, J. Z. Smith even concluded that his book was apparently a joke;[41] Mary Beard only commented laconically that Frazer in any case kept it to himself.[42] The problem remains that the explanation generally does not follow the theoretical handicaps the author himself gives. That is especially conspicuous in the theory of myths. Frazer used three different theories of myths in his work—the ritualistic, the cognitive, and the euhemeristic—without even making an attempt to standardize them. To call *The Golden Bough* a palimpsest (as Frazer does)—a manuscript in which various texts have been written down one on top of the other—is simply to apply a metaphor to the inconsistencies of the work. It hardly helps to understand it. We should at least not abandon the attempt to find the chord that touched his contemporaries, like Jane Harrison, so directly.

One of the many inconsistencies seems to be that in 1900, in the preface to the second edition, Frazer suddenly introduced the distinction between magic and religion, without modifying his account: "I have come to agree with Sir A. C. Lyall and Mr. F. B. Jevons in recognising a fundamental distinction and even opposition of principle between magic and religion. More than that, I believe that in the evolution of thought, magic, as representing a lower intellectual stratum, has probably everywhere preceded religion."[43]

It would be rash to see that as merely another theory adding nothing to the structure of the work, like the explanations of myths, and would underestimate the value of this distinction for the composition as a whole. For this distinction allowed Frazer to comprehend the most varied customs as part of a whole. With the term *magic*, Frazer grasped the possibility of naming and determining this unified whole. The distinction helped him to state Mannhardt's interpretation of peasant rites more precisely. They were really "originally magical rites designed to cause plants to grow, cattle to thrive, rain to fall, and the sun to shine."[44] Like science today, magic wants to influence the course of natural events. Religion, on the other hand, worships gods without such an intention.

Linking magic with Mannhardt's grain demon had a reverse effect on Frazer's view of magic and brought the element of social stratification that was so important to Mannhardt into magic. Frazer did see a progress from magic to religion, but assumed that this progress took place in the various social strata at a different speed. The upper classes could liberate themselves from magic and create space for both religion and science. In this sense, "religion" is an intellectual latecomer of the intellectuals. The lower classes, untouched by history in Mannhardt's sense, were cut off from this development, but were dependent on the upper classes for the development and were left behind, so to speak, in magic. Magic, science, and religion remained undifferentiated for them. Frazer's position can be understood in a model that posits that social processes of change taking place in the three dimensions of space, time, and social stratum. In Frazer's view, magic was superseded by religion in the time dimension, but that applied only for the social stratum of the educated classes. In the space of European peasantry, as well as in non-European cultures, it went on unbroken.

In the second edition of *The Golden Bough*, when Frazer took up the religion-magic dichotomy, he finally broke with Mannhardt's linguistic Aryan-Semitic classification that he had also assumed at first. The attraction of Müller's comparative mythology was gone by then. A sensitive review of the first edition of 1890 did not neglect to point out the connection: "Here we have two books [by Robertson Smith and Frazer] dealing with the primitive religion of the two great groups of nations from which civilisation has obtained its chief spiritual material, and both avowedly appeal to folklore for methods of investigation and for corroborative criteria. Both use freely the analogy of savage custom and ritual to explain those of Semites and Aryans."[45] The linguistic classification remained in Frazer but only in an attenuated form. In the second and later editions of *The Golden Bough*, it disappeared altogether, as can be understood by a change in the subtitle. The subtitle of the first edition, *A Study in Comparative Religion*, still alluded to the concept of comparative philology. The subtitle of the second and third editions, *A Study in Magic and Religion*, drew attention to a contrast between magic and religion that left the model of linguistic classifications.

The Varnish of Civilization

In a peculiar section of *The Golden Bough*, Frazer dealt with the origin of the supplies of men who agreed to be temporary kings so they could ultimately be slaughtered. It would be a fundamental error, Frazer explained, to think that other peoples attached the same value to human life as we do. There was sufficient proof that many of them were indifferent to life.[46] And he added a commentary that sheds a characteristic light on how he saw himself as a historian:

> We shall never understand the long course of human history if we persist in measuring mankind in all ages and in all countries by the standard, perhaps excellent, but certainly narrow, of the modern English middle class with their love of material comfort and "their passionate, absorbing, almost bloodthirsty clinging to life." That class, of which I may say, in the

words of Matthew Arnold, that I am myself a feeble unit, doubtless possesses many estimable qualities, but among them can hardly be reckoned the rare and delicate gift of historical imagination, the power of entering into the thoughts and feelings of men of other ages and other countries, of conceiving that they may regulate their life by principles which do not square with ours, and may throw it away for objects which to us might seem ridiculously inadequate.[47]

Frazer saw his task as a historian as leaving behind the narrow-mindedness of the British property-owning middle class. His description was assumed to be consciously committed in general to this principle. Indeed, in 1931, Ludwig Wittgenstein was angry at *The Golden Bough*: "What narrowness of spiritual life we find in Frazer! And as a result: how impossible for him to understand a different way of life from the English one of his time."[48] But this was neither Frazer's intention nor effect. His work was not calculated to justify petit-bourgeois prejudices. Instead, like Tylor, his description was influenced by the critical spirit of Matthew Arnold. He wanted to use the historical imagination to bring the thoughts and feelings of people from other times and countries closer to civilized Western European, pulling his readers into his description with suggestive metaphors. I shall examine two of them more closely: the metaphor of the voyage of discovery and the metaphor of life on the volcano.

A Voyage of Discovery

After Frazer claims that the shrine of Aricia had been a scene of a "strange and recurring tragedy,"[49] unparalleled in classical antiquity, he invites the reader to join him on a greater journey: "It will be long and laborious, but may possess something of the interest and charm of a voyage of discovery, in which we shall visit many strange foreign lands, with strange foreign peoples, and still stranger customs. The wind is in the shrouds: we shake out our sails to it, and leave the coast of Italy behind us for a time."[50]

The metaphor of a voyage of discovery is apt in view of the fact that Great Britain was a colonial power, whose worldwide possessions made it a depot of information about exotic cultures. Reports of all possible new finds streamed there on a massive scale: about buried ancient cities as well as about the most savage peoples of desert and forest.[51] In this situation, Frazer was in demand as an authority of the bizarre, as Mary Beard stated in an evaluation of contemporary newspaper reports about Frazer.[52] When an incomprehensible custom from a remote corner of the British Empire became known, the reporters immediately thought of the author of *The Golden Bough*. Finally, it was his endeavor to document "early modes of thought."[53] Like Charles Darwin, he had an unbounded interest in as many various forms of human thought as possible. He himself, however, had never set out on voyages, but had drawn his information from books and from scholarly travelers who risked their life to visit foreign peoples.

Frazer's imaginary voyage took the reader first to the sacred kingdom of primitive peoples. It became known in 1905 that the African people of Shilluk occasionally killed their king. Charles G. Seligman and his wife studied the kingdom of the Shilluk in the Sudan. When they returned, he wrote Frazer on December 3, 1910, with information that would surely delight him:

> Dear Dr. Frazer
>
> I am now writing up the material I collected in the Sudan during the first half of the present year. My Shilluk and Dinka information will please you, the Shilluks have Divine Kings, incarnating the spirit of the semi-historical, semi-divine founder of the nation who according to the genealogies lived from 20 to 26 generations ago. Until the last few years the king was ceremonially killed when he began to get old or invalidish, his grave becoming a very holy shrine. The king is killed by a special family in conjunction with some of the heads of the different districts into which the Shilluk country is divided. (I use the term district rather loosely.) If the stories and beliefs of the people themselves mean anything there was before this a period when anyone (of the royal blood?) who could get at the king and kill him became king. This is of course the merest outline.[54]

One year later, Seligman published his observations in a scientific journal. Although there is no doubt that the Shilluk killed their king as soon as they showed the first signs of old age or disease, it was difficult to obtain truly reliable information.[55] Frazer saw Seligman's report as confirmation that the incident of Aricia could be explained with overseas analogies.

> On the whole the theory and practice of the divine kings of the Shilluk correspond very nearly to the theory and practice of the priests of Nemi, the Kings of the Wood, if my view of the latter is correct. In both we see a series of divine kings on whose life the fertility of men, of cattle, and of vegetation is believed to depend, and who are put to death, whether in single combat or otherwise, in order that their divine spirit may be transmitted to their successors in full vigour, uncontaminated by the weakness and decay of sickness or old age, because any such degeneration on the part of the king would, in the opinion of his worshippers, entail a corresponding degeneration on mankind, on cattle, and on the crops.[56]

Magic as a form of thought operates on a misunderstood law of nature that things influenced one another through a secret sympathy. Like produces like (homeopathic or imitative magic): the weakness of the king necessarily has an effect on the vegetation and fertility of his people. Things that are in contact with one another affect one another: the frailty of the king weakens the divine spirit that dwells in him (contagious magic). On his "voyage" to distant lands, Frazer found an unending flood of illustrations that both laws—of similarity and of contact—control early thought throughout the world.

These bold assertions did not remain unchallenged. Edward E. Evans-Pritchard reexamined the especially illustrative case of the Shilluk and presented his results in a Frazer Lecture of 1948, "The Divine Kingship of the Shilluk of the Nilotic Sudan."[57] It turned out that there was not one case of a ritual murder of the king among the Shilluk that could be proved. But there were recurring political rebellions during which kings were killed. These murders had nothing to do with a particular form of thought, but rather with a particular type of change of ruler in a segmented society.

Life on the Volcano

Everything Frazer discovered on his "voyages" showed his own civilization in a different light. The importance of this reflex for Frazer is shown in his 1907 lecture, delivered when he was appointed to a chair in Liverpool. The lecture, *The Scope of Social Anthropology*, is a rare programmatic presentation of his views. The study of anthropology always refers knowledge of savage cultures to our own civilization. In Tylor the proof of survivals of past periods served to reveal what was exotic in our own time, while for Frazer, all of modern civilization rested on a foundation where light can be shed in a roundabout way through the study of primitive peoples. The more knowledge about savage people is available, the greater the chance of advancing this reconstruction. As with Tylor, the means for that was a conjectural historiography. From the reports of other cultures, one's own prehistory could be concluded. What Tylor struggled alone to prove with the existence of survivals achieved the status of certain knowledge with Frazer. Darwin's theory of development helped, with its important assumption that the development of the embryo recapitulated the whole history of human nature.[58] "By comparison with civilized man the savage represents an arrested or rather retarded stage of social development, and an examination of his customs and beliefs accordingly supplies the same sort of evidence of the evolution of the human mind that an examination of the embryo supplies of the evolution of the human body. . . . A savage is to a civilized man as a child is to an adult."[59]

But for Frazer, life in the childish culture of the primitives was ruled by the madness of magic. Warm-hearted associations such as childish purity and innocence are lacking. The survivals do not indicate the force of the human soul vis-à-vis the relentless reign of natural law, as in Tylor. For Frazer, they indicated a dangerous delusion that civilized society is not immune to either. Within one and the same nation, people are basically and permanently divided from one another. While educated classes have successfully liberated themselves from magic, superstitions go on living on their doorstep, unbeknownst to them. Most people in modern society, especially peasants, still live in a condition of intellectual savagery. The same explosive blend of magic, science, and religion that can be seen in non-European peoples still exists among the uneducated classes.[60]

Frazer observes the continuity of the savage in the civilized from another side, too: in the history of the cult of the dying and resurrected god. The Easter celebration of the Church continued an older cult of Adonis,[61] while Christianity preserved the form of a vegetation cult in the rural underclasses. The belief of these strata was structurally similar to that of primitive peoples. A universal, "catholic" belief in the effectiveness of magic threatened civilization in Europe.[62] While the educated upper classes understood that cult and control of nature have nothing to do with one another, most people had not yet made this separation. For them, life grows only out of death, the new only from the destruction of the old.

> A mass, if not the majority, of people in every civilized country is still living in a state of intellectual savagery, that, in fact, the smooth surface of cultured society is sapped and mined by superstition. Only those whose studies have led them to investigate the subject are aware of the depth to which the ground beneath our feet is thus, as it were, honeycombed by unseen forces. We appear to be standing on a volcano which may at any moment break out in smoke and fire to spread ruin and devastation among the gardens and palaces of ancient culture wrought so laboriously by the hands of many generations. After looking on the ruined Greek temples of Paestum and contrasting them with the squalor and savagery of the Italian peasantry, Renan said, "I trembled for civilization, seeing it so limited, built on so weak a foundation, resting on so few individuals even in the country where it is dominant."[63]

Frazer did not yield to superstition. He wanted to fight it with all means. The comparative method was to be a military battery to shoot down the walls of superstition. No matter how ungrateful it was and no matter how much sadness it caused to destroy the fundamentals of belief that had sheltered human hopes and wishes from time immemorial, new refuges had to be built.[64]

From the beginning, the admiration of writers and poets has remained unharmed by the massive criticism of Frazer's book by scholars of religion and anthropology. Frazer's work has exercised an immense effect on modern literature. The history of the effect of *The Golden Bough* has been described by the literary scholars J. P. Bishop (1948), J. B. Vickery (1973), and S. E. Hyman (1974). One small example is T. S. Eliot's *The Wasteland* (1922).

> After the torchlight red on sweaty faces
> After the frosty silence in the gardens
> After the agony in stony places
> The shouting and the crying
> Prison and palace and reverberation
> Of thunder of spring over distant mountains
> He who was living is now dead
> We who were living are now dying
> With a little patience

In his footnotes, Eliot wrote: "To another work of anthropology I am indebted in general, one which has influenced our generation profoundly; I mean *The Golden Bough*; I have used especially the two volumes *Adonis, Attis, Osiris*. Anyone who is acquainted with these works will immediately recognize in the poem certain references to vegetation ceremonies."[65] The desperate tone of this poem overwhelmed the intellectual youth of the 1920s, as A. Assmann has shown.[66] Frazer's topography of modern civilization appeared as a revelation to them. The history of religion had become the principal witness for the power of the irrational in a period when civilization was progressing inexorably to total destruction.

CHAPTER SEVEN

THE UNFATHOMABLE DEPTHS OF LIFE

IN THE MIRROR OF HELLENIC RELIGION

The Modern as the Dwelling Place of the Greek Gods

THE MEANING of the Greek gods in nineteenth-century culture can be understood in light of the quarrel between the supporters of the old and the champions of the modern at the end of the seventeenth century. This quarrel was triggered by the claim that modern culture, especially modern science and art, was superior to the old. After a few intellectual skirmishes the adversaries agreed that there must be a distinction between science and art. In art, there could be no measurable and undoubted progress, but in science there could be. Art must be judged by the aesthetic criteria of its own time, which is why ancient and modern art each possessed its own right to exist in the framework of its day. As a result of this resolution of the quarrel, the history of art was separated from the historical process of the progress of knowledge. The effect on the notion of the modern was fundamental: it was regarded as an age when the historical split of knowledge and art could no longer be mended. It was characterized by a "rift with the present."[1]

Ever since the fifteenth century, ancient literature and art had been celebrated in Europe as a source of a genuine humanism. This admiration is reflected in the history of the German word *antik*, which assumed a normative meaning in the late eighteenth century. Based on Winckelmann's work, Hellenism was especially regarded as a bright model of all classicism, whereas Latinism was relegated to the background.[2] Greece became a source of personal identity. In genuine Greek works, we can find "clarity of view, serenity of acceptance, ease of communication," said Goethe, and added: "Everyone is a Greek in his own way!"[3] But what did this experience have to do with religion, particularly ancient religion? Was it not outdated by the progress of science, or did it maintain an independent right to exist like art? Friedrich Schiller's poem "The Gods of Greece" answered the question of the place of Greek religion in the modern age. The poem was written in 1788, when Schiller was friendly with Wieland, and the

Greek gods appeared in it as creatures from a world that was not yet inanimate.

> Ye in the age gone by
> Who ruled the world—a world how lovely then!—
> And guided still the steps of happy men
>   In the light leading-strings of careless joy!
> Ah, flourish'd then your service of delight!
>   How different, oh, how different, in the day
> When thy sweet fanes with many a wreath were bright,
>   O Venus Amathusia![4]

According to Schiller, it was Christianity and natural science together that ended this harmony of the gods with nature.

> And to enrich the worship of the ONE,
>   A universe of Gods must pass away!

The poet linked the gods of Greece with a dramatic change in history: man was robbed of his harmonious relation with the world. Schiller described the Greek gods from the perspective of his own time, which had come under the yoke of Newton's (1643–1727) mechanical and rational view of nature. Thus the past received its meaning. Poetry changed a remote era into a memory, making people aware of such a loss. Judeo-Christian monotheism was to blame for the decline of this cheerful world, and the victorious one God was also responsible for the demon of the mechanized world. While bringing the Greek past into the Christian and scientific present, Schiller also showed his contemporaries the soullessness not only of the exact sciences, but also of the Judeo-Christian religion.[5] It is not surprising that this poem triggered a controversy. But it is surprising that Schiller felt compelled by it to revise and tone down his poetry.[6] Schiller's view was shared by many in the nineteenth century. As noted, Matthew Arnold called Hellenism as a witness against Hebraism, which he too considered the main culprit for the modern inanimate world and the narrow-minded petite-bourgeoisie. A few decades later, Max Weber again made the history of the Jewish-Christian religion the driving force of the demystification of the world. Thus there was a widespread view that the demystified world dated from the victory of Christianity, which had banished the quite different Greek experience of the world.

Another aspect of Schiller's poetry—that the dead gods of Greece could be resurrected as poetry—was also widely accepted. Poetry was entrusted with preserving the metaphorical spirit of religion that Herder had talked about. This was also a feature of the modern age.

A seminal idea for the nineteenth century was that extinct gods and rituals could be made accessible to the people of the inanimate age in the experience of art, and thus be protected from final extinction.[7] It was not by accident that the scholar of religion, F. Max Müller, saw the poetic language of Indo-European early history as the source of a genuinely pure religion. What Schiller opened up with poetry, Müller later hoped to achieve through a scientific comparative linguistics: a discovery of the impoverishment produced by the scientific worldview.

The normative view of antiquity that developed in Germany in the eighteenth and nineteenth centuries was linked with the word play of *culture versus civilization*. Culture, from the Latin *cultura*, had two meanings in every European language from its Latin origin: agriculture and the formation of the human mind. In addition, there was another component that made the meanings of both terms drift apart in Germany and France, without allowing these distinctions to be played off against one another too strictly.[8] In France, *culture* and *civilisation* were used interchangeably. But the German use of the term *Kultur*, by Herder, for example, emphasized the difference between progress controlling nature and the spirit of a people. In Germany, culture was spoken of consistently and often in the plural: different nations and periods had their own cultures, and there could be different cultures in the very same nation.[9] In *The Civilizing Process*, Norbert Elias showed that the different evaluation of the terms *civilization* and *culture* in France and Germany was linked with different social developments in both countries. In Germany the contrast between a Francophile courtly aristocracy and a Germanophone middle class was responsible for the emphasis in the German use of the words. The German bourgeoisie considered civilization as something useful, but only second class in comparison with spiritual, artistic, and religious expressions.[10] Thus, when culture was separated from the realm of progressive civilization, it could become a timeless abode of the Greek gods.

The Epiphany of Dionysos in the Nineteenth Century

Hellenism was a religion that lacked doctrinal systematization. Myths and cults led an independent life locally and were never subject to an official religious reform—like that of Josiah in ancient Judaism. Under the conditions of the new scientific-technological civilization, of the many gods of Greece, Dionysos (Latin: Bacchus) had the most meteoric career. Schiller celebrated him as a "bringer of joy." A hundred years later, the "bringer of joy" emerged in Friedrich Nietzsche as the self-destructive dionysian principle. Nietzsche claimed that he himself "was the first to grasp and discover the wonderful Dionysiac phenomenon" in "Ecce Homo" and "The Birth of Tragedy." Yet it is not hard to find proof that this is a rhetorical exaggeration. J. J. Winckelmann had developed his maxim of the classic as "noble simplicity and silent greatness" in a comparison of the level-headed Apollo with the passionate Dionysos.[11] And ever since the period of "Sturm und Drang," Dionysos had been seen as the embodiment of the impetuous creative force of the poet.[12] Against the crippling mechanization by cold intellect, the poetic genius brings the fullness of life into words. Romantic poets, philosophers, and archaeologists made yet another image of Dionysos. For all of them, he embodied the experience of the ecstatic absorption of man in the universe.[13] In the Romantic age, Dionysos gave up his privileged place as poetic genius and stood for the typical Romantic wish for unlimited flourishing of the internal creative force of man, even for death and self-destruction. Dionysos became the dionysian.[14]

All this had already transpired when Friedrich Nietzsche took up the material. Without a dissertation or the formal qualifications to teach, he was appointed professor of classical philology in Basel in 1869 at the age of twenty-four. In 1872, he published a work that was to allow him to move to a vacant chair in philosophy; meanwhile, he had become disgusted with philology. The *Birth of Tragedy* was to be the exhibit for his philosophical aptitude. In fact, it made him the most offensive philologist of his day.[15] Nietzsche described two contradictory principles in Greek religion: the Apollonian and the Dionysian. Two forms of art, visual art and music, were fed from these two sources. In addition, they stood for two human properties: Apollo for dream, Dionysos for ecstasy. To illustrate their effect in human life, Nietzsche went back to Schopenhauer, who had created a suggestive metaphor for men who had illusions about reality:

Even as on an immense, raging sea, assailed by huge wave crests, a man sits in a little rowboat trusting his frail craft, so, amidst the furious torments of this world, the individual sits tranquilly, supported by the *principium individuationis* and relying on it. One might say that the unshakable confidence in that principle has received its most magnificent expression in Apollo, and that Apollo himself may be regarded as the marvelous divine image of the *principium individuationis*, whose looks and gestures radiate the full delight, wisdom, and beauty of "illusion." In the same context Schopenhauer has described for us the tremendous awe that seizes man when he suddenly begins to doubt the cognitive modes of experience, in other words, when in a given instance the law of causation seems to suspend itself.[16]

Brooding on the image, one grows giddy. Schopenhauer saw the individuation of man as a baseless illusion, and therefore unreal and wrong. Only when the veil of Maya falls[17] does the egotistical distinction between individuals disappear. According to Nietzsche, only a self-destructive ecstasy in which man plunges into the raging sea can destroy this false appearance. "If we add to this awe the glorious exaltation which arises in man, from the very depths of nature at the shattering of the *principium individuationis* then we are in a position to apprehend the essence of Dionysiac rapture, whose closest analogy is furnished by physical intoxication."[18]

Bolder images are inconceivable to conjure up the bottomlessness of life beyond the apparently self-evident modern order: "Not only does the bond between man and man come to be forged once more by the magic of the Dionysiac rite, but nature itself, long alienated or subjugated, rises again to celebrate the reconciliation with her prodigal son, man. The earth offers its gifts voluntarily, and the savage beasts of mountain and desert approach in peace."[19] Against the illusion of a logic that thinks the individual can shape his individuality independent of the world, only ecstasy helps for a surrender to the raging life itself.

It is a long stretch between Nietzsche's words and Schiller's poetry. Dionysos, the bringer of joy, then the poetic genius, according to the model of ecstatic exaltation in life, finally became the principle of the annihilation of individuality. Thus Dionysos, in his exile in the modern world, to use a metaphor of Heinrich Heine (1853), gradually had to serve in other capacities. In Schiller, the fleeing Dionysos, expelled by the one Christian god along with the other gods, was granted freedom to reside in poetry. For Nietzsche, he can stay there only when men renounce the illusion of individualism and abandon themselves to the torrential flow of life.

Mysticism and Immortality: Rohde's Dionysos

Even if most of Nietzsche's colleagues kept quiet about him—with the prominent exception of Jane Ellen Harrison—his impact was considerable. In his monumental work, *Psyche: The Cult of Souls and Belief in Immortality among the Greeks*,[20] Erwin Rohde (1845–98) treated the figure of Dionysos in a way that was profoundly obligated to Nietzsche, although Rohde did not mention his friend's name.[21] Rohde considered Dionysos a stranger from Thrace in the Greek religion, who brought an internal difference to Hellenism that was good for it. Syncretism, a much-used category of religious history at that time, gave Greek religiosity a decisive impetus. Greek religion was able to develop a belief in the soul, as Homer's writings showed. Rohde used E. B. Tylor's *Primitive Culture* to support this position.[22] Yet Rohde could not comprehend that religions would nevertheless necessarily develop conceptions of a metaphysical identity of the soul, as Tylor had also assumed.[23] He did not believe that the Greek conception of the soul was capable of such a development. It would have required an external impetus, which came as the cult of Dionysos that immigrated to Greece.[24] The origin and spread of the belief in immortality was explained not by the independent and natural development of the idea of the soul, but by the diffusion of a special cult and thus a syncretism.

As closely as Rohde had studied Tylor, his interpretation of the development of the concept of the soul in one regard was fundamentally different from Tylor's. In letters to Otto Crusius, who was later to be his biographer, Rohde described how he had come up with the idea:[25]

> But there too—where Dionysos rages in—I did not have an inspiration . . . but at most yielded to a long pondering back and forth. It is not true that "immortality," strictly conceived, is taught by the Eleusinians. When Plutarch wants to say (Consul.ad.uxor. 10) what justifies his *hopes of immortality*, he definitely names the Dionysian mysteries. That alone would be enough to show the direction. There are a thousand others as well. But in the cult of Dionysos, the seed of belief in immortality cannot be sought anywhere else than in *ecstasy*, in its faces and revelations. That was the rough outline of my original consideration, and every more precise consideration and exposition only confirms the correctness of my approach from all sides. Speculation must enter the "dissolute giddiness" of the Dionysian consecrations in order to generate the *Greek* belief in immortality—I tell myself that a dozen times, especially when I speak of the Orphics.

Only ecstasy could have produced belief in the immortal soul. Initially, a cult of excitement existed, in which god and man were fused. In a second step, the Orphics turned ecstasy into a *doctrine* and established *sects* that tried to achieve *redemption* through asceticism and purification. Thus they created a religion of redemption that survived for centuries.[26] Belief in immortality emerged from ecstasy.

The reader of *Psyche* will hardly note the word *mysticism*, which suddenly pops up before him without any explanation. It looks like genuine Greek. But in fact, in Germany the word had long since taken on meanings that had little to do with its Greek origin. It was established in religious studies discourse at that time. When Rohde was teaching at Heidelberg, Ernst Troeltsch was one of his colleagues.[27] How well the two knew one another is not known, but both Heidelberg professors were in fact linked by the importance they ascribed to mysticism. In 1895, Troeltsch had published a large basic treatise, *The Autonomy of Religion*, justifying his claim to be considered the head of the School of Religious History, which was developing in the same decade.[28] Religion is an autonomous area of life, separate from morality and aesthetics and in tension with culture, it is based on a *sui generis* experience. In the course of development, a qualification of the world and an idealization of rejection of the world inevitably emerge from this experience. If religion with its opposition to the prevailing culture is socially successful, it even becomes an authority controlling culture. Troeltsch used the term *mysticism* to denote the experience that the visible world is not everything.[29]

To return to Rohde, his journal entries (titled *Cogitata*) show that, by 1877, he had similar ideas about mysticism.[30] If Troeltsch had heard his colleague Rohde's rector's address in Heidelberg in 1895,[31] he would have nodded in agreement with the following: "Morality is alien to mysticism; it is superfluous to it, which, in a fundamental estrangement from earthly life, does not know a practical mission of the conduct of life."[32] Like Rohde, Troeltsch wanted to overcome a moralistic determination of religious terms.[33] Rohde also thought that mysticism was an experience linked to a radical reevaluation of everyday life that led to a "devaluation of everyday life" and "an estrangement from this life."[34]

This proximity to Troeltsch corresponds with a difference between Rohde's view of Dionysos and Nietzsche's, which Rohde's biographer, O. Crusius, correctly pointed out.[35] Nietzsche saw Dionysos as the representative of an ecstatic life that obliterates all individuation, while Rohde saw him as the origin of individual immortality. Thus, for Rohde, mysticism offered the chance to save the self of the personality from destruction in the compulsion to conform to the world. In the background were two distinct views of the possible achievement of mysticism for the individual in society, which were both represented in the cultural philosophy of that time. Like many other intellectuals of that period, Nietzsche and Rohde were alarmed by the threat to the individuality of the person in a world of progressing civilization. Their solutions, however, went in different directions: Nietzsche voted for the annihilation of the illusionary self, Rohde for saving the genuine self through mysticism. With this view, Rohde was much closer to Troeltsch and (as we will soon see) to the *Relig-ionsgeschichtliche Schule* than to Nietzsche. Rohde's portrayal of classical Greek religion was based on a cultural discourse in which antiquity forfeited none of its normative nature. Nevertheless, doubts were expressed about whether modern civilization might refer to antiquity as if it were the most natural thing in the world. Rohde studied the history of ancient religion from this perspective, isolating in it what Tiele and Weber called a particular "direction" characterized by renunciation of the world and immortality of the soul. His description of Greek religious history was produced by a perspective that would be fundamentally misunderstood with the rubric of "cultural pessimism." In fact, it concerned the rescue of the individual person from his standardization by modern civilization. Moreover, the world-renouncing trends of Greek religion and philosophy described by Rohde had powerful historical and religious consequences in the investigation of early Christianity. Just as the cult of Dionysos wanted to cast sparks of ecstasy into the older intellectual concept of the soul, so Hellenistic religiosity was also to establish ecstatic elements in the Judeo-Christian religion. The representatives of the *Religionsgeschichtliche Schule* developed this approach.

The Mysteries of Life: Jane Ellen Harrison

In her memoirs of 1925, Jane E. Harrison described how the fossilized structure of classical philology even in England broke open in the 1890s. The very fact that a female scholar who openly took positions on the history of Greek religion that were diametrically opposed to established scholarly opinion signaled the beginning of a new era. Her words convey something of the turbulent mood of that time:

> We Hellenists were, in truth, at that time a "people who sat in darkness," but we were soon to see a great light, two great lights—archaeology, anthropology. Classics were turning in their long sleep. Old men began to see visions, young men to dream dreams. I had just left Cambridge when Schliemann began to dig at Troy. Among my own contemporaries was J. G. Frazer, who was soon to light the dark wood of savage superstition with a gleam from *The Golden Bough*. The happy title of that book—Sir James Frazer has a veritable genius for titles—made it arrest the attention of scholars. They saw in comparative anthropology a serious subject actually capable of elucidating a Greek or Latin text. Tylor had written and spoken; Robertson Smith, exiled for heresy, had seen the Star in the East; in vain; we classical deaf-adders stopped our ears and closed our eyes; but at the mere sound of the magical words "Golden Bough"

the scales fell—we heard and understood. Then Arthur Evans set sail for his new Atlantis and telegraphed news of the Minotaur from his own labyrinth; perforce we saw this was a serious matter, it affected the "Homeric Question."[36]

Jane Ellen Harrison (1850–1928) was one of the first women students in Cambridge; she studied classical languages at Newnham College, one of the two women's colleges.[37] In 1880, after passing the final examination—women were denied an official degree—she went to London, where she devoted herself to the study of Greek art and archaeology. There she became friendly with artists and writers who were excited about Hellenism for aesthetic reasons. During her time in London, she broke with the idealization of Greek classicism, an event that was increasingly to mark Harrison's scholarly work. After many vain attempts to receive a professorship in London, she returned to Cambridge in 1898 as a lecturer in Classical Archaeology at Newnham College, a position that allowed her to investigate a completely different Greece from the one that existed in the minds of her bourgeois contemporaries.

Jane Harrison sided with those who expected information about classical culture and literature from archaeology, an expectation that was not obvious at that time, but one which had to struggle for acceptance. Young scholars of antiquity were especially enchanted by archaeology. Back in London, Harrison had been engrossed by this new controversial field, and in 1888 she set off for Greece herself. When she arrived there, the excavations in Athens were explained to her on the spot by the German archaeologist Wilhelm Dörpfeld.[38] Dörpfeld's excavations and explanations had revolutionary consequences not only for her, but for a whole generation of young scholars of classical antiquity. With her own eyes she could see that, beneath the surface of Greek classicism, were older layers that indicated another history and culture of Greece than the familiar one. Thus, for example, the excavation of the big Dionysian theater in Athens seemed to reveal that it had no stage. Although this interpretation was soon challenged, it did raise questions about an obvious identification of the ancient with the modern theater, and the ritual premises of the ancient theater began to be considered.[39] If we can speak of a struggle for archaeology in this context, the mid-1890s were decisive. The victory of archaeology, however, logically entailed the next conflict, surrounding the issue of how the observed layers of ancient culture were to be interpreted. From 1895 on, the struggle raged around ethnology: about the value, methods, and results ethnology could have for the study of classical antiquity. In 1915, this battle was also decided, when the enlistment of ethnology was accepted by scholars of antiquity.[40]

When Jane E. Harrison came home from her trip to Greece, her observations of the excavations left their mark on the preface of her new book on Athens (1890). For the first time, she formulated a thesis that was to be a lasting inspiration for decades, and not only for religious studies:

> My belief is that in many, even in the large majority of cases *ritual practice misunderstood* explains the elaboration of myth. . . . Some of the loveliest stories the Greeks have left us will be seen to have taken their rise, not in poetic imagination, but in primitive, often savage, and, I think, always *practical* ritual. In this matter—in regarding the myth-making Greek as a practical savage rather than a poet or philosopher—I follow, *quam longo intervallo,* in the steps of Eusebius, Lobeck, Mannhardt, and Mr. Andrew Lang. The *nomina numina* method [Müller's comparative mythology] I have utterly discarded.

Observations of places of worship and rituals had led Jane E. Harrison to a conclusion similar to William Robertson Smith's: that rituals were the basis of myths. Her failure to mention Robertson Smith in this preface, even though she was to praise him in her later memoirs, might be explained simply by the fact that, when she wrote her preface in 1890, she did not know about him. Apparently, it was her personal experience of Greek archaeology along with her rejection of the idealization of Greek classicism that led her to the new view.[41] The study of antiquity awoke from its slumber. If Robertson Smith had destroyed the established image of the history of ancient Israel with his study of the history of sacrifice, Harrison's approach was just as revolutionary for classical Hellenism. Intellectual England of the nineteenth century had thought itself the resurrection of fifth century Athens, only more perfect. Harrison's studies were determined to hoist that belief on its own petard. Beneath the classical was a layer that indicated a completely different lifestyle from that of the bourgeoisie.

Jubilation over the Discovery of an Old Ritual of Mother and Son

In 1898, when Harrison returned to Cambridge, she got in touch with her old friends and like-minded scholars of antiquity, and created an unusually productive intellectual network,[42] like Émile Durkheim's in

France or Max Weber's in Germany. In 1900, she met Gilbert Murray (1866–1957), and in 1903 she met Francis Cornford (1874–1943). Later, Arthur Bernard Cook joined them.[43] All were excited about Frazer. Yet Frazer himself had no time for their careful theoretical positions, as shown by a correspondence with R. R. Marett. In his inaugural lecture as a reader in anthropology at Oxford in 1910, Marett had approvingly quoted Robertson Smith's thesis that rituals had preceded dogma in history. Marett sent a copy to Frazer, who immediately wrote back that Robertson Smith had never claimed that ritual was historically older than myth. On the contrary, Robertson Smith would have rejected such a claim as absurd. Marett had no trouble proving to Frazer that he was mistaken;[44] Frazer, however, wanted nothing to do with such theoretical arguments. Nor could he be persuaded to join the group, but went on writing his books as an individual workaholic. On the other hand, the Cambridge Ritualists, as they were later called, prepared their publications in a lively exchange of opinions among one another. One high point was no doubt 1912, when three classics appeared at the same time: Cornford's *From Religion to Philosophy*, Murray's *Four Stages of Greek Religion*, and Harrison's *Themis*, to which Cornford contributed a chapter entitled, "The Origin of the Olympic Games" and Murray a piece called, "The Ritual Forms Preserved in Greek Tragedy."

Now at last, the study of antiquity was wide awake. In the *Prolegomena to the Study of Greek Religion* of 1903, Harrison exposed the religion lying under the layer of the Olympic world of the gods and determined its internal consistency. For her as for Robertson Smith, the separate document of a remote time was a fragment that had to be added to the entirety of life at that time in order to be comprehensible. In the process, she broke with the belief in progress that had been linked with evolution by Herbert Spencer and others. Jane E. Harrison did not view the transition to civilization as a smooth increase in complexity. Instead she observed buried and forgotten initial forms. Beneath the official sacrifices of the Olympic gods, she discovered exotic rites. Believers did not enter into an exchange of gifts with the gods—as in the case of the heavenly gods. They performed acts intended to avert the rage of the gods and absolve themselves from impurity. In this world of earthly chthonish deities, goddesses assumed a high rank. Archaeology had helped in this discovery. A few years later, Harrison had not forgotten the moment when the archaeologist Arthur Evans showed her the impression of a seal ring:

> Somewhere about the turn of the century there had come to light in the palace of Cnossos a clay sealing which was a veritable little manual of

primitive Cretan faith and ritual. I shall never forget the moment when Mr. Arthur Evans first showed it me. It seemed too good to be true. It represented the Great Mother standing on her own mountain with her attendant lions, and before her a worshipper in ecstasy. At her side, a shrine with "horns of consecration." And another sealing read the riddle of the horns. The Minotaur is seated on the royal throne, and the Minotaur is none other than the human King—God wearing the mask of a bull. Here was this ancient ritual of the Mother and the Son which long preceded the worship of the Olympians: here were the true *Prolegomena*. Then when, some years later, I again visited Crete, I met with the sequel that gave me the impulse to *Thetis*, the *Hymn of the Kouretes* found in the temple of Diktaean Zeus. Here we have embodied the magical rite of the Mother and the Son, the induction of the Year-Spirit who long preceded the worship of the Father.[45]

Her interest in such finds was not purely academic. She made no secret of her growing antipathy to the classical Olympic gods. In 1885, before her sudden turn to archaeology, she had judged differently: at that time, the pre-Olympic religion seemed to be the "dark side of the Greek religion," the result of a contamination from the East.[46] On the other hand, in her first letter to Murray, part of an exchange of ideas about the emerging *Prolegomena*, in 1900, she called Zeus a "trickster."[47] The Olympians were too patriarchal for her. The family of the Olympians reflected ordinary patriarchal social relations.[48] One had to study the local cults to know the matriarchal world that was completely different from the patriarchal one. Harrison did consider the transition from the matriarchal to the patriarchal social structure as a certain progress since it did destroy the false magical prestige of the woman. But she saw the double-edged aspect of the transition when she noted that Hesiod had reinterpreted the earth goddess Pandora misogynistically because of his bourgeois attitude.[49] With the victory of the Olympians, intellect triumphed over feeling, cold rationality over female power. The patriarchal family that emerged from this victory had cut the primeval bond between mother and child. This description shows clearly that Harrison's portrayal of the pre-Olympian cult was hardly independent of her personal experiences as a woman in Victorian England.

If in the first part of the *Prolegomena*, Harrison had exposed the chthonic prehistory of the Olympians with archaeological means and style, in the second part she focused on the later overcoming of the Olympian world of the gods. With Dionysos and the Orphic mysteries, Greek religion had taken a decisive turn: instead of a cheerful and friendly superficial service to the Olympians, a religion worthy of the name now appeared. Dionysos alone adequately represents the emotionality, sexuality, and naturalness of man. Harrison gladly followed Nietzsche's ideas.[50] "The religion of Orpheus *is* religious in the sense that it is the worship of the real mysteries of life, of potencies (*daimones*) rather than personal gods (*theoi*); it is the worship of life itself in its supreme mysteries of ecstasy and love."[51] These words at the end of the book are followed by a quotation from Gilbert Murray that can serve as the credo of the Cambridge Ritualists. "Reason is great, but it is not everything. There are in the world things, not of reason, but both below and above it, causes of emotion which we cannot express, which we tend to worship, which we feel perhaps to be the precious things in life."

Harrison's concept of religion deserves attention since it consciously disregards all theological aspects. She herself was aware of the paradox of this approach. "To be an Atheist, then, to renounce eikonic theology is to me personally almost an essential of religious life." "When I say 'religion,' I am instantly obliged to correct myself; it is not religion, it is ritual that absorbs me."[52] A comparison of this view of rites with that of Robertson Smith reminds us that his view is associated with German historicism. Doctrine does not only come later than ritual, but is also rooted in something else: in understanding, reflection, and analysis. Ritual, on the other hand, is rooted in something more primeval. It is only this primeval quality that deserves the name "religion."

From the *Prolegomena* to *Themis* was not a very big step. In the meantime, Harrison had read Henri Bergson's *L'Évolution Créatrice* (1907):

> But when four years ago, I first read [Bergson's] *Évolution Créatrice*, I saw dimly at first, but with ever increasing clearness, how deep was the gulf between Dionysos the mystery-god and that Olympus he might never really enter. I knew the reason of my own profound discontent. I saw in a word that Dionysos, with every other mystery-god, was an instinctive attempt to express what Professor Bergson calls *durée*, that life which is one, indivisible and yet constantly changing. I saw on the other hand that the Olympians, amid all their atmosphere of romance and all their redeeming vices, were really creations of what Professor William James called "monarchical deism." Such deities are not an instinctive expression, but a late and conscious representation, a work of analysis, of reflection and intelligence. Primitive religion was not, as I had drifted into thinking, a tissue of errors leading to mistaken conduct; rather it was a web of practices emphasizing particular parts of life, issuing necessarily in representations and ultimately dying out into abstract conceptions.[53]

Even in the *Prolegomena*, she had emphasized that the ancient Dionysos was responsible not only for a transcendence of the individual vis-à-vis social constraints, as in Rohde, but also for a community, as in Nietzsche. Reading Durkheim had confirmed her in this. In *Themis*, she extended this line: the Olympian gods represented men who raised above life. On the other hand, the god of the mysteries represented what life really was. She interpreted rituals accordingly, as not simply an expression of emotions, but a visualization, a realization, a presentation, and a performance of them. As such, they were a community affair. A. van Gennep's *Les Rites de Passages* (1909) soon found its way to Harrison's desk, and in *Themis*, her search for buried and forgotten forms of life led again to ritual, this time understood as *drômenon*. The great events of life—birth, adolescence, marriage, death—were represented by rituals and thus became a *sui generis* reality.[54]

The Mirror of Hellenism

Studying the history of Greek religion seems to be quite different from investigating other ancient religions, perhaps because of the tacit basic assumption that the Greek past still had a brilliant future in present-day Europe. To understand the harsh struggle over the assumptions of archaeology and anthropology in the scholarship of classical antiquity, we will have to review the presence of Greece in the European educational canon.[55] Art history saw Greek classicism as the beginning of European art history, even if this was partially based on a misunderstanding of the ancient art objects.[56] The texts of the classics were read in the gymnasium attended by the children of the intellectuals and shaped their view of people and their world. There can hardly be any greater veneration shown by a society of its own free will for a culture that had long since passed away. In the case of the Jewish Bible, there was still a religious authorization that makes the permanence of this tradition comprehensible. But here, an educated class voluntarily chose a past culture as its normative ideal. The opposition articulated by Harrison and others against the image of classical Hellenism assumes this normative nature of Hellenism in the nineteenth century. The inanimate world created by Christianity and natural science had played a significant role in the process. The recollection of antiquity was to help allow the emergence of a culture untouched by the flaws of rational civilization. Greek education was a proven means to break away from the enormous consequences of modernization. They thought they were living in a revived Greek classicism.

But as the mechanization of nature and the discipline of individual life progressed, the more receptive did bourgeois culture become to internal differences in the ancient model. The ancient civilization seen to be resurrected in the present suddenly looked like the external varnish over a passionate worship of life itself. Archaeology and anthropology became the favorite means of tracing other fixed points in the history of Greece than those of bourgeois morality and aesthetics. The new methods were to help show the exotic quality of Greek culture and to systematize it by comparison. Hellenic religion contained a great deal that was scandalous, and did not seem suitable as a moral model to many bourgeois of the nineteenth century.[57] F. Max Müller had wanted to do away with this indecency in Greek culture with his nature mythology, but this attempt had ceased to be attractive long ago. The search for suppressed and forgotten forms of life in the past and for alternatives in one's own culture began to converge.

In the process, it was no accident that people focused on the history of religions. Hardly any of the participating scholars of ancient culture appear to have been personally religious, but the focus of *religion* was chosen because it promised to open the door to a world beyond the flat classical surface. It could be used not only to cast doubt on moral and aesthetic norms, but the interpreters also hoped to capture a different life and to sensitize themselves to it. The Greek myth that Müller had defended at the barricades of bourgeois morality with his nature mythology had become the key witness to the lifestyles that suddenly contrasted advantageously with those of the bourgeoisie. Instead of needing explanation, the myth now even seemed suited to justify deviant norms. In an extremely fortunate formulation of Walter Burkert, from an *explanandum*, myth had become an *explanans*.[58] The offensiveness of Greek traditions was seen as a legitimate provocation not only of the past classicism, but also of the present neo-classicism. The past stages of the history of Hellenic religion became indications of lifestyles that eluded and contradicted civilization. What some bourgeois categorically rejected and spurned as irrational was celebrated by others as an irreplaceable insight into the hidden dimensions of human nature.[59]

Nietzsche impressively described this special function of the Greek:

> *The Greeks as interpreters.*—When we speak of the Greeks we involuntarily speak of today and yesterday: their familiar history is a polished mirror that always radiates something that is not in the mirror itself. We employ our freedom to speak of them so as to be allowed to remain silent about others—so that the latter may now say something into the thoughtful reader's ear. Thus the Greeks make it easier for modern man to communicate much that is delicate and hard to communicate.[60]

CHAPTER EIGHT

THE PRODUCTIVE FORCE OF WORLD REJECTION

N THE two decades before and after the turn of the century, not only was classical scholarship on the move, but the scholarship of early Christianity also began to stir. And just as Jane Harrison had great hopes for a breakthrough, so did Wilhelm Bousset, Albert Eichhorn, Ernst Troeltsch, Hermann Gunkel, William Wrede, and other young scholars in theology. As young postdoctorates and lecturers, called the "small faculty," they shook up the Göttingen theology faculty in the 1890s, doing away with the liberal theology of their elders. This so-called Religionsgeschichtliche Schule did assume that the liberal biblical criticism was correct and they did hold onto Julius Wellhausen's reversal of Law and Prophets, as well as the two-source theory of the Synoptic Gospels.[1] Their difference with liberal theologians resulted instead from the intention to interpret both Jesus and Paul in the context of the culture of that day and thus to consider their difference systematically vis-à-vis their own time. The representatives of this school saw their primary task as reconstructing the existence of the early Christian religion genetically from contemporary contexts. They saw this more as a model of genealogy than analogy,[2] but expected diffusion rather than development. They explained similarities with other religions by influence rather than by independent development. Note that in the 1890s, the evolutionary theory that had started from a universal equal development of all human ideas and institutions had increasingly been challenged. According to the critics, the assumption of similar causes everywhere and always for similar phenomena was wrong and often overlooked the fact that similarities can emerge from the contact of cultures. It was hardly accidental that similarities between peoples increased with geographical proximity and decreased with increasing geographical distance. The strength of this model vis-à-vis the evolutionary model can be discovered clearly in the arguments of the German-American anthropologist Franz Boas, who found good reasons to replace the comparative method with the investigation of historical relations between neighboring cultures.[3] In the 1890s, this model of anthropology won increasing numbers of supporters and displaced the assumption of parallel, independent developments and inventions presented by Edward Burnett Tylor. Now, influence and diffusion were also attractive in researching the history of the Judeo-Christian religion.

Jesus in the Context of Apocalypticism

The turning point in research on the earliest Christianity can be studied in Johannes Weiss (1863–1914), a scholar who was at home on both sides of the emerging boundary between the liberal theologians and the Religionsgeschichtliche Schule. He was personally very close to Albrecht Ritschl (1822–89) and had married Ritschl's daughter. On the other hand, he sensed that Jesus' preaching and Ritschl's interpretation of the Kingdom of God were two quite different things.[4] Ritschl had understood the Kingdom of God as a kind of moral authority, like Kant's categorical imperative. The Kingdom of God is achieved through the disciples of Jesus doing the will of God. Weiss subjected his father-in-law's view to a more precise examination. In *Die Predigt Jesu vom Reiche Gottes* (Jesus' Proclamation of the Kingdom of God, 1892), he explained his reasons for coming to a completely different finding. Reading the brief text conveys the relentless ferocity of its destruction of fond assumptions. Weiss relied on the words of Jesus from the Bible text, which demonstrated that Jesus' ethics were completely conditional on His expectation of the impending end of the world. Only this explains why Jesus saw wealth as an irreconcilable foe of God and preached that all those who parted with it might have the hope of being saved from the approaching judgment (Matthew 19:21).[5] Jesus raised even more, equally radical demands: anyone who "does not hate his own father and mother and wife and children and brothers and sisters, yes, even his own life, he cannot be my disciple" (Luke 14:26).[6] Jesus demanded things that were simply impossible under ordinary circumstances, and that made sense only under the assumption that the Kingdom of God was at hand. Jesus' demands did not come from an ideal of human community and had nothing to do with generally valid moral norms. They came from the dreadful seriousness of the present view of the end of days. "The greatest crisis of world history is at the gates. The most blessed salvation and the most awful doom lie hidden in the dark of the nearest future. Once more, at the eleventh hour, is the decision about his own fate given to everyone. The time is short."[7] There is only one salvation: everyone had to repent and atone if they did not want to perish in the messianic judgment (Luke 13:3, 5). Weiss's discovery posed a new choice for the study of the life of Jesus: to understand Jesus either eschatologically or not at all.[8] Many years later, Rudolf Bultmann still remembered how great was the shock of his discovery: "Then, however, it came as a shock to the theological world. I still recall how Julius Kaftan in his lectures on dogmatics said, 'If the Kingdom of God is an eschatological matter, then it is a useless concept so far as dogmatics is concerned.'"[9]

Yet even the author himself was uneasy about the effect of his claim, and by the second edition of his book in 1900, he clearly weakened it: "The first edition of this work was rebuked for connecting Jesus' ethical preaching too closely with the eschatological proclamation. Jesus' worldview was too one-sided, his judgment of earthly life was placed in the harsh light of the impending end of the world, and therefore the portrayal of the ethics turned out much too negative, ascetic, and escapist. I must admit that in a certain sense."[10]

Even before this retraction and not especially impressed by it later, Wilhelm Bousset had used Weiss's discovery to determine more precisely the historical religious context of Jesus' tidings. An understanding of Jesus and his disciples was possible only if they were placed in the history of contemporary religions in Palestine, a step that had an impact on the reevaluation of ancient texts. Some texts that had previously not been considered important were suddenly granted a high status as historical sources. These were books that had been known in synagogues and in early churches, but had later been removed from official Jewish literature as well as from the canon of the Roman Catholic Church. Thus, apocalyptic writings between the second century B.C. and the first century A.D. had lost their official validity in synagogue and church except for the apocalypse of Daniel, but had not vanished. Various other old Christian churches would not give up these writings and saw them as further revelations of the impending end, and thus many of these texts were preserved as translations into Ethiopian, Syrian, and Slavic.[11] Growing interest in the historical religious context of Jesus and his disciples led to a systematic tracking down and editing of these texts, which were translated into German for the first time by E. Kautzsch in 1898–99, with the title *Apokryphen und Pseudepigraphen*. Since the texts from Daniel, Henoch, 4 Ezra, and Baruch contained revelations that had allegedly been issued and written down in the dim and distant past—but in reality only shortly before they became known—they demonstrated how widespread expectations of the End had been in Palestine at that time. Bousset correctly assumed, as the later manuscripts of Qumran confirmed, that these texts were even more key than the canonical ones for the history of the Jewish religion in the first century A.D.

In 1919, in a later review of this new perspective, Bousset described how the discoveries of these texts had contributed to a reevaluation of early Christianity. Bousset and the other representatives of the Religionsgeschichtliche Schule used them to take early Christianity out of the context of the Jewish "religion of law" and put it in the context of "late Jewish" religious history. Before rabbinic Judaism became the spokesman, apocalypticism had prevailed.

> Only three or four years ago we heard our teacher Ritschl say that the dignity of the New Testament scriptures compared with their successors comes from their direct contact with the texts of the Old Testament and only thus can they be understood. How our scholarship has changed since then! It has taken two giant steps beyond that situation. First, it was clear to us that Ritschl's statement was wrong since there is still a large, unresearched land between the Old and the New Testaments, late Judaism. And as we set about this research, it became clear to us that the most important basic notions of Jesus' preaching, the Son of Man and the Kingdom of God first came to light in this later time and its literature, that the growth of early Christianity in the world cannot be understood without a knowledge of Diaspora Judaism, its religious worship and its liturgy. And as soon as our eyes grew accustomed to the new discoveries that arose here, our scholarship needed to take a second big step. We discovered that we could not understand Paul and John in many essentials without precise knowledge of the world of Hellenistic religion, the world in which Christianity conquered its new homeland, especially by Paul.[12]

The great discoveries of written monuments in the East stimulated research even more. If Robertson Smith and Wellhausen had seen the old Arabic religion as an analogy to the old Israelite religion, the newly uncovered Jewish and Babylonian texts probably would allow connections between Israel and its neighbors.[13] The new discoveries provided one more reason to stop seeing breaks in the tradition as consequences of independent development, but rather to consider them as diffusion. Late Judaism had not been an independent continuation of the Old Testament religion, but was rather a new model with the stamp of contemporary pagan religions.[14] Syncretism had become typical for the religious historical context in which early Christianity had taken shape. The "hybrid religions" of Judaism and Hellenism had appeared first and foremost in the Apocalypticism. The Jews who were fond of Hellenism were the "leaven, which induced and advanced the process of fermentation in Hellenistic culture."[15] From this merger, the miracle of the Gospel could finally rise.[16]

Along with the scholarly motives for this new interpretation, the impact of a civic ideology should not be ignored. The tendency to consider a non-Israelite "pagan" influence in ancient Judaism systematically revealed an anti-Semitism that was rife among the bourgeoisie.[17] Despite their legal equality and their successful economic emancipation from the ghetto, German Jews were refused recognition as fellow citizens with equal rights. Prejudices of German citizens against the Jews were not limited to the political arena, but left deep traces in historiography. The category of syncretism was designed to dissociate Christianity from Judaism, and to indicate that injection of hellenistic ecstatic religiosity which Judaism urgently needed if it was to liberate itself from its stiff religiosity of law. The newly discovered historical context of early Christianity allowed Bousset to redefine Jesus' relationship with Judaism. Not obedience to the Law, but expectation of the End of Days formed the focus of his preaching. But even here, Jesus distinguished himself favorably from Jewish views of his time. While the God of the apocalyptic texts had been a remote and transcendent monarch of the world, Jesus regarded Him as a close Father in Whom man could place all his hopes. Instead of awaiting the Kingdom of God with fear and terror, Jesus and his disciples awaited it with joy.[18]

Fitting early Christianity into this context essentially changed its character. What Wellhausen had done for early Israelite history happened again in the study of the late history of ancient Judaism. The "Law" was neutralized by an historical operation. The newly discovered texts became the "main bridges between the Old and the New Testaments."[19] The snag in this rearrangement was recognized and criticized directly by the Jewish scholar George Foot Moore. For the reconstruction of the *Religion des Judentums im späthellenistischen Zeitalter*, Bousset referred almost exclusively to the Apocrypha and Pseudepigrapha and only secondarily and occasionally to the recognized and authorized texts of the rabbinical schools and the synagogue. This was as if the history of early Christianity were written exclusively with the apocryphal Gospels, the acts of the Apostles, and the Apocalypses.[20]

For Bousset, the *Apocrypha* and *Pseudepigrapha* represented the keys to a genuinely fervent popular religion. They were also distinguished favorably from the sources of educated Jewish scribes. This perspective was especially important to Bousset and the other representatives of the Religionsgeschichtliche Schule, and distinguished them from the previous literary criticism. "How often is the unwritten more important than the written!" exclaimed Hugo Gressmann, explaining that it was religious experiences that counted, not their literary expression. Since all literary material had to consider the intellectual assumptions of hearers and readers, attention was focused on the oral tradition, which always was much closer to religious experience than written texts.[21]

> The literary critic does not usually remember that there is also an unwritten history, and that one has to go beyond literary texts if one wants to grasp the impelling motives. How often is the unwritten more important than the written! "It is precisely what is vital, historically effective, i.e., significant in it . . . what never has its ultimate basis in books, but rather in persons, their experiences, and in the history they are rooted in" [Gunkel 1895, *Schöpfung und Chaos*, 238]. The historian who observes men and relationships pushes aside the philologist who studies books; the scholar should be both in the same person.[22]

One logical assumption of this theory, that religion ultimately eluded a rational grasp, is directly and clearly avowed in Heinrich Hackmann, a less prominent member of the Religionsgeschichtliche Schule.[23] Bousset also saw religion as an exclusively irrational force.[24] A similar claim accorded completely with Dilthey's vitalism, which valued experience higher than its expression, and saw the interpretation of an author as hermeneutically more informative than his intention.

Paul in the Context of Gnosticism

What Apocalyticism was to be for Jesus—the primary context of all his words and actions—Gnosticism and mystery religions were to be for the early Hellenistic communities and for Paul. In his history of dogma, Adolf Harnack argued that the missionary success of Christianity among the Greek-speaking pagans had been bought at the price of its hellenization. Bousset agreed but raised the obvious question of whether the process had not begun much earlier than Harnack thought, that is, back in the time of the New Testament.[25] Harnack had exempted early Christianity from such considerations, rejecting the notion that Gnosticism might have been an independent movement that could have influenced Christianity. In a review of Bousset's book, *Hauptprobleme der Gnosis* (1907), Harnack's description of Gnosticism was extraordinarily disparaging. Gnosticism deserved study only as a problem of church history. "But, aside from its church historical significance—in terms of world history and the universal history of religion—it did not have any significance, was not a factor, but rather a passive element, eternally obsolete, a hodgepodge of fossils, a storeroom and rubbish heap."[26] Bousset and other historians of religion naturally saw it quite differently, as a religious movement independent of Christianity, which influenced its early history even if it is not mentioned directly. Decades later, Hans Jonas commented on the reason why Gnosticism had attracted the attention of historians and philosophers of religion:

> Something in Gnosticism knocks at the door of our Being and of our twentieth-century Being in particular. Here is humanity in a crisis and in some of the radical possibilities of choices that man can make concerning his view of his position in the world, of his relation to himself, to the absolute and to his mortal Being. And there is certainly something in Gnosticism that helps one to understand humanity better than one would understand it if one had never known of Gnosticism.[27]

Bousset concluded from the new studies that Gnosticism must have been a phenomenon of religious history independent of Judaism and Christianity.[28] Important additional discoveries of texts allowed him to seek its origin in the East. In the gnostic view, the world fell into two dualistic parts: into the good kingdom of light and the bad kingdom of darkness. The good spirit-soul of man is held and enslaved by the power of fate, of the seven planets, in this world. To free itself from this imprisonment and begin the journey to Heaven, it needs the redeeming wisdom. A redeeming god would come down from the upper world to bring the necessary knowledge of truth and pave the way to the Kingdom of Light above. Bousset considered this image a blend of Greek, Babylonian, and Persian elements.

Gnosticism, which is less a doctrine than a specific religiosity, helps to explain some facts of early Christianity that are otherwise hard to grasp.[29] These include the extremely early verified cultic worship of Jesus and the idea of His pre-existence. A previously existing doctrine of a redeemer god from Heaven had been transferred to the person of Jesus. Early Christianity had been molded by this popular religious movement, but had also corrected its views.[30] In a passionate lecture, Bousset later characterized Gnosticism as a religion that wanted to remove the shackles of rational contemplation, so its adherents could savor direct experience in a state of ecstasy.[31] If Christianity had followed this Hellenistic model completely, it would have vanished, but that fate was avoided because of rational theology. Like a good gardener, the task of ecclesiastical theology was to prune the wild shoots of religion and channel the impetuous stream, providing a language to communicate about religion.[32] Richard Reitzenstein's studies of ancient mystery religions reached a similar conclusion. The reference system for the interpretation of early Christianity, especially of Paul and John, was no longer the ethical religiosity of Judaism, but Hellenistic religiosity.

The Category of the Salvation Religion

When Bousset adopted the term *salvation religion*, it already had a long and choppy history. Surprising as it may sound, its genealogy was philosophical and led from Hegel through Schopenhauer to two German philosophers of religion at the end of the nineteenth century. Eduard von Hartmann (1888) and then Hermann Siebeck (1893) both conceived of the salvation religion as an independent stage in the history of religions. Siebeck's explanations demonstrated clearly why salvation religion as a separate category of religions was interesting.

Siebeck began his philosophy of religion not with a definition of religion, but with a reference to its *actuality*. Aside from the content and nature of religion, agreement could be achieved on its "position in cultural life." Religion was an independent cultural factor along with "language and customs, morality and law, family and government, school and upbringing, art and technology, science and practice."[33] Unlike the phenomena mentioned, religion takes "a position toward the total value of the culture that is critical and thereby *problematic*."[34] That is, only religion can claim its right to deny the finality of the secular and pass a rejecting judgment on the whole world. "It looks as if, through the existence of religion, the unity of cultural life experiences a split that would not have existed otherwise."[35] Starting from this premise, Siebeck developed a division of historical religions into three categories. *Natural religions* considered gods as saviors from external evil. *Morality religions* saw gods as guarantors of social norms and also took a positive attitude to the world. Only a reflection that succeeded the morality religion leads to another attitude to the world. *Salvation religions* focused on the contradiction between the existence of God and the reality of evil in the world. Only now can the notion of God serve the denial of the world.[36]

A few years later, when Cornelis Petrus Tiele delivered his Gifford Lectures, he attacked this view. Siebeck's first two categories did concur with Tiele's own division, since he also distinguished natural religions from ethical religions. Nevertheless, Tiele rejected salvation religion as a distinct category. If salvation is understood generally as liberation from evil, it applies to all religions and is then too big as a category. But in the strict sense, the only religions that reject the world were Buddhism and Pauline Christianity, which leaves the category too small. Then Tiele added a comment that showed he knew and understood the assumptions of German religious philosophy: "In fact, his [Siebeck's] classification is closely connected with his conception of religion as 'world-negation' [*Weltverneinung*] which is really applicable to one set of religions only, and with which on the whole I cannot agree."[37]

Siebeck's conception of salvation religion has special consequences. Since the typical feature of all religions is denial of the world, he saw the sequence of natural, moral, and salvation religions as an inexorable development affecting the view of man himself. In morality religion, the predominant issue was a social community, in which the individual remained subordinate to society. Only in salvation religion could he face the world as an independent, individual person. Only in that religion does the spirit come into conflict with the world, both theoretically and practically.[38] Thus Siebeck explained that individuality was a product of the history of religions. To define such a development more precisely, Siebeck distinguished between a *subjective* and an *objective* aspect of religion.

> The subjective aspect of religion, as distinguished from the objective aspect, can be defined as the existence of religious thoughts, feelings, moods, and forebodings, that appear as the contents of both the individual and the community awareness. . . . The objective side is the existence of some oral and some written handed-down doctrines, dogmas, commandments, and prohibitions, promises, and an equal sum of actions, some symbolic and some directly graphic, which all serves to exhibit a community filled with the same religious spirit and to strengthen and reinforce it.[39]

Siebeck referred critically to Kant's metaphor of the "vehicle" of pure religion. Unlike Kant, Siebeck also saw subjective religiosity as bound to the objective handicaps of scripture, doctrine, and ritual. This reevaluation of the "vehicle" as representation of the spirit ultimately goes back to Hegel. So, distinguishing a subjective from an objective religion did not correspond to the two religions as we know from Hobbes, Rousseau, Kant, and others. Instead, Siebeck—following Hegel—assumed that subjective and objective sides need one another. There is no subjective religion that is not carried by objective forms, just as there are no concrete forms without subjective spirit. For this mediated religion, Siebeck used the term "religiosity," an interface between the individual and religious tradition. Salvation religion establishes a socially effective subjective principle. By means of it, it evokes an internal rupture of culture and provide religious lifestyles with an inherent value vis-à-vis otherwise valid norms.

Siebeck clearly developed an approach that was continued a few years later by Ernst Troeltsch, Max Weber, and Georg Simmel, each with a different perspective, even though they were apparently not directly dependent on Siebeck.

Siebeck's position, which was long ignored, shows clearly that, a few years before the Religionsgeschichtliche Schule, *salvation religion* had already become a cultural and philosophical term that increased in importance with the rise of this new trend. Ernst Troeltsch especially assigned the term a cardinal function in the theory of religion, combining historical and normative perspectives in his argumentation. Troeltsch was aware of the problems arising from a radically historical examination of Christianity.[40] Although the new discipline of the history of religions—which had emerged from the cooperation of the study of antiquity, Oriental philology, and anthropology—was still incomplete, it was already affecting theology. That is, if all religions including Christianity were purely historical phenomena, there is only one single source for normative knowledge: the history of religions itself.[41] Like Siebeck, Troeltsch also assumed that religion was not a purely internal and spontaneous product of human consciousness, but—aside from such exceptions as the founders of religions— was conveyed by firm external traditions. He considered religions a historical force of the standardization of morality and worldview. As a result, normative knowledge can be gained only through a comparison of religious traditions. Troeltsch found the measuring rod in a general tendency of the history of religions to "spiritualization, internalization, moralization, and individualization." If Christianity is placed in such a trend, it assumes a leading role. "It alone, among all religions, by breaking on principle with any kind of nature religion, fulfilled the drive toward salvation, as, in this connection, it had fulfilled the drive toward a purely internal general validity."[42] In his well-known 1902 lecture, *Absoluteness of Christianity and the History of Religions*, Troeltsch expatiated on this view. The history of religions constantly shows that religions tend to be independent of their natural ties to nature, place, and society. The more highly developed they are, the more they break with the natural and social world, making man independent of existing reality, even of the nature of his own soul, and confronting him as an autonomous individual with reality. This happens most consistently in salvation religions.[43]

The postulate of an autonomy of religion was both necessary and fundamental for this cultural critical version of religion. Back in 1895–96, Troeltsch had said that religion was an independent area of life. As a "deep and vigorous belief," it exists "in a certain tension with culture." An experience of God that could not be more closely defined forms the "original fact of consciousness."[44] Whether religions could hold their own vis-à-vis modern science was not a question in view of these premises. They could! Salvation religions that turned the soul against the world assumed the subjectivity and personality of individuals. It was not culture in general, but only the religion in it that could ensure the subjectivity of man in the world, especially the mechanized world. Religion was thus something other than an ethical ideal; it was the basis of practiced subjectivity. The autonomy of religion and an irreducibility of the individual were two sides of the same coin. Only religion can protect culture from a permanent descent into materialism and save the human personality.[45] This view was even more persuasive at that time because research in religious history provided it with resounding proof. The more firmly Christianity was placed in the religious historical context of its time, the clearer the categories expressing a distance from the world emerged: eschatology, apocalypticism, mysticism, and asceticism. The more early Christianity was examined in purely historical terms, the more normative knowledge did this observation produce. The history of religions sanctioned the view that the Christian religion was a force that could separate man from the culture that was overwhelming him.

In the entry titled "Salvation" in the concise dictionary of theology and religious studies, *Religion in Geschichte und Gegenwart* (Religion in History and the Present), Troeltsch clearly described why the term "salvation" was a bridge from the general history of religion to the existential problematic of "meaning":[46]

> All areas of religion that are allowed to develop a deep and rich ethical and religious content, somehow result in belief in salvation. The stronger and more homogeneously the deity rises to the embodiment of everything good and perfect and to the quintessence of all true and eternal reality, the greater is the distance of man and the yearning to overcome this distance, the clearer the impediment standing between God and man emerges as world. Either the world now becomes a principle of appearance and error, of ephemerality and suffering, or of sin and alienation from God.[47]

As examples along with Christianity, Troeltsch listed Hinduism, Parsism, the Greek religion, the "dark gnostic-syncretic Near Eastern religion movement," and the Israelite religion. Only Islam and Judaism, which broke with Christianity, lacked ideas of redemption and remained essentially moralist. Note how this system of religion dissociated Judaism from Christianity, with a perspective relevant to the culture of the modern age. Compared with Judaism, Christianity increased the distance between God and the World and thus established individualism as a real force. This had been a special and unique achievement of Christianity that Judaism had not been able to attain, nor could the other great existing salvation religion, Buddhism. Buddhism regarded God not as a first cause of the personal value of freedom, but as a realm of the impersonal, where the idea of personality turns out to be an error and an illusion. In terms of Troeltsch's view—which was indebted to Hegel—the two salvation religions, Christianity and Buddhism, produced two contrasting concepts of human subjectivity: one created a tension of the human self with the existing forces of the world, while the other provided for an extinction of the self in oneness with the divine.[48]

With the category of "salvation religion," Troeltsch, Bousset, and other historians of religions systematically distanced themselves from the old liberal Protestant theology, especially that of Ritschl. If the older liberal theology supported a harmony between culture and religion, the distance from the world now became a distinguishing feature of Christianity. Friedrich Wilhelm Graf clearly hit the pivot and crux of this consideration, which also gave rise to Weber's sociology of religion: "The 'historians of religion' and the theologians associated with them radicalized the tension between religion and 'world' in the eschatological character of the original Christian kerygma into a contrast that is constitutive and normative for the nature of genuine Christianity."[49] These scholars decisively rejected the view of Christianity as an almost spontaneously intuitive religiosity. Christianity was also a historical religion. To grasp its spirit required classifying it in the history of religions. Eschatology, apocalypticism, and asceticism were valid as authentic forms of expression of this Christian redemption religion. Thus, the religious history of ancient Christianity approached discoveries that Rohde had attained in observations of Hellenism. But in this theological context, they assumed a normative authority.

Franz Overbeck, the theologian and close friend of Nietzsche, proclaimed triumphantly that the fundamental nature of Christianity was "ascetic." This was the root of its force, because "the ascetic impulse is as deeply embedded in mankind as the opposite. Without consideration of this fact, no culture is possible among men. Asceticism and libido must develop in the same freedom."[50] This was not a lone voice. The decades when the Religionsgeschichtliche Schule was taking shape were full of admiration for apocalyptic expectation and mystical escape from the world. Representatives of the Religionsgeschichtliche Schule wrote the history of early Christianity from the perspective of rejection of the world, and no longer from morality. They replaced Kant's philosophy of religion with Hegel's (and Schopenhauer's), and thus met the horizon of expectations of many contemporaries.

CHAPTER NINE

COMPETING MODELS OF THE RECAPITULATION

OF THE HISTORY OF RELIGIONS

The Pre-Animism of Robert Ranulph Marett

IN RELIGIOUS studies, the new century began with a thunderbolt. In 1899, Robert Ranulph Marett (1866–1943), an Oxford philosopher who loved ethnology,[1] was invited by the British Anthropological Society to deliver a lecture at its next session in Dover.[2] Because the program seemed too insipid to those in charge, they wrote Marett asking him to spice it up with something exciting. At the time, Marett was on the island of Jersey, separated from his books by the English Channel. Fortunately for him, his wife, who checked religious historical sources for him, had a few excerpts with her. "On these I fell hungrily, resolved to suck from them their last drop of juice. My paper entitled 'Preanimistic Religion' was the outcome of this squeezing process."[3] The Dover lecture was enthusiastically received, and the publisher of *Folk-Lore* offered to include it in his journal, where it appeared in 1900 with the title, "Pre-animistic Religion."[4] Yet Marett was haunted by the suspicion that what was a tremendous success in Dover would fail at home in Oxford.[5]

As a philosopher, Marett had seen the dilemma of the comparative study of religion more sharply than many of those directly involved in the work of comparison and classification. Marett saw that pigeonholes had to be found for the "vast and chaotic piles of 'slips' which their observation or reading has accumulated."[6] They had distinguished magic from religion, ritual from myth, mysticism from ethics. E. B. Tylor's well-known phrase, "belief in spiritual beings," was too rigid and intellectual to appropriately capture the differentiation of all these facts. Marett's suggestion of "pre-animistic religion" seemed to promise a remedy. The understandable idea of animation had to be preceded by something else—a psychological fact. A feeling of awe 'drives a man, ere he can think or theorize upon it, into personal relations with the supernatural."[7] According to him, this feeling was the common matrix of all facts of the history of religion and still formed the common base beneath the endlessly fluctuating objects. *Animatism*,[8] as Marett called it, was to provide an experimental formulation whose value was in the practical study of religion. In the argument with Tylor's "animism," Marett did seem to be pushing the search for the beginning of religion even farther into the dark prehistory of man. In fact, his argument was not aimed at an origin of religion at the beginning of human history, but rather at a psychology of religion.

Marett suspected that contemporary scholars of religion were already operating tacitly with these kinds of assumptions.[9] In his autobiography, he pondered his great success that had surprised even him.[10] At the time of the lecture, he did not yet know Émile Durkheim. When he later discovered the French sociologist and his colleagues, Marett bought all the volumes of *L'Année sociologique* himself, since no library in Oxford had them. In Volume 7, he discovered the treatise by Hubert and Mauss, "Outline of a General Theory of Magic," from 1902–3. Hubert and Mauss had analyzed magic as Marett had, and discovered in the Melanesian *mana* a basic phenomenon from which magic and religion had been formed. Without knowing one another, the Durkheim School in France and Marett in England had shot at the "same bird." They shot, as he unselfishly admitted, with a wider caliber, but he had shot first. Marett described his great success with a certain astonishment. Wilhelm Wundt in Leipzig promptly granted him a prominent place in his *Elements of Folk Psychology*, and even spoke of "Marettian pre-animism."[11] From then on, his place in the footnotes of the industrious German scholars was secured, he added ironically. Konrad Theodor Preuss even supported his thesis with evidence from Central America.[12] Support also came from America, where William James[13] signaled his agreement with Marett, and John Napoleon Brinton Hewitt[14] collected North American source material in his 1902 essay, *Orenda and a Definition of Religion*, which was grist to Marett's mill.

The God Material

Marett later characterized his conception with the metaphor of "plasma": magic and religion had emerged from a "common plasma."[15] Elsewhere, he even spoke of "theoplasma or God material."[16] The elementary religion was represented best by *mana*,[17] the raw material of all religions.[18] Thought, emotion, and behavior was still undifferentiated in this state. It was only a later development that led to their differentiation.[19] The starting point of the history of religion and the remaining structural element beyond all differentiation was an amorphous experience of power. Thus Marett found an authority from which religion had naturally emerged and was constantly reemerging in every individual. Elementary religion was an ever-possible experience independent from the everyday world.[20] Marett thought that man constantly carries the possibility of religion within himself.[21] Even a completely exotic type of religious experience could therefore be translated into one's own experience, and only when that happened was it adequately recognized.[22]

Marett could therefore do without a *Survival* theory, which he saw as superfluous.[23] In Tylor, *Survivals* had been those irrational views and acts in modern society that had analogues in primitive cultures and hence must have been early stages of our own culture. Marett replaced them with a fundamental experience of power, which was only secondarily molded into ideas. A psychology of religion replaced intellectual explanation. This new aspect allowed Marett to integrate religious historical facts systematically into a scholarly model. That was influenced by W. Robertson Smith, who had proved the link between *holy* and *impure*.[24]

In his autobiography, Marett's astonishment at the success of his lecture can still be felt. Even in our own day, it is astounding. The idea that the seed of religion was an experience of power was accepted into the theory of religion by Nathan Söderblom, Rudolf Otto, and Gerardus van der Leeuw, and both Max Weber and Émile Durkheim referred to it. Ever since 1900, all important trends of the analysis of religion have accepted Marett's pre-animism, all of them subscribed to the view that positive religions were formed in their history from one original, essential religion, which remained in human life as an unspecific experience. The unanimity of scholars, who otherwise attacked one another, is even more astonishing since the grounds for pre-animism were rather weak. According to Robert Henry Codrington, the discoverer of *mana* in the Melanesian religion, *mana* works only under the direction and control of a person—a living human being, a ghost, or a spirit. In all known cases, the effect of *mana* was based on its connection with a person and not with an impersonal experience of power. Yet Marett's definition eliminated this internal connection with the personal. With complete justification, *mana* could have been interpreted as a special form of animism.[25] Thus, the triumphal march of pre-animism existed in tension with its ethnological grounds. But then what was the real reason for the great success?

The Crisis of Historicism and the History of Religion

To explain the success of pre-animism, we must turn to the crisis of historical thought at that time. Historicism, as an idea that the norms of contemporary acts can be inferred from history, had become especially powerful in Germany between 1792 and 1815. Referring to the theory of a timeless natural law, the French Revolution wanted to create a supernational reasonable political order. When it ended in terror, belief in the existence of such a natural law was shattered. In Germany, during the wars of liberation, when demands for a creation of a national Civil Code and a legislative jurisdiction of the German people arose, they were opposed by Friedrich Karl von Savigny (1777–1861), a representative of the Historical School of Law: "The Historical School assumes that the material of the law is given by the entire past of the nation, but not arbitrarily, not either one thing or another at random, but rather emerges from the deepest nature of the nation itself and its history."[26]

The law of a nation comes from its customs and habits, but not from a formal legislative act, thus making historical knowledge extremely relevant for practical political acts. Political legitimacy depended on this knowledge, which was provided by historians who wrote history from the perspective of the nation-state. Since the state was an original regime of the people, its history could give information about it.[27]

Nevertheless, what had initially been a strength of national historiography after the failure of the French Revolution turned into its weakness in the second half of the nineteenth century. The processes of modernization permeated trusted and customary legal and political relations. Historicism that could provide an orientation in political questions could no longer offer help to understand the processes of social changes. Historical knowledge was suddenly suspect. Friedrich Nietzsche described the situation drastically in 1874: "Now not only does life no longer rule and control knowledge about the past, but also all the border markings have been ripped up, and everything that used to exist has come crashing down onto people. . . . No generation ever saw such an immense spectacle as is shown now by the science of universal becoming, by history."[28]

If historical knowledge had previously been expected to provide an orientation, now the opposite was true. In 1902, Hugo von Hofmannsthal expressed his disappointment: "My case, in short, is this: I have completely lost the ability to talk or think coherently about anything."[29] After World War I, the accusation of the futility, even harm of historical knowledge culminated in a revolt against historical thinking in general. At that time, Ernst Troeltsch ruthlessly revealed the symptoms of the crisis in lectures and in an article in the *Neue Rundschau*. Along with the "disappointment of a suffering mankind that no longer trusts intellectual progress," historicization had also pulled government, law, morality and art into the flow of the historical process. The arbitrariness of the historian who selected a few facts as representative from the vast abundance of sources and ignored others as inconsequential could not be overlooked. When historical research became more modest and philosophical in reaction to this arbitrariness, the suffering grew worse. Moreover, when sociological perspectives were included in historical research, that also contributed to making large syntheses impossible, since the problems now considered would challenge only the specialists.[30] The crisis of historicism reached its climax in the 1920s, but it had begun in the last quarter of the nineteenth century.

In *Geschichte des Historismus* (History of Historicism), Friedrich Jaeger and Jörn Rüsen showed how an uneasiness with the prevailing view of history had been articulated in Germany, especially since the 1890s. A "call for cultural history" and for a reconstruction of life even of the "broad masses" were the signals.[31] In the 1890s, the historian Karl Lamprecht (1856–1915) had demanded a historiography to close the growing gap between individual and politics through a study of culture. The historian, he argued, must use laws to explain the material of history, just as the scientist explains the phenomena of nature. Yet, instead of leading to a renewal of research attempts, this venture led to a bitter quarrel over methods. Things turned out badly for Lamprecht. His own historiography was hardly convincing of the need for such a drastic change of perspective. The academic study of history in Germany returned to historicism with its national focus, along with an idiosyncratic drawing of boundaries between disciplines. The study of history was assigned to deal with the individual, while other sciences, like sociology and economics, were to investigate general laws of human behavior and thought.[32]

To get a better understanding of the different solutions, Georg G. Iggers compared the problem in Germany and France. French historians had no reservations about adopting scientific methods in the study of history and investigating collective facts in history, but that fit into a different internal political situation. Compared with Germany, liberal intellectuals in France participated much more in political power and could successfully oppose conservative images of history. In Germany, the worldview of the political elites played a part in drawing the distinctive boundaries between history and sociology differently. While boundaries between disciplines remained open in France and research was devoted to the investigation of collective mentalities, in Germany those boundaries were sealed for several decades.[33] The study of history focused on nation, politics, and law, while society and economics fell within the realm of sociology. Between these two powerful giants of scientific knowledge, religious studies was dwarfed. The history of religions was guaranteed a disproportionate significance only because it was an argument in the critical cultural discourse.

Many intellectuals saw national historiography failing and unable to provide any knowledge for orientation, and turned their attention to the history of religions, which seemed to promise reliable information about human life before modern society. The more the new great forces of industrialization of economics, the introduction of science in education, the objectification of power, and the individualization of life were distrusted and seen as threatening human life, the more interest there was in the history of religions. Modern society invaded the life of the individual and the nation as a whole with tremendous force, and whether that incursion constituted a liberation or an irreplaceable loss could best be judged, it was thought, in light of the history of religions. The highly regarded works of the early research on religion had produced important insights about the extreme age of religions, the structure of religions in the simplest communities, the differences between the history of Semitic and Indo-European religion, the permanence of the concept of the soul, the existence of magic in modern culture and its tension with official religion, the meaning of ritual for the formation of communities, as well as the consequences of world-denying religions for the history of culture. All that was available. Moreover, the descriptions of these finds were already written from the perspective of the present and focused on religion as a human lifestyle whose passing away people experienced.

What was lacking was a theory of religion that could clarify the meaning of the past history of religion for human life today. A modern concept of religion was needed to enable the countless discoveries of the history of religion to be grasped systematically and to allow a description of their meanings for life even under the conditions of modern civilization. Intellectuals saw the history of religion as a possible key witness to the extent of the human damage wrought by modern civilization. The theory of pre-animism met this expectation. It was broad enough to cover an endless quantity of religious historical documents, and it was principled enough to identify a specific kind of experience in all of them. It provided a model that could definitely be compared with Haeckel's "biogenetic formula." Now a universal principle of formation that also structured life in the present could be perceived in the various findings of religions. This was the real reason why pre-animism was attractive, but it is not sufficient to explain its success. That was achieved by a theory of knowledge.

Support from the Theory of Knowledge

At that time, philosophy in Germany took a serious turn that was not confined to the national borders. In 1894, in a rector's address in Strassburg titled "History and Natural Science," Wilhelm Windelband (1848–1915) had assigned philosophy the task of advancing the theory of knowledge. Philosophy was not to be limited to study only its own history, nor was it to turn into psychology, but was instead to devote itself to the process of acquiring knowledge, to penetrate its structure, express it in a general form, and determine its boundaries: "Never has a productive method emerged out of an abstract construction or purely formal considerations of logicians for they are assigned only the task of giving a general form to what has been successfully developed in practice and then determining its meaning, its cognitive value, and the limits of its application."[34]

The usual division of empirical science into natural science and the humanities could no longer satisfy him. A division of our total knowledge could only be done according to formal criteria of knowledge, not according to the outdated scheme of nature-spirit. Hence, Windelband suggested a new subdivision of empirical studies into those that sought in reality what was general in the form of a natural law, and those that sought in reality individual facts or events. The former was the science of laws (natural science) and the latter was the science of events (history); the former was nomothetic, the latter idiographic. It was not the content of knowledge that justified the distinction between the two, but rather the treatment of reality. Windelband gave religion its place in history. In a lucid article of 1902, he reviewed the history of the philosophy of religion once more: Kant had changed the point of view of the philosophy of religion from theoretical reason— knowledge and cognition—to practical reason—ethics. Schleiermacher had then transferred it to aesthetic reason. Windelband disagreed with all these operations and found them too one-sided. The philosophy of religion should not seek holiness in a special sphere, but had to start from that basic relationship, common to cognitive, ethical, and aesthetic awareness. This was the contradiction between Should and Must, norm and natural law. In human consciousness, both norm and anti-norm exist. Human conscience gives man the possibility of revolting against current norms and referring to transcendent ones instead. If these transcendent norms are called *holy*, that means these norms are ultimately absolute and incontestable. They are holy since they are neither products of the personal soul nor of empirical social awareness, but rather because they are the value content of a transcendent reality.

Religious History As Differentiation of Systems of Meaning

Along with Wilhelm Windelband, Heinrich Rickert (1863–1936) paved the way to a theory of religion based on the same theory of knowledge. Both belonged to the so-called Southwest German School, which was part of the broad current of neo-Kantianism. The issue of contention with other contemporary philosophers, especially Wilhelm Dilthey, was the process of understanding. Rickert did not assume that understanding was based on a direct empathy with a different life. He considered life and the cognition of life as two fundamentally distinct facts.[35] Cognition resulted from conditions Rickert defined as transcendental categories: when we apply laws to the world, we know it as nature; when we apply values and meaning to it, we know it as culture. Life that is strange to us relates to the world as we do, and in the process refers to a system of meaning. These systems of meaning (meaning and value) are not real themselves, but exist only as a claim to validity. Thus, understanding can only be directed to an "unreal meaning," but not to life itself.[36]

Max Weber (1864–1920) adopted the relevant observations of Windelband and his student Rickert, whom he had known while in Freiburg. "In what sense are there 'objective valid truths' on the basis of the study of cultural life?" asked Weber in 1904. Cultural life means that man refers to the world and confers meaning on it. This meaning cannot be gained from the observation of natural laws, and worldviews cannot be a product of progressive empirical knowledge. To account for the possibilities of typical meanings requires a study of the history of religions, as in Weber's later writings—"Sociology of Religion" (1913), contained in *Economy and Society*, and the introduction to *The Economic Ethic of the World Religions* (1915). They combined Marett's pre-animism as a case of the extraordinary with Windelband and Rickert's category of history and interpreted the history of religion as a systematization of possible meanings in view of a world without meaning. The genealogy of modern culture is located in religious history.

Like Max Weber, Émile Durkheim (1858–1917) also combined Marett's pre-animism with a Kantian theory of knowledge, and in *Elementary Forms of Religious Life* (1912), he also referred to Marett. In reality, the totem cult is devoted not to animals or plants, but to a vague force in them. After Durkheim had defined primitive totemism as a material power and a moral force, he drew conclusions for the emergence of religious thought in general. Back in 1899, Durkheim had indicated the need to give up a concept of personality in the definition of religious facts. One year later, Marett proved the existence of a pre-animistic stage in the history of religion, yet Marett understood historically what could be challenged (and is inaccurate).[37] In reality, it refers to social morality taking precedence over individual identity. Animism and dynamism were two genuine forms of the one elementary religion.[38]

Religious History as Expressing Experiences

Like Windelband, the German philosopher Wilhelm Dilthey (1833–1911) had tried to delineate the studies from one another. His approach was less principled than Windelband's. Along with natural sciences, a large group of other kinds of studies had formed all by itself: history, economics, legal and political sciences, the study of religion, of literature and poetry, of music, philosophy, and psychology. The common denominator for all of them was that they referred to human life, and this common ground established a characteristic way of cognition. While the natural sciences studied man as an object of nature, these studies established another set of facts: man experiences his life, expresses this experience, and shares it with others. Dilthey consistently distinguished three fundamental aspects that form the basis of this study: the *experience* of life, the *expression* the individual gives to his experience, and the *understanding* of this expression by others. Closely linked with one another, they form the structure of the humanities.[39]

In this epistemology, "life" was the fundamental term, which justified the special constellation of object and subject in the humanities; thus Max Scheler characterized this philosophy in 1913 as "philosophy of life":

Life is not something that "adapts" itself or is "adapted." To live is rather a tendency to *shaping*, to *formation*, even to the lordly overwhelming and inclusion of a material. . . . For Nietzsche, "life," down to the smallest detail, is something like a daredevil enterprise, a metaphysical "adventure," a bold thrust in *possibilities* of being that is successfully shaped into a being—to what then considers all possible "science." Life—that is the place of the existence, where existence and nonexistence are *decided* at the very first.[40]

Like Dilthey, Scheler also mentioned Friedrich Nietzsche and Henri Bergson as other representatives.[41] The philosophy of life, as Scheler elucidated its intention, was not an application of philosophy to life, but rather a philosophy from the abundance of experiences of life. He traced the special tone the word "life" assumes here back to Nietzsche, who had protested the basic concept of evolutionary biology that life was an adaptation of internal to external relations. Scheler turned that into a proper agenda.

Dilthey was an avowed opponent of a mechanical view of human life. Modern philosophy had applied basic concepts of mechanics to the human soul and degraded it to a machine of external perception and discernment, thus losing sight of the internal context and the autonomy of mental processes. As for the forms of experience, without any claim to systematic completeness, Dilthey distinguished between art and literature, religion, philosophy, the sciences. These were "worldviews" or, as he sometimes said, "cultural systems." For Dilthey, religion—*pace* Friedrich Schleiermacher—expressed the experience of the "mystic" unity of man with the infinite. Thus, in two objects, in religious experience and its expression, religion was scientifically accessible. "Religion is a psychological context which . . . [is] given in the religious experience and the externalization of that in a double manner. The experience always remains subjective; only the understanding of religious creations after the experience enables an objective knowledge of religion."[42] Understanding the history of religions generates in one and the same process both reliable historical knowledge and a practical life orientation. Under standing is not an external act, but a "direct intuition, as if soul disappears in soul, creative as conception in mating," as Johann Gustav Droysen expressed it in 1882.[43] Looming behind Dilthey is Schleiermacher, whose revival Dilthey promoted with his biography, *Leben Schleiermachers*.[44]

Here, it is instructive to glance briefly at Ernst Cassirer, who used the term "symbolic forms" a few years after Dilthey in a similar context. These were "basic forms for 'understanding' the world." Unlike Dilthey, however, Cassirer did not want to grant "expression" priority over more abstract means of representation like description or concept. His view of individual forms of symbolic representation of the world was based not on unmediated experience, but rather on language. This correction was Cassirer's reaction to the rising irrationalism that preferred a supposedly healthy feeling to critical thinking.[45]

What Dilthey had developed remote from the history of religion, Rudolf Otto (1869–1937) established firmly in religious studies a few years later. The phenomenology of religion continued the approach and also postulated a kind of preverbal religious experience that preserved its right to existence independent of modern civilization. Marett's pre-animism was the main evidence for Otto's "pre-religion." Mystical, internal religiosity could be clearly separated from knowledge and ethics and maintained its own right to exist in modern culture. The study of the history of religions could generate an experience of one's own life that would be dismissed from modern civilization.

By ascertaining a common form in all phenomena of the history of religion, Marett and his supporters made it possible to describe the facts of religious history so that distinctions can be discerned as differentiations of an elementary structure. A nearly indefinable feeling of awe and anxiety had formed in religious worship or magical divine compulsion, in contemplative mysticism or world-renouncing asceticism, in concepts of the soul or notions of power. *Survivals* were then replaced all down the line with an approach to religious history that saw the past as present options. No congenial personal belief in metaphysics was necessary. Religious studies identified options in religious historical facts that could still be chosen today, like experiences that were still available. At a time when modernization was pressing forward, this religious historical knowledge was in great demand. Henceforth, the way the history of religion was written was permanently determined by this systematic turn to the present. Searching for *Survivals* was over. The sources of the history of religion opened insights into human mental and social life that were independent of the demands of modern civilization.

CHAPTER TEN

RELIGION AND THE SOCIAL BOND

THE GREAT French sociologist Émile Durkheim (1858–1917) was convinced that the key to grasping the internal cohesion of a society dominated by a division of labor was to be found solely in religious history. He came from a Jewish family in Alsace and in 1879 was a student at the École Normale Supérieure in Paris, where he attended lectures by N. D. Fustel de Coulanges, among others, and later visited Germany—ultimately because of the defeat of France in the Franco-Prussian war of 1870–71.

That defeat left deep wounds in France and generated an intense search for causes. One of the weak points the French discovered was their own university system. Germany's victory had been a victory of science, said Ernest Renan. If France wanted to rise from the disaster, it had to learn from the example of German universities. Such views were widespread. Thus, the Ministère de l'Instruction Publique offered a stipend to talented young French academics to visit Germany and learn more about the latest scientific progress there. One of those chosen was Émile Durkheim. Influential sponsors sent him to study in Germany for a year in 1885–86, where he attended the universities of Leipzig, Marburg, and Berlin.[1]

Right after he returned to France, Durkheim reported his observations in Germany in *La Philosophie dans les universités allemandes* (Philosophy in German Universities). He reported with amazement on the large number of courses that were all dealing with similar or even the same subjects. He listed thirteen of them in philosophy for the 1886 summer semester in Leipzig, which was not an exception, but was repeated one semester after another. In the next winter semester of 1886–87, in Leipzig, there were three courses in logic and five in the history of philosophy. How meager was the offering of French universities in comparison! Yet he soon became aware that most of these courses were poorly attended.[2] On the other hand, he was very impressed by the positivism of the Leipzig philosopher and psychologist Wilhelm Wundt.

Religion as an Object of Observation
at the University of Leipzig

Even before Nathan Söderblom was appointed to the first German chair for the history of religion at the University of Leipzig in 1912, there was a lively interest in religion there. In his invaluable study of the history of religious studies at Leipzig, Kurt Rudolph has shown how many various courses there were in religious studies, long before the establishment of a chair in the history of religions in Leipzig.[3] The kind of interest in religion can be inferred from a small story that took place in Leipzig in December 1877, and shows that this interest in Leipzig—unlike other places in Germany—was empirically directed.

An American physician named Henry Slade had given up his practice in the United States because he had discovered extraordinary forces in himself. As a spiritual medium, he went to London, where he presented his miraculous abilities for sale. He was indicted and even convicted of fraud, and was released only because of an irregularity in the proceedings. Slade then went to Berlin, where the police urged him to leave the city at once.[4] Leipzig professors heard of the man and recognized their chance to test spiritualism scientifically and determine whether there is a spirit realm that can tangibly affect our reality. This curiosity can be explained by a belief in science in the 1860s and 1870s in Germany and England that boasted of being able to explain everything on the basis of natural causes. The response was doubt about such optimism among the bourgeoisie. Hence the interest in a scientific clarification of the issues.

The astrophysicist Professor Dr. Fr. Zöllner invited Slade along with famous colleagues of the universities of Leipzig and Göttingen to his home. Before their eyes, Slade placed a small pencil between two slates and tied it all up. The slate was placed on the corner of a gaming table. While the gentlemen were busy with magnetic experiments—another of Mr. Slade's abilities—according to an eyewitness, "Writing suddenly began between the untouched slates. When we separated the slates, the following words were on one of them: 'We feel to bless all those that try (?) to investigate a subject so popular as the subject of Spiritualism.'"[5] Professor Zöllner published these and other incredible phenomena in a scientific journal, and remained convinced to the end that it could not be sleight of hand, but genuine phenomena of spiritual reality. When the lecturer H. Ulrici discussed Zöllner's treatise in a journal, he himself became caught up in the matter, collecting written eyewitness reports from professors at the scene so he could "cite them among those considered convinced of the reality of spiritual phenomena after the results of the Leipzig sessions."[6] The facts were so well authenticated that there could be no doubt: "Clearly, with regard to them, the generally prevailing, one-sided mechanistic (materialistic) view of nature and explanation of nature are insufficient."[7]

Not all professors who had seen the experiment with the slate were convinced that it was a spiritualist phenomenon. One of the skeptics was Wilhelm Wundt. Ulrici called on him and the other skeptics to explain their doubt. It was "their duty as prominent representatives of science to explain publicly what they saw and why they doubt the objectivity of what they themselves saw."[8] Wundt did not need much urging to respond with an open letter, *Der Spiritismus*.[9] Was the reality of spiritualist phenomena not to be doubted, he asked, only because outstanding representatives of natural science claim to have observed them? What were the characteristics of scientific authority? Isaac Newton, who discovered gravity, wrote apocalyptic texts. Did they therefore deserve our belief? Slade's experiments could convince only those who were convinced of his trustworthiness in advance. A lawyer would have been less trusting and would have compared his performance with that of a capable magician.

The story shows clearly that, years before the establishment of a chair, scientists in Leipzig had been concerned with religion and had treated it empirically and critically. One of those who had made religion an object of observation had been Wundt. It was to be momentous for the history of the study of religion that Durkheim and Wundt crossed paths nine years after those events.

Émile Durkheim's Encounter with Wilhelm Wundt's Empirical Study of Morality

In 1879, Wilhelm Wundt established the first "Seminar for Experimental Psychology" in Leipzig. "He is the first psychologist in Germany who has broken almost every connection with metaphysics," stated Durkheim in his report. When Durkheim was in Germany, Wundt's book, *Ethik. Eine Untersuchung der Thatsachen und Gesetze des Sittlichen Lebens* (Ethics: An Investigation of the Facts and Laws of the Moral Life), appeared in October 1886. It was unproductive, wrote Wundt in the preface, to base moral philosophy on metaphysics. Awareness cannot be grasped directly, but can be studied only by indirect means of observation. Psychology was the appropriate means, provided it was not limited to the individual, but was expanded to a national psychology.[10] However, as Durkheim noted in his article on the situation of philosophy in Germany, Wundt's view was relatively singular in Germany,[11] where the neo-Kantian view prevailed that the realm of facts and that of value, "being" and "should" were heterogeneous areas. Thus, Wundt's positivism was much better suited to France than to Germany. Durkheim himself had seen that even intellectual Germans first heard of Wundt while visiting Paris. Durkheim gave his French colleagues a detailed description of the kind of research done in Wundt's seminar, by concentrating on precise and limited problems that could be observed. Yet even outside of Germany, Wundt was also controversial.[12]

In a second article published in the famous *Revue philosophique*, Durkheim introduced *La science positive de la morale en Allemagne* (The Positive Science of Morality in Germany). Unlike current moral philosophy, in Germany, morality had been an object of empirical and historical investigations for some time. Durkheim was an enthusiastic reviewer of Wilhelm Wundt's brand new book, and it was obviously hard for him to distinguish between his own view and Wundt's. To categorize Wundt's achievement, Durkheim put it in the context of German economy and jurisprudence and compared these with English approaches. While the Manchester School saw the national economy only as the sum of all individuals involved in it, German scholars (Wagner and Schmoller) had understood the national economy as a *sui generis* reality. Economic behavior was only superficially a decision of the individual. In reality, it was subordinate to moral constraints of which the actors were usually unaware. A reflection on history shows that this morality has undergone changes. For example, demographic factors forced a more intensive use of land, and people gradually understood the benefit of private property, and in view of that, private property had become a holy right.[13] The integration of the individual into the larger social body is carried out through the morality that controls social acts. These moral rules emerge under the pressure of collective restraints and elude the direct consciousness of the actors.[14] Thus, social acts cannot be explained by private intentions or personal motives. Wundt correctly abstained from deducing morality from consciousness. It was most important for the reviewer Durkheim to prove that moral norms had changed in the course of history. "There are as many ethics as there are social types, and the ethics of inferior societies is no less an ethic than that of cultivated societies."[15] Durkheim agreed with all this, even admired it. He found fault with Wundt only because Wundt could not explain the essential feature of morality—*its obligatory character*: "Wundt recognizes this characteristic in principle, but he also had to say where morality gets such authority and in whose name it issues orders." Durkheim thought he knew: "It is in God's name, if it is considered to be a divinely given duty. It is in the name of society, if it consists of a social discipline."[16]

In this early essay, Durkheim, the outsider, obviously dissected the view in German science that morality was not the content of consciousness, but rather of social reality, and could be discovered only through observation of acts. Durkheim's later claim in 1907 that for a long time, Wundt had not been as important to him as W. Robertson Smith and his school must be taken with a grain of salt. Tensions between Germany and France were too great at that time for such proximity to be tolerated. There were dangerous affinities, as W. Lepenies put it.[17] On the other hand, there is a great deal of evidence that Durkheim's preoccupation with German philosophy had provided him with an assumption that was fundamental for his later work.

Durkheim's Problem: The Division of Labor and Social Cohesion

After Durkheim returned from Germany in 1887, he received a special teaching post for social science and education in the philosophy faculty of the University of Bordeaux. At this time, he completed his postdoctorate and defended it in the Paris faculty of philosophy. He was then appointed adjunct professor at Bordeaux, and in 1896, he received the first professorship in France in social studies and was appointed *professeur de science sociale*.[18] He remained there until 1902, when he was appointed to the Sorbonne, where he became full professor in 1906.

Durkheim's first major work, his thesis, *The Division of Labor in Society*, focused on a current phenomenon. France was in the middle of a period of rapid social change. In 1870, only 23 percent of the working population were industrial laborers; by 1914, it was 39 percent.[19] This was paralleled by a shift of political power from a privileged upper class to a bourgeois middle class.[20] When Durkheim selected this change as his subject, he focused on the division of labor, the great innovation of modern society. In societies without a progressive division of labor, the social role of the individual was set by tradition and convention. Every violation of that was considered a crime against the gods and was punished accordingly. Criminal law had to guarantee conformity. Durkheim called this type of social integration mechanical solidarity. The British social anthropologists M. Fortes and E. E. Evans-Pritchard later turned that into "segmentary" solidarity. This society was short-lived. Conditioned by demographic factors (population growth) and the intensification of communication and transportation, the division of labor advanced. Competition increased in reaction to the specialization of economic occupations. Gradually, the social integration of the individual no longer took place on the basis of equality, but rather of the difference of occupations. Instead of mechanical solidarity, another type of integration prevailed: organic solidarity. The expanding area of private agreements was controlled by a contract law that put conventional criminal law in its place.

In the society characterized by the division of labor, men are strangers to one another, although, on the other hand, they rely on one another functionally. Durkheim pointed out the paradox of this fact. He was more interested in intensifying it than weakening it: "This work had its origins in the question of the relations of the individual to social solidarity. Why does the individual, while becoming more autonomous, depend more upon society? How can he be at once more individual and more solidary? Certainly these two movements, contradictory as they appear, develop in parallel fashion." This is the problem we are raising.[21]

Can a society characterized by the division of labor produce a moral bond between its competing members? This formulation of the problem clearly contradicted the popular opinion that the individual was a kind of monad and society was secondary. Durkheim saw it precisely the other way around: "Collective life did not arise from individual life; on the contrary, it is the latter that emerged from the former. On this condition alone can we explain how the personal individuality of social units was able to form and grow without causing society to disintegrate."[22]

Durkheim was not the first to pose the question of the moral bond in modern society. The problem had been generated by the French Revolution, which had deprived the individual of the place allocated to him in the traditional hierarchy and order, and replaced it with the contract between citizens. Several thinkers in England and Germany, and especially in France itself, had already considered the long-term social consequences of that.[23] Many feared that individualism would undermine the cohesion of society. Durkheim saw it quite differently, and his reference to religion was hardly accidental.

Religion and the Social Bond

Only at first glance is it surprising that, in the search for the sources of morality, Durkheim's sociology hit upon the history of religion. Other French thinkers had paved the way for him. J.-J. Rousseau thought a society had to have a *religion civile*. One of Durkheim's teachers in Paris, the ancient historian N. D. Fustel de Coulanges (1830–89), in *The Ancient City* (1864), had supplied the classical example of how religion established social relations. In antiquity, religion had been a driving force for social relationships. The cult of death, which was closely connected with the cult of the household gods, engendered the domestic community and family bonds, even the institution of property; religion was also involved in the formation of ancient city communities that consisted of several clans.

> We should not lose sight of the excessive difficulty which, in primitive times, opposed the foundation of regular societies. The social tie was not easy to establish between those human beings who were so diverse, so free, so inconstant. To bring them under the rules of a community, to institute commandments and insure obedience, to cause passion to give way to reason, and individual right to public right, there certainly was something necessary, stronger than material force, more respectable than interest, surer than a philosophical theory, more unchangeable than a convention; something that should dwell equally in all hearts, and should be all-powerful there.
>
> This power was a belief. Nothing has more power over the soul. A belief is the work of our mind, but we are not on that account free to modify it at will.[24]

Thus, even before Durkheim, the ancient state had become a convincing example that religion can be socially productive.[25] However, the assumption was that it consisted not only of doctrine, but mainly of obligatory acts. Durkheim shared this unequal evaluation of doctrines and rites of religion with regard to their social impact. Durkheim's concern with a religion beyond the ecclesiastical domain was not only dependent on philosophers and historians. It also reflected a new path. In 1885, religion became the subject of an academic section of its own, "Science religieuses" at the École Pratique des Hautes Études, established by Parliament and independent of ties to the Church.[26]

With regard to the social bond in the society characterized by the division of labor, Durkheim developed an approach in which the history of religion was relevant, even if he regretfully stated: "At the present time we do not possess any scientific conception of what religion is."[27] At any rate, Durkheim at least knew where he had to look: religion was only another word for social obligation. With the increasing division of labor, the area in which the individual acted autonomously also expanded. The list of those traditions that were obligatory for everyone and whose offense was punished emotionally by the community constantly shrank. Religion withdrew from the law, but not completely. The retreat stopped at the individual's right of self-determination. Little by little, political, economic, and cognitive areas and functions broke away from religious ones. The area of religion had become smaller, and the individual was increasingly less controlled from outside. It was this remnant of collectivity that formed the last common moral basis of the society characterized by the division of labor.

Social philosophers on both the left and the right had lamented this development of individualism as social decay, but had not agreed on the appropriate therapy: Should governmental restraint be deployed or should the return to tradition be preached as a kind of moral rearmament? Durkheim could not share that pessimism. For him, the change produced the basis of a new kind of social integration: "As all other beliefs and practices assume less and less religious a character, the individual becomes the object of a sort of religion."[28]

At the end of his study of the division of labor, Durkheim replied negatively to the opening question of whether a society characterized by the division of labor had to dissolve into a cloud of isolated atoms. He mentioned two circumstances that militated against that: the duties that arise for the individual from his functions and the government he depends on. The morality of the society characterized by the division of labor seems to be shaped all by itself in these words. Yet that was not the whole spectrum of Durkheim's views. Both these approaches could not explain either the shaping of individual morality or the idea of the moral *autonomy* of men.

In *The Division of Labor*, Durkheim rather tentatively presented another view. That is, he was not yet sure if a cult of the individual could really form a genuine social bond or if it might be a destructive superstition. What he still seemed to lack at this point was the sort of distinction between religion and magic that Robertson Smith had assumed: religion as a public ritual as opposed to magic as a private selfish abuse of supernatural power. Thus, after 1895, Durkheim's thought inevitably fell into the gravitational pull of the work of Robertson Smith and his school. In 1906–7, when Durkheim was suspected of surreptitiously smuggling German thought into his sociology and thus into the Sorbonne, he defended himself in a November 8, 1907, letter from Paris that gives important information about the genesis of his work:

It is claimed that I found in Wundt the idea that religion was the matrix of ideas of morality, legality, etc. It was 1887 when I read Wundt, but it was not until 1895 that I became clearly aware of the central role of religion in social life. It was in that year that I first found the means to tackle the study of religion sociologically. That was a revelation for me. The lecture of 1895[29] marks a line of demarcation in the development of my thought. All my earlier research had to be redone and brought into harmony with the new views. Wundt's *Ethik*, which I had read eight years earlier, played no role in this change of direction. The reason for it was exclusively the historical study of religion I had carried out and especially reading the works of Robertson Smith and his school.[30]

When Durkheim wrote this, it was dangerous for a French scholar to be too enamored of German scholarship, especially if, like Durkheim, he wanted to be loyal to the Third Republic. A survey of Durkheim's writings before 1907 leads inevitably to the conclusion that Durkheim played down Wundt's significance for the formation of his own thought, while increasing Robertson Smith's. That is, his early writings lack any clear indications that Durkheim was as impressed by Robertson Smith as his letter suggests.[31] Durkheim mentioned Robertson Smith by name for the very first time only in 1902 in an article on "Totemism,"[32] and it is striking that the name occurs without any emphasis and quite *en passant*. Before Robertson Smith, he was familiar with J. G. Frazer. In 1886, the librarian of the École Normale Supérieure, Lucien Herr, had called his attention to Frazer's article "Totemism" in the *Encyclopedia Britannica*.[33] The first mention of Frazer is in Durkheim's study *Suicide* (1897), which does not mention Robertson Smith. In the second volume of his journal, *L'Année sociologique*, in 1897–98, when Durkheim presented a sociological definition of religion, *De la définition des phénomènes religieux*, he adopted Frazer's view of magic as a belief in effective rites and words.[34] Robertson Smith's name still does not show up, even though implicit allusions to him can be discovered. Then Durkheim distinguished two kinds of religion: a free, private, self-chosen religion, on the one hand, and on the other, the one the individual receives from tradition, which applies to the whole social group and must be practiced by every member of it.[35] Robertson Smith had presented and explained this distinction in his *Lectures on the Religion of the Semites* (1889). All public social institutions had developed from a religion practiced by one group. If the term "revelation" deserves anything Durkheim could have learned from Robertson Smith "and his school," it is the recognition of a public religion distinct from a private one.[36] Durkheim's colleagues, Hubert and Mauss, also supported this distinction (1902–3) and distinguished sharply between religion and magic according to the attendant circumstances of ritual acts: in the former they happened publicly and were religion, while in the latter they were secret and magic. Religion was a public matter, magic a private one.[37]

Something else also shows that Durkheim did in fact take a great deal from Robertson Smith. While Durkheim's students were reserved about Smith's theory of sacrifice, Durkheim himself accepted it without reservations in his *Elementary Forms of Religious Life*. He saw sacrifice as originally a social performance whose participants constituted a moral community by consuming the holy totem animal. In 1907, when Durkheim distanced himself from Wundt and emphatically declared his support for Robertson Smith, that corresponded completely with his scholarly development, yet political considerations also played a role.

Is There a History of Religion of Autonomous Individuals?

The origin of the cult of the individual became clearer to Durkheim from his position in the Dreyfus affair. Intellectuals demanded a reopening of the case against the Jewish officer Alfred Dreyfus, who had been unjustly convicted of treason in 1894. In 1898, when the debate about the "Manifesto of the Intellectuals" created quite a stir,[38] Durkheim also began to speak publicly and supported the right of the individual. In his article *L'Individualisme et les intellectuels* (1898), he argued against the accusation made by the anti-Dreyfusards that the intellectuals would plunge the country into anarchy and that individualism was to blame for their destructive attitude. T. W. Adorno reproached Durkheim for deifying the collective,[39] but here Durkheim defended individualism and the intellectuals, unequivocally supporting the party of individualism, which is not to be confused with egotism, but must be traced back to Kant, Rousseau, and the Rights of Man. Far from an egotistic cult of self, it taught that the human being was holy. Individualism was an absolutely obligatory morality, even a religion, in which man is both believer and god. Thus Durkheim drew a surprisingly clear boundary between the rights of the government and of the individual. This can be clarified with three core sentences: "There is no reason of state which can excuse an outrage against the person." "This cult of man had for its first dogma the autonomy of reason and for its first rite freedom of thought." "Not only is individualism distinct from anarchy, but it is henceforth the only system of beliefs which can ensure the moral unity of the country."[40] In these remarks, Durkheim completed his considerations in *The Division of Labor* with a historical argument that individualism was older than the Enlightenment and went back to Christianity, which shifted the center of moral life from outside to inside and made the individual the sovereign judge of his own acts. And he drew a conclusion from that which was also relevant for the Dreyfus affair: "Thus the individualist, who defends the rights of the individual, defends at the same time the vital interests of society."[41]

Durkheim's argument must be examined closely to discover why a thinker like Adorno could misunderstand it fundamentally. It was not the most natural thing in the world for a French sociologist of this rank to conceive the function of government not nationalistically, but morally, as a guarantee of the individual right to freedom.[42] And it was even more unusual for a sociologist to reject individualism methodologically, but nevertheless make it the subject of sociology.[43] The subject of Durkheim's study was the individual, but the way to the individual led through the observation of collective facts. He excluded a direct look into consciousness. Here the influence of Wilhelm Wundt can be seen again: morality is a matter of the collective, not of the individual.

Reasons for Suicide: Religion as Social Fact

The study of suicide that appeared in 1897 was to be convincing evidence that religion is a social fact that can define the individual in his behavior even without his knowledge. Here, Durkheim reversed the cardinal question of *The Division of Labor*. Instead of asking, "What establishes the social bond between people in a society based on the division of labor?" the question now was: "What leads people in a society based on the division of labor to cut the social bond?" S. Lukes obviously struck the nerve of Durkheim's intention when he pointed out that this study was intended to celebrate the triumph of Durkheim's sociological method. Suicide per se was an absolutely individual act. Yet comparisons of its occurrence show that, even in this act, the individual is dependent on a social reality outside himself.[44]

Sensational as the intention still seems today, it hardly was at that time. Even before Durkheim, suicide had been a topos of conservative French social philosophers. When people cast off traditions, they thus gave up social protection and in desperate situations could become the victim of their own isolation. In a short essay on suicide in 1819, Lamennais wrote: "As man moves away from order, anguish presses around him. He is the king of his own misery, a degraded sovereign in revolt against himself, without duties, without bonds, without society. Alone, in the midst of the universe, he runs, or rather he seeks to run, into nothingness."[45] Someone who thinks like that sees suicide less as an individual problem than as a social one. Ultimately, the unconnectedness in the society torn apart by the division of labor must be to blame for suicide. Of the three mottos of the French Revolution—"Liberty, Equality, Fraternity"—these thinkers saw "Liberty" as man's leading enemy. If they had looked over the border at Germany at that time, they would have witnessed another kind of objection. Contemporary Romantic thinkers saw the word "Equality" as the primary problem, undermining the uniqueness of the individual person. The Romantic idealization of suicide is thus seen as a consistent counterpart to the view of French thinkers of suicide. For the Romantics, suicide was mainly an expression of human freedom, not of social unconnectedness.

Durkheim was aware that there was a connection between religious denominations and the suicide rate. Statistics showed that there was a higher rate of suicide among Protestants than Catholics. In his fundamental investigation of 1882, *Die Moralstatistik in ihrer Bedeutung für eine Socialethik* (The Significance of Moral Statistics for a Social Ethic), Alexander von Oettingen had emphasized that the number of suicides among Protestants was three times that of Catholics. And he shared the opinion of other scholars that current Protestantism was more favorable to the predilection toward suicide than Catholicism.[46] Durkheim presented a coherent explanation for this surprising fact. He formed three logical types of social circumstances under which suicide occurs: suicide because of social isolation; suicide because of collective pressure (for example, the death of soldiers or the burning of widows in India); or suicide because of economic crises or situations with disappointing expectations (anomie). In von Oettingen's statistics, war played no role. After investigating the possible correlations, Durkheim concluded that the higher rate among Protestants was explained by the individualism of their religion. Catholics were more integrated into a community. Jews had an even lower rate of suicide, since constant persecution had created an especially firm solidarity among them. Since the breakdown of religious authority follows higher education, Durkheim pointed to another correlation: between education and suicide. The only exception were the Jews, for whom education was simply a means to be better equipped to cope with modern society.[47] All this led Durkheim to conclude that religion either promoted or restrained suicide, but it could work only prophylactically and protect people from the impulse to suicide if it formed a community. Dogmas were secondary: "The essential thing is that they be capable of supporting a sufficiently intense collective life."[48]

It is irritating that Durkheim firmly eliminated an explanation for other reasons than sociological ones, since suicide can also reasonably be seen as the symptom of mental illness. Note that suicide is statistically very rare. This presents particular problems that undermine

Durkheim's ingenious explanation. Assume—as Durkheim would calculate—that Country A has a suicide rate of 450 people per million, and Country B has a rate of 50 per million. This might be considered an immense statistical difference. But if the numbers are reversed, the picture looks this way: in one country, out of one million people, 999,950 do *not* commit suicide, while in the other country, 999,550 do *not* commit suicide. Can it logically be argued that there are general factors that protect 999,950 people in one case and only 999,550 in the other? The critics of Durkheim's study quickly found this weak point.[49]

Durkheim presented his study of suicide as proof that an investigation of society has to deal with facts that are not close at hand, but must first be found. People voluntarily perform many acts and yet also obey a constraint. He summarized such acts, which are neither subordinate to a law of nature nor spontaneously voluntary, into their own category: *faits sociaux*, social facts. They comprise "ways of acting, thinking, and feeling that present the noteworthy property of existing outside the individual consciousness. These types of conduct or thought are not only external to the individual but are, moreover, endowed with coercive power, by virtue of which they impose themselves on his individual will."[50] This category of acts was the subject of his 1895 book, *The Rules of Sociological Method*. Here, too, Durkheim dissociated himself from psychology. The doubt that man may trust his own consciousness was too profound. Most human acts cannot be known through self-reflection or empathy, as shown clearly by the case of individualism. In many cases, social facts are not organized in institutions, but are scattered diffusely in society. All of Durkheim's sociological interest was aimed at this category.

Religion As a Matrix of Collective Life

In the preface to the first volume of the journal he had founded in 1897, *L'Année Sociologique*, Durkheim cited as an urgent task of the journal to provide information about specialized studies in law, religion, morality, and economics, "for they contain the materials sociology must use to emerge."[51] In the preface to the second volume of 1897–98, he appealed directly to the reader concerning religion: "The special priority we have granted this kind of phenomena may be surprising. But they are the seed that produces all others. In principle but still not clearly, religion contains all the elements which gave rise to the various manifestations of the collective life by separating, establishing and binding with one another in a thousand ways."[52] Durkheim ascribed priority to religion in the investigation of all those social acts he denoted with the term *faits sociaux*. At that time, he seemed obsessed with this idea. One of his colleagues wrote to a friend that Durkheim wanted to explain rules of marriage, criminal law—in short, everything—by religion.[53]

Durkheim was interested exclusively in the results produced by religion in society. Consequently, he did not define religion, but rather religious facts (*faits religieux*): obligatory beliefs connected with acts. If religion was defined merely as belief or as religious experience—a swipe at F. Max Müller—one lost sight of the fact that religion was not produced and maintained by the individual, but by the collective. For Durkheim, the strangeness of religion was based on this circumstance. Religion was proof that the collective life of our own society is necessarily mysterious and alien to us:

> Society has its own mode of existence which is peculiar to it; correspondingly, its own mode of thought. It has its passions, its habits, and its needs, which are not those of the individual, and which leave their mark on everything it conceives. It is not surprising, therefore, that as mere individuals, we do not feel at home with these conceptions which are not ours and which do not express our nature. That is why they are shrouded in an air of mystery which disturbs us. This mystery, however, is not inherent in the object itself which they represent; it is entirely the result of our ignorance. It is a provisional mystery like those which science invariably clears up step by step as it advances. It stems uniquely from the fact that religion belongs to a world which human science has only just begun to explore and which to us is still unknown. If we can succeed in finding the laws of collective conceptualization, these strange *représentations* will lose their strangeness.[54]

To understand our own social life, we have to study religion. The history of religion is no longer *explanandum*, but is rather *explanans*.

Totemism

Durkheim saw the religions of the simplest peoples as an entrée into the unknown world of the collective. A study of them could eliminate the usually disturbing factor of diffusion. At the beginning of all development, the blueprint of all religions could be recognized most clearly. These people were still close to the motives of their own acts, while the psychological distance between motivation and act in progressive societies has become greater and more opaque. Since religions in primitive societies contained not only moral, but also cognitive patterns of interpretation, investigating them also allows a glance at the origin of our own categories of knowledge, since the forms we still use to shape our knowledge came from them.[55]

Durkheim's scientific objectives urgently required a precise description of the religion of primitive societies, and he thought he found it in recent publications about the indigenous peoples of Australia. In 1899, two British ethnologists, B. Spencer and F. J. Gillen, had published an extraordinarily sound ethnography of the Aranda and other Australian tribes, which Durkheim had immediately reviewed in the third volume of his journal in 1898–99.[56] In the fifth volume of *L'Année sociologique* of 1900–1901, Durkheim devoted a special article to totemism, intensifying even more—*hinaufschrauben*—the significance of the available report about a totemistic religion: "Everything concerning totemism has compelling consequences in every area of sociology because totemism is the origin of many institutions."[57] In this article (a prelude to his last major work, *Elementary Forms of Religious Life* [1912]), Durkheim gave the findings of the British ethnographers a different interpretation from the one given by the British fieldworkers themselves. Durkheim felt obliged to do the review since Frazer had said that the new discoveries would require a revision of the previous view of totemism.[58] Neither the prohibition of eating the totem animal nor the command of exogamy was part of totemism, since neither occurred in Australia. On the other hand, Durkheim presented the view that the material revealed an older stage when both had indeed been a component of totemism.[59] In their next book, Spencer and Gillen cautiously commented critically on Durkheim's interpretation.[60] Yet in a personal letter, Spencer registered his reservations without mincing his words. It was difficult, he admitted, to write about such things without creating false impressions in the reader, but Durkheim's article was larded with errors.[61]

Durkheim had staked everything on "totemism," just as it was starting to dissolve into its individual parts as the result of more precise individual investigations. This process of dismantling the conglomerate of "totemism" ended in 1910 with a convincing article by A. A. Goldenweiser.[62] Two years later, when Durkheim's *Elementary Forms of Religious Life* appeared, it relied on a forty-year-old construct devised in 1869–70 by the jurist J. F. MacLennan, and that belongs in the context of a process A. Kuper called *The Invention of Primitive Society* (1988).

The Holy Soul

Yet it would be wrong to consider Durkheim's book ruined. Both quantitatively and qualitatively, the materials and interpretations of his study reached far beyond totemism. According to him, the history of religion was to help answer the question of how a collective social morality emerges in a society. Of the scholars of religion we have discussed so far, Durkheim is the first who systematically posed the question of religion in a society characterized by the division of labor. In reality, he was not seeking religion, but rather the sources of collective life in a society torn apart by the division of labor.

Durkheim began his last book with a definition of religion that refined his previous definition of 1899.[63] The compulsory nature of religious convictions which then formed its core could materialize only when religion was a group concern, an aspect neglected by the previous definition. This also produced another view of available theories of religion. E. B. Tylor's animism and F. Max Müller's natural mythology were both based on totemism, not vice versa. Totemism, in turn, was based on social facts and expressed experiences the individual had in and with collective assemblies. The totem (animal or plant) represented this assembly. Worshiping it was socially productive, changing the many individuals into one community with its own supernatural reality. Durkheim's words sound like a kind of miraculous transubstantiation transforming a number of individual people into a religious community. The fortifying and invigorating act of the society could still be seen in assemblies where people declared themselves willing to make the kind of sacrifice they would not do under normal circumstances, as for example in the French Revolution on August 4, 1789. The history of religion of the most primitive societies provided the key to understanding how the independence of society with regard to the individual is achieved.

This book did not lose sight of the individual either, as is clear especially in Durkheim's analysis of the idea of the soul.[64] Just as there is no society without religion, so there is no member of society without a soul. Yet the origin of this soul is not in the experiences of dream, illness, and death, as Tylor thought. Durkheim replaced Tylor's individual explanation of the concept of the soul with a social conception originating in the duality of man, who as individual was one with the collective represented by the totem. In Australian tribes, souls were reborn and embodied according to the totem principle. While the totem principle existed in the person himself, it retained its own value. We can observe how Durkheim drafted a model of communicating tubes between the sacralization of society and the "autonomy" of the individual. The structure of moral autonomy is embedded in the religion of elementary societies. Modern society has only filled in what primitive religion previously shaped.

In an article of 1914, Durkheim once again focused on this collective dimension in man. Human existence was double: in terms of the body, man was a sensual, individual, egotistical creature; in terms of the soul, he was a moral, social, reasonable creature. He had the freedom to act against his own inclinations—an idea first propagated by Kant—and this was what made him a moral creature. It was this antagonism between duty and inclination that was expressed in the body-soul duality. A man becomes a person by obeying the general moral law; he becomes an individual by following his physical instincts. Therefore, it is the body that achieves the individualization of the individual, while the soul accounts for his autonomy with regard to the natural. The more man frees himself from the sensual, the more he becomes a person.[65]

Marcel Mauss: The Endangered Category of the Person

Durkheim never recovered from the death of his brilliant son André, who was killed in the Balkans in 1916; he died on November 11, 1917, at the age of 57. His interest in the issue of the autonomy of human individuals was pursued by his colleague and nephew Marcel Mauss.[66] Ever since the establishment of the journal *L'Année sociologique* in 1896, Durkheim had attracted younger scholars to his journal, first in Bordeaux and then, after 1902, in Paris. There were about forty of these junior colleagues, who came from various disciplines and followed traditional academic careers. Since there were hardly any positions for sociology in France at that time, the collaboration of scholars from various disciplines was a necessity that Durkheim turned into a virtue. His view of social facts assumed the participation of many disciplines. These scholars formed a dedicated community, even though the first and only time they met together in person was in 1912.[67] Politically, they shared Durkheim's devotion to the Republic and his rejection of clericalism.

A series of individual studies indicates the productive nature of this collaboration. In *Essai sur la nature et la function du sacrifice* (Essay on the Nature and Function of Sacrifice, 1899), Hubert and Mauss explained that the typical sacrifice was always annihilated instead of the sacrificer, whose relation to the gods was fundamentally changed by it. The sacrifice expressed the power that controlled relations between the individual and the sacred sphere. Another example of the seminal nature of Durkheim's approach was Mauss's *Essai sur le don* (The Gift: Forms and Functions of Exchange in Archaic Societies, 1923–24) which centered on what appeared to be a purely economic institution but was really a moral one. It can be proved that, in some primitive societies, goods were not exchanged out of necessity. In the gift as such was a force (*mana*) that bound the giver and the recipient. It was the gift itself, and not some agreement, that produced the obligations.

The school came to an end twenty years after Durkheim's death in 1938 with Marcel Mauss's essay, *Une catégorie de l'esprit humain: la notion de personne, celle de 'moi,' un plan de travail* (A Category of the Human Mind: The Notion of Person; the Notion of Self).[68] Mauss once again accepted Durkheim's assumption that the categories of the human spirit and the categories of the person had a history. In most human societies, they were understood as a role. The emergence of an autonomous individual from the category, independent of his role, resulted from a unique development, combining Greek philosophy, Roman law, and Christian theology, with India and China also forming bases. However, in the course of history, these had disappeared. Therefore, the category of the person was unstable, tricky, and precious, and still to be developed completely. This historical approach was to be elaborated three decades later by Mauss's student Louis Dumont.

Durkheim's confidence in the moral foundation of individualism in primary social structures was gone, along with confidence in the guarantee of the individual by the system of the social division of labor. The tyranny of Communism and National Socialism had destroyed it, as Mauss expressed his painful awareness in a letter to S. Ranulf on November 6, 1936:

> Durkheim and after him, we, I think, are the founders of the theory of the authority of collective representation. What we did not foresee was that great modern societies . . . could be as suggestible as the Australians in their dances, and could be set in motion like a group of children. This reversion to the primitive had not been a subject of our considerations. We made do with a few allusions to the state of the masses, even though it was something altogether different. We were satisfied to prove that the individual could find in the collective spirit the foundations and nourishment for his freedom, his independence, and his critical awareness.[69]

In 1939, when Mauss was asked to publish his letters, he asked to append an addendum: "I believe that all this is a tragedy for us, an exaggerated verification of the things we indicated and the proof that we should have expected this verification through evil rather than through good."

The end of his school hardly put an end to Durkheim's impact. In the analysis of religion in the twentieth century, Durkheim remains extremely important. For example, observations collected by anthropologists which confirmed that rituals contribute to social integration. Since Durkheim had linked this effect not only with the fact of community behavior, but also with the cognitive dimension of rituals, he also paved the way for scholars studying the symbolic representation of reality. In the science of history, the *Annales* school is indebted to him for a basic impetus, since their basic notion, *mentalité*, was shaped with his help,[70] and is now the guiding concept of an extraordinarily productive cultural historical investigation.

CHAPTER ELEVEN

THE GREAT PROCESS OF DISENCHANTMENT

Max Weber's Search for the Conditions of Capitalism

MAX WEBER'S surprising thesis that a basic element of modern culture was a product of religious history had nothing to do with any personal or scholarly proximity to theology, although Weber's family included theologians, and he was close to one of them, Otto Baumgarten. Yet Max Weber, who was born in Erfurt in 1864 and died in Munich in 1920, studied something entirely different. In 1882, he enrolled in Heidelberg in jurisprudence. In 1884, he went to Berlin, where he received a doctorate for a work on trading societies in Italian cities. In 1892, he did a postdoctoral essay on *Die Römische Agrargeschichte in ihrer Bedeutung für das Staats- und Privatrecht* (The Meaning of Roman Agrarian History for State and Private Law). In 1893, Weber was appointed professor of economics at Freiburg. In 1896, he received a chair in that subject in Heidelberg, where he lived until 1918; but in 1903, he retired from his professorial duties for health reasons. Thus the subject of religion had to find entry into his thoughts through another path, and amazingly, that path was economic issues.

In 1891–92, the *Verein für Socialpolitik* (Association for Social Policy) did an empirical survey of the situation of farmworkers in Germany and commissioned respected scholars to evaluate the data. Weber was assigned the East Elban material, a part of the survey eagerly awaited at that time because development was taking place on the estates of East Elbe that caused some concern. If the estate owners wanted to emulate the standard of living of the urban upper middle class, they could no longer maintain their previous economic way of production. If they did nothing, they were in danger of declining to the status of simple farmers. To avoid that, they had to become entrepreneurs and rationalize their enterprise. But they also had to put increased pressure on the *Instleute* who were dependent on them, and this could have undesirable consequences, because these *Instleute* were of German origin and could exchange the patriarchal regime of the estate for the freedom of being hired workers. In fact, a considerable number of them had already migrated to industrial regions elsewhere and were replaced by Polish farm workers, which posed an obvious long-term danger for the German policy of nationality in that region. Thus, Weber described a dilemma: if the estate owners made the leap to entrepreneurs, they inadvertently undermined German presence in the east,[1] an evaluation that indicated Weber's interest in the conditions and consequences of a change to a capitalist economy.

External Conditions for Capitalism

Weber did not see the emergence of a capitalist economy as self-evident, as he explained in a lecture of 1896 on the "social reasons for the decline of ancient culture."[2] The fall of Rome was generally ascribed to the mass migrations, but Weber saw the process differently, in terms of a gradual social change in the Roman Empire. Initially, ancient civic communities were based economically on slave labor. Because of their advantageous position on the coast, these cities could engage in trade. After the second century A.D., because of the *Pax Romana*, when the supply of slaves dried up and the economic focus shifted inland in the Roman Empire, a self-sufficient estate economy gradually displaced the trade and industry of the cities. When even government officials and soldiers could no longer cover their needs through taxes but through barter, little remained of the capitalistic trade economy at the end of Antiquity. The cities disintegrated into villages, the culture once again became rural.[3] It was this reversal of development that allowed the dramatic devastation of the mass migrations.

Weber returned to this reconstruction in his later works, and extended it with more source material in his *Agrarian Sociology of Ancient Civilizations*.[4] A comparison of Antiquity and the Middle Ages showed that the two had developed in diametrically opposed directions. Ancient capitalism had been practiced by the citizens, who equipped themselves for military service and supported a military expansion of their cities for their own economic interests. Thus, ancient capitalism had established itself politically, unlike Medieval cities, which were founded by princes as commercial cities, where citizens had to struggle tediously and gradually for political autonomy. The development of the civic community of the Roman Empire was the reverse. With the rise of standing armies and the professional bureaucracy in the Roman Empire, the cities gradually lost their independence. Thus, it was the progressive bureaucratization of the Roman Empire, and not the mass migration, that was primarily responsible for the depoliticization and disarmament of the ancient cities and the decline of the social foundation of capitalism. Only where freedom of trade was guaranteed, as later in the European cities, could capitalism develop permanently.

It was Weber's credo that the kind of social integration determined capitalism's chances of survival. An intensely expanding political power, either in Antiquity or in the modern age, seemed especially dangerous to him: "The bureaucratization of society will overcome capitalism in our society too, just as it did in Antiquity."[5] This problem continued to plague Weber: "Faced with this superiority of the tendency of bureaucratization," he asked in 1917, "how is it *still possible* to rescue *some* remnant of 'individualist' freedom of movement in *any* sense?"[6]

A Religious Ethos Overcomes Traditional Economics

Political conditions were necessary but not sufficient for the establishment of capitalism. What else had to be added is the subject of Weber's famous essay, "The Protestant Ethic and the Spirit of Capitalism," which appeared in 1904 and 1905 in two parts in the *Archiv für Sozialwissenschaft und Sozialpolitik* (Archive for Social Science and Social Policy). Later, he revised and expanded it when it was included in the *Gesammelten Aufsätze zur Religionssoziologie* (Collected Essays in the Sociology of Religion).[7]

Weber did not discover the connection between Protestantism and capitalism. He assumed that the "greater relative participation of Protestants in the ownership of capital, in management, and the upper ranks of labour in great modern industrial and commercial enterprises" was known and secure.[8] In 1892, Eberhard Gothein had noted it in his *Wirtschafsgeschichte des Schwarzwaldes und der angrenzenden Landschaften* (The Economic History of the Black Forest and the Adjacent Districts): "The same fact is forced on anyone who pursues the traces of the development of capitalism in any country in Europe: the Calvinist diaspora is also the nursery of the capitalist economy. The Spanish expressed it with bitter resignation: heresy promotes the spirit of trade."[9]

Other contemporary scholars had made similar observations.[10] The question was only how these connections were to be explained. In 1902, Werner Sombart indicated one difficulty: "The fact that Protestantism, particularly in its Calvinist and Quaker variety, essentially promoted the development of capitalism is so well known it does not need to be established. Yet if anyone would object that the Protestant system of religion was ultimately much more an effect than a cause of the modern capitalist spirit, it will be hard to show him the error of his view except with an empirical proof of *concrete historical connections*."[11] What Sombart here considered proof, Weber tried to realize two years later.

The fact that Weber did not discover the connection, but only wanted to explain it, has certain consequences for our understanding of Weber. Richard van Dülmen expressed it clearly:

> Weber was not interested in the fact of a connection between Protestantism and capitalism or in an influence of Calvinism on the development of modern capitalism as such, as Gothein and Sombart had already formulated it; his probing interest concentrated exclusively on *how* the connection was to be thought and reconstructed more precisely. The fundamental novelty of Weber's thesis resides in this dimension; the intellectual dynamic is based in this endeavor.[12]

Impending capitalism needed the support of an internal power, an ethos, because it first had to bring down a powerful opponent: *traditionalism*. Weber had explained how this worked economically with the example of piece rate. Increasing the piece rate often had the remarkable effect of not making the laborer work *more*, but against all expectations, *less*, responding to the increase of the piece rate by reducing the daily output. Higher income was obviously less of a stimulant than was less work. This led Weber to far-reaching conclusions:

> A man does not "by nature" wish to earn more and more money, but simply to live as he is accustomed to live and to earn as much as is necessary for that purpose. Wherever modern capitalism has begun its work of increasing the productivity of human labour by increasing its intensity, it has encountered the immensely stubborn resistance of this leading trait of pre-capitalistic labour.[13]

This dogged resistance, which Weber almost ascribed to human nature, did not fade away by itself. It had to be broken.

"The Impact of Religion in Areas Where It Is Not Sought"

The assumption that religion could have played a role in the rise of capitalism does not seem very reasonable to us. Many would guess the opposite, that capitalism was a result of the emancipation from religion—but not Weber. Moreover, he had an example for such an achievement of religion right before his eyes in the history of law, which convinced him, even if this example was controversial. His Heidelberg colleague, the scholar of national and international law

Georg Jellinek, had wanted to prove that modern human rights had not emerged from the religious criticism of the Enlightenment, but rather from the Reformation. It was religious nonconformists of the seventeenth century who first supported the fundamental right of the freedom of belief and conscience, even before the Enlightenment. A direct model for the Declaration of the Rights of Man adopted by the French National Assembly on August 26, 1789, was the American Declaration of Independence of 1776. That the individual citizen had an innate right, not granted by the state, had been produced from the Reformation idea of a freedom of religion and conscience.[14] In 1904, Jellinek discussed "The Religious and Metaphysical Bases of Liberalism" in the scholar's club called "Eranos" that also included Weber. Years later Weber acknowledged that Jellinek's proofs of a religious impact in the genesis of 'human rights' had encouraged him "seeking the impact of religion in areas where it is not sought."[15]

Friedrich H. Tenbruck noted that the sympathetic welcome of such a proof had to do with a special feature of German sociology. Around the turn of the century, a "protest against the usual belief in progress" had emerged. "The rebellion against economics, which produced the German Society for Sociology, was fueled not least by the conviction that the progress of reason was not a natural law, that the emergence of Western rationality was not to be explained by human intelligence. Weber shared this conviction with Troeltsch, Simmel, and others. . . . This may be the most important reason for the well-known characteristic of German sociology that had to devote itself to the search for the nonrational, social, anthropological, and especially historical conditions of rationality."[16] Its representatives shared a "front against the concept of 'natural laws,' and even more so against a simple, 'positivistic' study of external facts." Social reality was constituted by meaningful actions and not through general external laws.[17] This beginning of sociology in Germany shows clearly why Weber searched the history of religion in order to explain why economic actors broke with tradition.

His use of the history of religions as source of meaning was also intended to illustrate how "ideas become effective forces in history."[18] He constantly criticized historical materialism, which resulted from a fundamentally different view of historical progress. Only an authority beyond tradition could blast tradition, an authority to be sought in the subjective side of economics. Like every other social behavior, economic behavior requires a meaning adequate for it. This view was fundamental for Weber's sociology. Conduct that refers to the behavior of others can be successful only if all parties are attributing to it the same meaning. Regular social interactions materialize only when the parties agree about the validity of a system of meaning, a worldview. Meaning is anything but self-evident. Yet, in this context, everything depends on the binding force of such a worldview. Only if absolute validity is ascribed to it is there a good chance of a regular success of interaction. These considerations led Weber to turn his attention to religions and their history. In the history of religion, he assumed a system of meaning that guides the economic behavior of the individual.

Religious Sources of the Capitalistic Ethos

In the *Protestant Ethic*, Weber claimed that, independent of the capitalist system, there was a methodical conduct of life that was adequate for it. Capitalism owed its driving force to this "spirit." But where can this be ascertained, and how can it be observed? It was Weber's tremendous scientific nose that tracked down appropriate sources: English Puritan devotional texts of the seventeenth century that had come directly from pastoral practice. They constantly opposed the idea that salvation can be achieved through works. It was exclusively God's sole and unfathomable will that decided who was saved and who was not. Since no believer could ever be sure about it, all he could do was follow his obligation unswervingly in daily life, do his best, and prove himself worthy of his calling. Success may be considered the first sign of a state of grace. But you could not slack off. Idleness or pleasure were temptations to be resisted. Only relentless professional work and renunciation would preserve the chance of salvation. Thus, the theological theory of predestination had an unexpected practical consequence: it motivated an innerworldly asceticism that despised the uninhibited *consumption* of property, but exonerated the *acquisition of property* from the scruples of a traditional ethic.[19] The preachers had surely intended something quite different from this, but their sermons could have such consequences among the laity under special conditions, and could promote a conduct of life that undermined the traditional type of economic behavior.

By interpreting religious terms as categories of conduct of life, Weber gained access to the interpretations of meaning of those social classes who were the first to overcome traditionalism. *Innerworldly asceticism, spirit, calling, probation* indicated an ethos that demanded an economy independent of traditional needs. These notions granted an insight into the awareness of a Puritan merchant class. A Puritan search for salvation had been one of the driving forces in the revolution of the economic order and had burst the shackles of tradition on the acquisitive striving. Religion had become the impetus to a behavior that was no longer oriented toward traditional needs. If an entire social class followed it and thus had or acquired power, this could delineate a new course of development for a whole society. In his later writings on the sociology of religion, when Weber believed the *charisma* of individuals could break through the constraint of everyday life, he compressed in this term a view of religion that was fundamental for the *Protestant Ethic*. Thus he wanted to explain the conspicuous fact that the seed of capitalistic development fell on Calvinistic and Puritan ground.

It is not surprising that Weber's bold claims were not all approved by his professional colleagues. Historians objected that Weber had used English Puritan texts dating after 1660, a period when many Puritans had become disappointed with politics and had retreated to their professional functions.[20] The Puritanism described by Weber was hardly typical for Puritanism in general.[21] Finally, the whole thing suffers from a discrepancy: Weber wanted to explain a German fact of the nineteenth century—the statistically unequal distribution of capital property among Lutherans, Calvinists, and Catholics—with English devotional texts of the seventeenth century.[22] Weber's claim that Calvinism released an activism in its followers and that Lutheranism, on the other hand, evoked a quietism came from the arsenal of nineteenth-century denominational polemics.[23] Thus, there were many good reasons to object to Weber's thesis. Weber defended himself vigorously, reacting to some criticism with hard-hitting responses. The debate raged between 1905 and 1910, when Weber wrote his concluding article on the subject. His thesis, he concluded, had stood the test.

The Discovery of the Special Feature of Western Rationalism

In 1911, as soon as the battle was over, Max Weber resumed his studies of the sociology of religion more intensely. He set out on the Herculean task of exploring how the great world religions of Confucianism, Hinduism, Buddhism, Islam, Christianity, and even Judaism were related to the economic ethic. A survey of all of Weber's work shows why he undertook that mammoth endeavor.

In 1909, in an arrangement with the publisher Paul Siebeck, Weber planned to develop a *Handbuch der politischen Oekonomie* (Manual of Political Economy), later named *Grundriss der Sozialökonomik* (Outline of Socioeconomics). Weber's contribution to that is now known as *Wirtschaft und Gesellschaft* (Economy and Society). Amazingly, the first outline in 1910 lacked a separate treatment of religion, but included merely a section of *Wirtschaft und Kultur (Kritik des historischen Mater-ialismus)* (Economics and Culture [Critique of Historical Material-ism]).[24] Yet this was soon to change. In a letter of July 3, 1913, Weber thanked his friend from his Freiburg days, Heinrich Rickert, for an offprint and announced that he would soon return the favor by send-ing him the manuscript of "*my* systematics of religion." And in late November, he repeated that he would like to send him his "*(empirical)* casuistry of contemplation and active religion," but it was only three-quarters typed. Weber wrote to his publisher P. Siebeck on December 30, 1913, that he had worked out a description that related all major forms of community to economics: from family and household to en-terprise, group, in ethnic community, and religion. In brackets he ex-plained what could be expected from the section on "Religion": "in-cluding all great religions of the earth: sociology of the doctrines of salvation and religious ethics—what Troeltsch did, now for *all* reli-gions, only essentially more concise." A table of contents published in 1914 announced the division of the entire manual. The part Weber wrote was titled "The Economy and Social Orders and Powers," and the following subjects were treated: "Categories of Social Orders"; "Household, Oikos, and Enterprise"; "Neighborhood, Kinship Group, Local Community"; and "Ethnic Communal Relations." "Religious Groups" came fifth in the series. Weber expatiated on "The Class Basis of Religions; Religions of Culture, and Economic Ethos."[25]

These outlines show that Weber was interested in religions in the plural, and why he was. The assumption is obvious that not only Protestantism, but all great religions if they were socially established and supported by classes, had an impact on the course of economic development. The special social course of the West in comparison with the East might also be explained with the history of religions. In 1915, when the first essay of the *Wirtschaftsethik der Weltreligionen* (Economic Ethics of World Religions) appeared, Weber commented in a footnote at the beginning that the new essays were designed to appear at the same time as the treatise on "Wirtschaft und Gesell-schaft" in the *Grundriss der Sozialökonomik* and were intended "to in-terpret and complement the section on the sociology of religion (and, however, to be interpreted by it in many points)."[26] Weber's research in the history of religion had a systematic component. The text of this section characterized by Weber himself as "a systematics of religion" was edited by Marianne Weber as the section, "Sociology of Religion" from *Wirtschaft und Gesellschaft*. Weber's untimely death foiled his plan to revise it before publication.

Weber's Systematics of Religion

The systematics of religion in *Wirtschaft und Gesellschaft* is not light fare. It does not reveal either its internal context or its place in religious studies at the time. To know both of them better, I shall transform the description as casuistry into a systematic account of the history of religions.

Religion was a communal action that wanted to achieve an earthly goal through the use of supernatural forces. The supernatural forces first manifested themselves in things (fetishes) and abilities (ecstasy), before they were objectified as soul, spirit, and gods. Priests established a cult to influence the gods—unlike sorcerers who wanted to compel them. When believers noted the ineffectiveness of the cult, the priests either explained it by the independent existence of evil powers or interpreted the misfortune that afflicted the community as god's punishment for the violation of ethical norms.

Prophets elaborated this latter interpretation and replaced the cult with conduct of life as a means of achieving salvation. Ethical prophets demanded obedience to the commandments of the otherworldly god. Exemplary prophets demanded worship of the holy person or mystical contemplation. Thus they created the prerequisite for a systematic conduct of life of the laity. Divergent developments in the history of religion came from the difference of two types: exemplary prophets appeared mainly in India, ethical prophets in the Near East, where the concept of a personal, otherworldly, creator god prevailed.

The supporters of a prophet formed communities. If these lasted, they were led by priests who established doctrines and influenced the conduct of life of the laity through sermons and spiritual welfare. Yet they also had to consider membership in social classes. Because peasants were dependent on unpredictable nature, not many of them supported a rational ethic. Aristocrats supported prophetic religiosity at a time when waging war against unbelievers was awarded a religious bonus. State officials scorned irrational religiosity, appreciated it at most as a means of taming their subjects. Privileged bourgeoisie were also usually averse to otherworldly religions and were receptive to a religiosity of salvation only if they were depoliticized. Only where the citizens engaged in crafts and trade did they support a rational ethical community religiosity, as among the petit bourgeois of Western cities, but not in Chinese and Indian cities. Unprivileged groups like slaves and the proletariat could also support a religion of salvation. Their awareness of being chosen was based on the expectation of a future mission and retaliation. Ancient Judaism was an example.

But what was definitive for the history of religions was the support of intellectuals, promising redemption from external or internal needs. The more ethical the concept of God became, the more urgent was the problem of theodicy: how to reconcile the power and justice of God with the imperfection of the world. There were three consistent solutions. The Protestant doctrine of predestination taught that there was no way of knowing why one person was chosen and another not. To balance God's omnipotence with His justice rendered Him a *deus absconditus*. Another solution was offered by dualism, which ascribed the imperfection of the world to an independent evil force. A third solution was the Indian theory of the transmigration of souls. Guilt or merit were each balanced directly in the subsequent life.

Salvation could be either an act of the redeemed or a gift of grace. If it was the work of the redeemed, it could be attained by a specific conduct of life consisting either of an active ethical behavior or of a mystical escape from the world. There were several reasons for this distinction: the Middle Eastern conception of an otherworldly creator god; the intellectual religiosity of Asian religions; the legalization of the relation to God in the west; the rejection of ecstasy by the Romans; the bureaucratic organization of the church. But salvation could also be pure grace, and then salvation was transmitted sacramentally or achieved through belief. If salvation took place on the basis of predestination, signs of election were expected in the success of an appropriate conduct of life.

Only if the religiosity of salvation became an ethics of conviction did it explode the validity of established norms and revolutionize the everyday conduct of life. Hence, conflicts with the existing ways of life arose and created an awareness of their autonomous laws, but also established ethical alternatives to them. A religious ethic opposed economic rules since these could not be regulated charitably. Yet asceticism could contribute unintentionally to the accumulation of wealth. Mystical religiosity could impose the demand for brotherly love. There was a similar tension about political behavior, where a religiosity of salvation entailed either apoliticism or revolutions of faith. It also conflicted with sexuality, making hostility to sexuality a means of the search for salvation. But it could also be sublimated to the erotic. Finally, the religiosity of salvation was in conflict with art as a power of enchantment. As long as world religions remained directed at the world, like Judaism and Islam, they did not produce any methodical conduct of life. Buddhism did reject the world, but also rejected rational purposeful behavior in it. Only Protestantism prepared an end of the otherworldly search for salvation and established a methodical conduct of life in this world.

Weber's explanations indicate a good knowledge of contemporary religious studies, and one of his sources for that was his personal contacts in the Eranos. In 1904, that club of scholars was founded in Heidelberg by the New Testament scholar Adolf von Deissmann. A letter signed by all professors participating told of its purpose.[27] At the monthly meeting of the "meal of friends" (the meaning of the Greek *eranos*), the participants included the philosopher Wilhelm Windelband, the systematic theologian and philosopher of religion Ernst Troeltsch, the national and international jurist Georg Jellinek, the economist and cultural historian Eberhard Gothein, and the economist Karl Rathgen. At that time, religious studies was primarily an interdisciplinary undertaking that was not limited to the few academic chairs in the subject. Plausibly, throughout many years in Eranos, Weber not only provided stimulation but also received it. At one meeting of the group in their home, Marianne Weber reported that Max "enjoys this opportunity for mental exchange, in which they inflame one another and thus can always melt their own knowledge again."[28] The album indicates meetings until January 1909.

In his introduction to "Wirtschaftsethik der Weltreligionen" (Economic Ethics of World Religions, 1915), Weber outlined a systematic account of the history of religion. Primitive notions of spirit and gods were similar everywhere. The development in world history differentiating between an ethical and a mystical concept of god resulted from a sublimation influenced both by psychological connections as well as by a couple of historical motives. Fundamental facts of this account came from religious studies at that time.[29] Weber's interpretation of religion did not follow Tylor's animism, but rather Marett's pre-animism. The raw material of the history of religions was formed of experiences of power, not ideas of the soul. According to Weber, this raw material underwent a similar development, as Cornelis Petrus Tiele had assumed.[30] Natural religions, which assumed terrifying powerful beings in the world and had undertaken to control them with magical means, had been replaced by ethical religions promulgated by prophets. "But the substitution of ethical religions for nature-religions is, as a rule, the result of a revolution, or at least of an intentional reform," wrote C. P. Tiele.[31]

Another element of Weber's construct also came from this source: the claim of two conflicting conceptions of god in the history of religion. Following F. Max Müller, Tiele had distinguished two conceptions of god: the "theanthropic" and the "theocratic." In the former, the deity was immanent in human nature; in the latter, it confronted man as a remote power. In this context, Tiele, like Weber, used the familiar terms of *stages* and *directions*. Natural religions and ethical religions were different stages in the history of religions. "Theanthropic" and "theocratic" denoted divergent directions in the history of the Indo-European and Semitic religions.[32]

Weber's interpretation of salvation religiosity, on the other hand, came from a quite different source. Tiele had rejected the thesis of Hermann Siebeck (1893) that religion must be linked with rejection of the world and that *salvation religions* had to be treated as a distinct class of religions. But on this point, Weber followed Siebeck, not Tiele. This choice allowed him to focus on the subjective side of religion, "religiosity," and to capture it with terms like "personality," "practical religion," and "irrationality." In terms of *the religiosity of salvation*, Ernst Troeltsch was obviously important. Weber's way of processing the history of religion was similar to Troeltsch's, as he wrote in a letter to the publisher in December 1913. Both Weber and Troeltsch saw experience of the world as inexplicable and meaningless as the driving force of all religious development. In his 1919 lecture, "Politics As a Vocation," Weber revealed a view that could have come from Troeltsch: "This problem—the experience of the irrationality of the world—was the driving force of all religious evolution. The Indian doctrine of Karma, Persian dualism, the doctrine of Original Sin, Predestination, and the Deus Absconditus, all these have grown from this experience."[33] Weber's system of religion revolved around the assumption that religious systems of interpretation had emerged gradually from the experience of helplessness: dynamism from the unpredictable nature, religious ethic from the failure of cultic means, and theodicy from the lack of a proper balance of retaliation.

The Momentum of Disenchantment

In about 1911, Weber resumed his sociological study of religions and—as his subjects indicate—expanded it to include comparative religious studies. The idea that this was a kind of cross-check of *The Protestant Ethic*, as has often been assumed, cannot be maintained. Fortunately, Marianne Weber's biography contains an important reference indicating that the study was motivated by a discovery: the special nature of the rationalism of Western culture.

> The process of rationalization dissolves the magical notions and increasingly "disenchants" the world and renders it godless. Religion changes from magic to doctrine. And now, after the disintegration of the primitive

image of the world, there appear two tendencies: a tendency toward the rational mastery of the world and one toward *mystical* experience. But not only the religions receive their stamp from the increasing development of thought; the process of rationalization moves on several tracks, and its autonomous development encompasses all creations of civilization—the economy, the state, law, science, and art. All forms of Western civilization in particular are decisively determined by a methodical *way of thinking* that was first developed by the Greeks, and this way of thinking was joined in the Age of Reformation by a methodical *conduct of life* that was oriented to certain purposes. It was this union of a theoretical and a practical rationalism that separated modern civilization from ancient civilization, and the special character of both separated modern civilization from Asian civilization. To be sure, there were processes of rationalization in the Orient as well, but neither the scientific, the political, the economic, nor the artistic kind took the course that is peculiar to the Occident.

Weber regarded this recognition of the special character of Eastern *rationalism* and the role it was given to play for Western civilization as one of his most important discoveries. As a result, his original inquiry into the relationship between religion and economics expanded into an even more comprehensive inquiry into the *special character of all of Western civilization.*[34]

Note primarily the term *disenchantment*. Its importance to Weber can be measured by the fact that, in 1920, he inserted it directly and as an "alien element" into the second edition of *The Protestant Ethic*:[35]

This, the complete elimination of salvation through the Church and the sacraments (which was in Lutheranism by no means developed to its final conclusions) was what formed the absolutely decisive difference from Catholicism. That great historic process in the development of religions, the elimination of magic from the world which had begun with the old Hebrew prophets and, in conjunction with Hellenistic scientific thought, had repudiated all magical means to salvation as superstition and sin, came here to its logical conclusion.[36]

Taking the cue of *disenchantment* as a connecting thread may be the easiest way to know what his discovery could mean. It surfaced back in 1913 in a theoretical scholarly article that is also important for the systematics of religion: "Some Categories of Interpretive Sociology," where Weber separated "sharply the subjectively intended meaning from the objectively valid meaning (thereby deviating somewhat from Simmel's method)."[37] Rational behavior can be embedded in the conduct of life of a subject without having to be objectively adequate.

Weber's term *disenchantment* is closely connected with this distinction. The objective "proper" world of facts on the one hand and the subjective world of rational conduct of life on the other are independent of one another. Religious history is responsible for turning this independence into a principle. Since the claim that the course of the world is somehow a *meaningful* process could not be maintained, the problem of unjust suffering had the tendency to progress gradually to an ever-broader devaluation of the world. For Weber, the history of religions tended inevitably toward a devaluation of the world, which elicited an awareness that the world and its ways of life obeyed autonomous laws. In the history of religions, the distinction of the world of facts from the world of meaning is elaborated. Just as worldly asceticism created the ethos of capitalism, so disenchantment created the practical postulate of the autonomous laws of secular orders.

Options in the Disenchanted World

A requirement for disenchantment as a drive of Western development was that it joined with an ethics of conviction. "Action oriented toward conceptions of magic, for example, is often subjectively of a far more instrumentally rational character than any non-magical religious behavior, for precisely in a world increasingly divested of magic, religiosity must take on increasingly (subjective) irrational meaning relationships (ethical or mystical, for instance)."[38] The disenchantment of external orders produced freedom for subjective meanings. When Weber described the tension between the ethics of world-denying religions and the autonomous laws of purposive economic and political behavior, he illustrated each of them with examples of how meaningful ethical alternatives might have been possible in the spheres of autonomous orders. They and their rational dynamics had formed the typical Western culture.

This Janus face of Western culture was the subject of Weber's talk, *Wissenschaft als Beruf* (Science As Calling, 1917/1919). His claim made this talk so exciting: that increasing rationalization does not mean an increasing general knowledge of the conditions of life:

> It means something else, namely, the knowledge or belief that if one but wished one *could* learn it at any time. Hence, it means that principally there are no mysterious incalculable forces that come into play, but rather that one can, in principle, master all things by calculation. This means that the world is disenchanted. One need no longer have recourse to magical means in order to master or implore the spirits, as did the sav-

age, for whom such mysterious powers existed. Technical means and calculation perform the service.[39]

Paradoxical as it may sound, Weber did not attribute the postulate of scientific knowledge to some kind of experience, but rather to religious history. This was achieved by his concept of disenchantment. In that rationalized world—and this is the reverse of disenchantment—the individual was forced to give meaning to the world himself. No knowledge of experience can help with that. Hence, daily life itself becomes the stage of the battle for the final attitude to the world. It was precisely the successful disenchantment that created that freedom in the objective orders of life where the history of religions goes on under different conditions.

In his *Sociology of Religion*, Weber linked this continuing religious history with intellectualism. "As intellectualism suppresses belief in magic, the world's processes become disenchanted, lose their magical significance, and henceforth simply 'are' and 'happen' but no longer signify anything. As a consequence, there is a growing demand that the world and the total pattern of life be subject to an order that is significant and meaningful."[40] Thus, disenchantment reproduced the problem that had given a driving force to the whole history of religions. If autonomous laws prevail in secular orders, the individual has to establish subjectivity independent of reality with reference to its own values. If, on the one hand, reality is reduced to mere factuality, on the other hand, meaning becomes a matter of personal decision and intellectual honesty.

In the early text of *The Protestant Ethic* (1904–5), there hardly seemed to be space for values other than the rational ethic of calling. At that time, Weber's assessment of the rational lifestyle ended in the dreary vision of an iron cage. After Weber's discovery, that seems to have changed. At least, the disenchantment of the world itself clearly makes that option, which had once been realized in the history of religions, available on the level of subjective life. While mysticism in *The Protestant Ethic* was more a remnant category—a passive counterpart to active asceticism—that changed both in *The Sociology of Religion* and in *Economic Ethics and World Religions*.[41] Mysticism was now promoted to an alternative of equal rank. Both asceticism and mysticism were valid as equally legitimate consequences of a methodical life in a disenchanted world. The formal rationalization of the world into secular orders with autonomous laws was accompanied by a plurality of divergent rationalizations of conduct of life.[42] The individual was entirely responsible for how he led his life strictly on the basis of subjective decisions. In this context, note the special nuance of the term conduct of life as distinct from behavior, which Werner Gephart correctly pointed out.[43] Conduct of life draws its consistency not from a success in interaction, but from the tempering of expectations in the face of inevitable disappointments. Both asceticism and mysticism are such tempered conduct of life. The pluralism of individual decisions creates the precondition for the continuation of the history of religion in the modern world.

Religion of the Intellectuals

The continuity of religious history led Weber to concentrate on the phenomenon of the intellectuals. A brief survey of the history of the term at the end of the nineteenth century is better than any definition to assess the significance of this construct. The traces of its genesis clung to the term for a long time. The word *intellectuels* emerged in France in connection with the Dreyfus case. After it was proved that the conviction of the Jewish captain Alfred Dreyfus for treason was a miscarriage of justice, and the real culprit turned out to be a French aristocrat, Major Ferdinand Esterhazy, a retrial was demanded. This was opposed by the conservative, anti-Semitic camp in France, since the credibility of the state was at stake. In the fierce quarrel that ensued, members of various professions, including many academics, artists, and journalists, published an appeal in a Paris newspaper on January 14, 1898, one day after Émile Zola published his famous open letter to the president of the republic, "*J'accuse.*" This appeal had far-reaching consequences and was soon characterized as a *protestation des intellectuels* (a manifesto of the intellectuals). At that time, the word was newly coined, perhaps by Georges Clemenceau, the spokesman of the Dreyfusards, but possibly also by their opponents.[44] From the first, the term *intellectuel* was ambivalent. The anti-Dreyfusards regarded the supporters of the appeal as abstract, anti-national, Jewish, decadent, and incompetent. All these features were compressed into the new term.

Yet those who were defined by the word in France adopted the term, and as intellectuals claimed that their political intervention and support for the republican, democratic ideal of a government of law was dictated by reason alone. They saw the vilification as a bid for identification, what Dietz Bering calls an "ideological polyseme."[45] The term *intellectual* derived its energy from the conflict of loyalties experienced by intellectuals in modern central European nation-states over whether to follow the national interests of their state or the universal demands of reason. Three decades later, in 1927, Julien Benda spelled out this dilemma in his famous manifesto, *The Betrayal of the Clerks*, and accused the nationalistic intellectuals of a betrayal of reason. But this problem had been discussed in France as far back as 1898 when Émile Durkheim advocated priority of the principle of reason over loyalty to the state at that time. In the fervent debate, appealing to reason, he defended the right of the intellectuals to challenge the authority of the state. Newspaper reports soon carried the term to Germany, where the pejorative meaning got the upper hand. Not only the political right, but also the Social Democrats judged the phenomenon of "intellectual" as negative. "In France, in 1898, the positive term of intellectual was opposed only by the fascistic invective. But in Germany, there was a double attack. Here, the *Marxist party* was also dominated by unequivocal tendencies to push 'intellectuals' into an insult."[46]

When Max Weber adopted the term *intellectual*, he did not follow the pejorative evaluation. Not only did Weber come in direct contact with the educated classes called intellectuals, but was himself a "political intellectual."[47] Aside from Eranos, another more informal circle coalesced around Weber in Heidelberg, where he lived and worked (after 1903, no longer as an official professor, but as an honorary member of the faculty). Heidelberg was not only the most liberal German university but also the most international one. Anyone who was persecuted or intolerable elsewhere "was possible in the city on the Neckar," wrote Paul Honigsheim in his essay "Max Weber in Heidelberg."[48] Many of these intellectuals visited Weber on Sunday afternoon for discussions. The regular and irregular participants of this circle included Georg Lukàcs and Ernst Bloch.[49] While studying the sociology of revolutionary intellectuals like Lukàcs, the scholar Michael Löwy was surprised to find himself thrust into the Weber circle in Heidelberg.[50] As indicated by Weber's recently published correspondence, he had lively exchanges of thoughts with other contemporaries, many of whom sympathized with a romantic criticism of capitalism that Weber also touched on, for example, in the gloomy prognosis of the iron cage at the end of *The Protestant Ethic*.[51]

The terms *religiosity of salvation* and *intellectualism* surfaced in Weber's texts after his discovery of 1911. As Weber stated in *Wirtschaftsethik der Weltreligionen*, we can have no real idea today of how important the intellectual classes once were in the history of religions. Sublimating the possession of sacred values into a belief in "redemption" had been their work. It was the age-old idea of liberation from distress, hunger, drought, illness, and ultimately from suffering and death. "Yet redemption attained a specific significance only where it expressed a systematic and rationalized 'image of the world' and represented a stand in the face of the world." Following these words, Weber formulated his famous thesis that (material and ideal) interests ruled, and not ideas of human behavior. "But," he added, "very frequently the 'world images' that have been created by 'ideas' have, like switchmen, determined the tracks along which action has been pushed by the dynamic of interest."[52] What Enlightenment critics of religion had judged as the mere consolation of a hereafter or a compensation for worldly failures and blows of fate, Weber made into the driving force of the systematics and the rationality of relations to the world. Religious concepts of the world, suspected as ideology, were in reality a fundamental and permanent element of the history of culture.

Weber used *religiosity of salvation* and *intellectuals* for his systematics of religion. The experience of the irrationality of the world was the fixed point from which he regarded and compared the great world religions. "The metaphysical conception of God and of the world, which the ineradicable demand for a theodicy called forth, could produce only a few systems of ideas on the whole—as we shall see, only three. These three gave rationally satisfactory answers to the questioning for the basis of the incongruity between destiny and merit: the Indian doctrine of Kharma, Zoroastrian dualism, and the predestination decree of deus absconditus. These solutions are rationally closed; in pure form they are found only as exceptions."[53] Because the problem was fundamentally insoluble, the history of religions continued unimpeded in contemporary society. Thus, there were still current options with the status of consistent foundations of conduct of life in the disenchanted world. On the other hand, however, religious history of the disenchanted world was not the same as that of the traditional world. The more intellectuals made the "meaning" of the world problematic, the more did "meaning" shift to the subject. The transmitted religions became maxims of a conduct of life that achieved validity on the basis of a subjective decision. In this form, the history of religion continues: "Many old gods ascend from their graves; they are disenchanted and hence take the form of impersonal forces. They strive to gain power over our lives and again they resume their eternal struggle with one another."[54] But the character of conventional pluralism changed. The individual is forced to decide. Pluralism turned into an antagonism of values, according to W. Schluchter.[55]

Weber's claim of a correlation between intellectualism and the religion of salvation was also an echo of discussions in the Weber circle. A need for salvation did not originate only in the social situation of the underprivileged or—as another source—from the practical rationalism of the bourgeoisie. There was also a third source that bubbled up abundantly in Heidelberg: "intellectualism as such, more particularly the metaphysical needs of the human mind as it is driven to reflect on ethical and religious questions, driven not by material need but by an inner compulsion to understand the world as a meaningful cosmos and to take up a position toward it."[56] The problem of "meaning" had its solid communicative place in Weber's circle. Paul Honigsheim recalled that Tolstoy and Dostoevski had been in conversations in the Weber house, "present in the flesh, one might almost say."[57] When reflecting on the "West," Weber first often looked "East," noted Hubert Treiber.[58] This can also be felt in Weber's talk *Science as Vocation*. When he said that science was incapable of solving any question of meaning, he makes Tolstoy get up and ask on behalf of everyone: "What shall we do and how shall we live?"[59]

The Disenchanted Gods

Though *asceticism* and *mysticism* are both equally justifiable in theory, in practice they are completely opposite consequences of the postulate of the irrationality of the world (W. Schluchter).[60] They were a still valid legacy of the history of religions. "The decisive historical difference between the predominantly oriental and Asian types of salvation religion and those found primarily in the Occident is that the former usually culminate in contemplation and the latter in asceticism."[61] Weber thus continued and systematized Tiele's version of the two different conceptions of god (both a personal, demanding Creator god; and an impersonal essence accessible only through contemplation). Under the conditions of the disenchanted world, the gods themselves can be disenchanted and receive power over human life as practical principles. The same intellectualism that propelled the disenchantment of the world can also include the gods and can make them into sublime values. As such, they justify current options. And Weber seemed to agree that these values "have retreated from public life either into the transcendental realm of mystical life or into the brotherliness of direct and personal human relations."[62] In any case, he did not consider it very likely that a real religious revival could emerge from them.[63]

Weber diagnosed "characteristic escapes from the world" among European intellectuals of his day: an escape to loneliness or to nature, a world-escapist Romanticism, an escape among "peoples" untouched by human conventions (the Russian Narodniks). This escape was carried out through contemplation or asceticism, and sought either individual salvation or revolutionary change of the world. Weber followed his assessment of contemporary tendencies of intellectuals with a recapitulation of religious history: "All these doctrines are equally appropriate to apolitical intellectualism and may appear as religious doctrines of salvation, as on occasion they have actually appeared. The distinctive world-fleeing character of intellectualist religion has one of its roots here."[64] Current tendencies in the German bourgeoisie had their equivalents in phenomena of religious history. He regarded the renunciation of politics by the intellectuals, their depoliticization, which went along with their turn to eastern religions, as a lesson of ancient religious history.[65]

Weber's interpretation of contemporary intellectuals was linked to his image of Indian religiosity: "Wherever an intellectual class strives to fathom the 'meaning' of the world and their own life by thinking, and after the failure of this direct rationalistic endeavor—then experientially to raise this indirect rationalistic experience to awareness, it will lead the way somewhere to the silent, next-worldly realm of cumbersome Indian mysticism."[66] These words do not refer to Indian philosophy of course, but to his contemporaries.

Both Weber and Durkheim, strangers to the history of religion, trained themselves in the field in order to trace the genealogy of parts of modern society. Both did this from an angle that revealed a critical distance from modern civilization. Durkheim was concerned that the society characterized by the division of labor could destroy the social bond between individuals. He was appeased only by the knowledge—drawn from the religious history—that individualism was guaranteed by the collective and had its roots in a deification of the human soul in elementary religions. Weber's different concern was whether modern civilization could still maintain individual freedom. His analysis of the history of religions, which was directed paradigmatically to the religion of salvation, concluded that the charismatic force of the supernatural was not broken. In the actual world, conduct of life distinct in principle remained. However, he saw this freedom as a new danger. His interpretation of the condition of European intellectuals is quite similar to Julien Benda's and can be read as a preformulation of Benda's thesis of betrayal. But in Weber's view, it was not the abstract, disinterested, unimpassioned reason of the Enlightenment that was betrayed, but rather a rational ascetic conduct of life that emerged from one of the three rational theodicies (i.e., Protestantism). The intellectuals were in danger of betraying this specific Western settlement of the problem of meaning.

CHAPTER TWELVE

RELIGION AS EXPERIENCE OF THE SELF

I N GERMANY, the twentieth century began with an emotional discussion of culture. In the shape and with the force of industrialization, bureaucratization, and scientization, modern society had become increasingly palpable in the life of every individual. Intellectuals paid special attention to the fate of "culture," which was considered threatened by the advancing external civilization. On the other hand, the urgency of the social question receded. "The previously dominant sociopolitical discourse [was] increasingly superimposed and widely removed by a new cultural critical discourse," as one study described the shifts of the problem of awareness of the German bourgeoisie.[1] Culture became an "emotion-laden watchword" with which philosophers reacted to the "concern for the threatened freezing of the soul."[2]

In the struggle waged by intellectuals against the advancing technical civilization, philosophers also called on religions for support. Man had paid for the gradual spread of technique and control of nature with a loss of inwardness, with a "loss of soul," as the respected philosopher and Nobel laureate Rudolf Eucken put it. Yet inwardness could not be discarded without resistance, and as proof Eucken pointed to the revival of religion, where the subject was again the real carrier of life. This change showed that "realism" could not triumph over "idealism." Eucken did not welcome the rise of religion per se, since obsolete things were also restored; but he did see it as an unmistakable sign that the outcome of the conflict was still open. "The revival of religion forms the strongest evidence for the rise of the problem of the inner man."[3] His book, *Der Wahrheitsgehalt der Religion*, which first appeared in 1901 and went through several editions, developed this theme broadly.

A few years later, Emil Hammacher presented similar considerations in another widely read book. The main enemy of man as subject was the metaphysical character of the Enlightenment. "All modern problems of culture have the same cause; they come from the inadequacy of the world view taught by the Enlightenment of the eighteenth century, and the inability of all previous attempts to overcome it."[4] The Enlightenment inserted calculating reason and the principle of utility between man and the world, and thus destroyed the human personality.[5] Christianity was also to blame for this distortion. Only the "experience of genuine mysticism" could liberate man from the constraint of rationalism.[6] Note that this reasoning judges mysticism to be the means of overthrowing the rule of reason over man and achieving a lifestyle without rationalist damage, by blending the essence of man with god.

Mystic Reading

Such cultural criticism resonated widely among the German bourgeoisie at that time, and the publisher Eugen Diederichs exploited that market.[7] The existence of his publishing house was not an end in itself, but emerged in response to a necessity. In 1908, he titled his ideas as "Paths to German Culture." One of the paths he suggested went through "living religion," "a real tautology," he added, "for religion always bears the principle of life within it, it appeals to life as a whole. We would not have to talk about religion today if the overestimation of intellectual knowledge, the one-sided preference of working life, hadn't obscured the voice of the inner demon."[8] The publisher saw the crisis of modern society as mainly a crisis of religion. Christianity, an accomplice in rendering life shallow and mechanical, was a poison that must be removed from the body of society.[9] This withdrawal treatment was to be complemented by a dose of new religion. The series *Die religiösen Stimmen der Völker* (The Religious Voices of the Nations) was intended to do that. In it, "the religious documents of all positive religions from the aborigines, Confucianism, Buddhism, Parsism, and Hellenism to Islam and the Talmud are displayed in convenient volumes expounded by prominent experts." In addition, the writings of Henri Bergson were to "constitute the speculative substratum for the modern religious consciousness."[10]

A special task in this therapy was assigned to "mysticism," which included not only medieval mystics, but also Tolstoy, Kirkegaard, and other modern religious authors. The publisher regarded mysticism as "a thoroughly worldly point of reference of a critical and reasonable debate with the modern age" (Gangolf Hübinger).[11] One still impressive document of the new literary mysticism was the collection *Ekstatische Konfessionen*, edited by Martin Buber in 1909. In his preface to this small tome, Buber surprised the reader with a provocative assertion. "At first, man explained with the name God primarily what he didn't understand about the world, but then, more often, what man didn't understand about himself. Thus, ecstasy—what man could understand least about himself—became God's highest gift."[12]

These words struck the nerve of the time. Man—as seen in vitalistic philosophy—lives, as it were, in the blind spot of himself.[13] An awareness of the history of religions could help him close the gap between life and consciousness. Religious experience leads to regions that are inaccessible to reason and where genuine life resides.

The extent to which this new mysticism had penetrated is demonstrated by the fact that in the first edition of *Religion in Geschichte und Gegenwart* a separate entry was devoted to it, dealing with the issue of establishing mysticism in the present.

> The need to internalize and absorb our scientifically and technologically directed modern culture going into tremendous detail has led fine minds back to M [mysticism], which had fallen completely into disregard and almost into oblivion in the second half of the nineteenth century. This remarkable process was heralded literarily in many ways: in theology, through a renewed interest for the young Schleiermacher; in philosophy and natural science through a revival of Fechner and a glorification of Indian Buddhism. The publisher Diederichs was especially involved in the excavation of mystical texts of all ages and nations. But these new editions and their characteristic introductions by the new mystics (especially W. Bölsche and H. Büttner) reveal clearly that this new movement is absolutely independent and is not a direct continuation of old mysticism. Instead, it was born out of a growing protest of minds against the total spirit of our time, that is against a desolate materialism, on the one hand, and against a one-sided religion of reason or will on the other (W. Hoffmann).[14]

As Diederichs said, living religion is the voice of a culture that is free from the overestimation of intellectual knowledge and the one-sided preference for the business life. This critical version of the relation of religion and culture long survived its initial formulation and has extended throughout religious studies in the twentieth century. This can be seen in Buber's collection of texts, reissued by Peter Sloterdijk in 1993 as number 100 in *Diederichs Gelbe Reihe*, a series that has followed in the footsteps of its predecessor, according to the publisher's prospectus.

William James and the Experience of the Freedom of the Self

Buber's approach was similar to that of the American philosopher William James (1842–1910), who, like Buber, was considered a representative of the so-called "vitalism." James had delivered the Gifford Lectures in Edinburgh in 1899–1900—one year after C. P. Tiele—and had published them in 1902 as *The Varieties of Religious Experience*. Among the many autobiographical reports James incorporated literally in his book as sources, one reproduces a coded experience of his own that dates from the early 1870s. Someone who had been in a state of pessimism and depression was suddenly overwhelmed by anxiety. For days, he kept thinking of an epileptic he had seen sitting in a madhouse. "He sat there like a sort of sculptured Egyptian cat or Peruvian mummy, moving nothing but his black eyes and looking absolutely non-human. This image and my fear entered into a species of combination with each other. *That shape am I*, I felt, potentially." He could not get rid of the feeling of the uncertainty of life. He wondered "how other people could live, how I myself ever lived, so unconscious of that pit of insecurity beneath the surface of life."[15]

James's journal shows that he relieved his depression by reading Charles Renouvier, a French thinker in the tradition of Kant, and saw no reason why Renouvier's definition of free will—holding onto a thought because I decide to, while I could have other thoughts—had to be the definition of an illusion. At any rate, he assumed for the time being that it was not an illusion. And his first act of free will was to believe in free will. The existence of freedom can be examined only by practicing it. James drew conclusions from that for all human knowledge. The pragmatism so closely linked to his name thus understands truth as nothing but a verification. It is not an objective fact, but must be established by the subject.

James's account incorporated abundant autobiographical reports revolving around these sorts of elementary experiences: documents from the past as well as reports from the present. Those from the present are particularly interesting, using widely circulated bourgeois narratives. Who doesn't know them from his own circle of friends? "Quite early in the night I was awakened. . . . I felt as if I had been aroused intentionally, and at first thought someone was breaking into the house. . . . I then turned on my side to go to sleep again, and immediately felt a consciousness of a presence in the room, and singular to state, it was not the consciousness of a living person, but of a spiritual presence." For James, such reports document an elementary human mental fact: the reality of the invisible.[16] In view of such experience, the visible world appears as *maya*, illusion, with an abyss gaping beneath.[17]

James devoted a separate chapter to "mysticism," which he still knew as a curse word. He used it to denote a special state of consciousness that could not be expressed properly in words, which also revealed a knowledge unfathomable to the discursive intellect, and was ephemeral and attacked passive people.[18] James designed a smooth transition for this state of consciousness, beginning with almost everyday incidents, continuing with experiences of anesthesia and ending with a methodical cultivation of mystical states in the great religions.[19] In all these cases, man experiences that he has a self beyond all natural causality, which provides release from the constraint of everyday life.[20]

Rudolf Otto's "Pre-religion" as an Argument against Rationalism in Religion

In 1911, the systematic theologian Rudolf Otto (1869–1937) traveled to Morocco. He later described precisely and empathetically what he experienced in a small synagogue:

> It is the Sabbath and already dark, and already in an inconceivably dirty corridor, we hear the "Benschen" [blessings] of the prayers and Bible-readings, that singsong nasal chanting that the synagogue bequeathed to the church and the mosque. In vain does the ear strive at first to separate and grasp the words and wants to give up the effort, when suddenly the tangle of voices is unraveled and—a solemn fear runs through the limbs—rises in unison, clear, and unmistakable:
>
> > Kadosh kadosh kadosh Elohim Adonai Zebaoth
> > Male'u hashamayyim ve'ha-arets kvodo!
> > [Holy, holy, holy is the Lord of Hosts
> > The whole earth is full of his glory.][21]
>
> In whatever language they sound, these most majestic words that have ever crossed human lips always grip the deepest ground of the soul, stirring and touching with a mighty thrill the mystery of the supernatural that sleeps beneath.[22]

Otto's description depends more on philosophical reflection than appears at first glance, since it contains his answer to the gnawing problem of historicism. Ernst Troeltsch, one of Otto's companions, had clearly grasped the theological consequences of historicism. His "Review of a Half Century of Theological Scholarship" (1909) had mercilessly explained how historical research inevitably had to destroy the plausibility of all theological statements. Otto saw only one way out of the dilemma of the immense variety of competing religious claims to truth. The a priori elements of all religions were to be determined by a comparative consideration of the entire history of religions, which would provide solid criteria for the very nature of religion. The religious experience was to be promoted to the position once occupied by revelation. As with the natural sciences, the authentication of religion should be referred to by experience.

Exactly one hundred years after F. Schleiermacher's *On Religion: Speeches to Its Cultured Despisers* first appeared in 1799, Otto produced a new edition. His explanation was intriguing: the speeches deserved our attention because they were an "original and daring attempt to lead an age weary with and alien to religion back to its very mainsprings."[23] It was a "broadside" aimed against the approach to religion as intellectualism and morality. "Alongside knowledge and action, Schleiermacher aimed to prove that religion was a new, unique, and independent area of human existence and the spiritual life, and that it possessed its own special worth with respect to knowledge and action; further, that religion should not be stunted."[24] The speeches were a program in a "struggle against rationalist culture and the Philistinism of rationalism in the state, church, school, and society." It demanded a leaning toward fantasy, melancholy, presentiment, mysticism; a bias in favor of the historical and positive "becoming" in contrast to the "natural"; a championship of the individual, and a preference for the strange and the curious as over against "universal reason."[25] In the history of the theory of religion, Otto's claim is known as *autonomy*. Religion may be described and explained neither according to cognitive nor normative claims to validity. It was independent of that and could not be "reduced" to it.[26]

Otto countered the Neo-Kantianism of Wilhelm Windelband, who had denounced such an approach as one-sided in 1902,[27] with an older version of Kant's philosophy of religion that went back to Jakob Friedrich Fries (1773–1843). "Today, we are again seeking on all sides for a 'religious apriori.' Supernaturalism and historicism fail to give a measure and principle of the truth in religion. Religious history is growing immeasurably."[28] J. F. Fries had regarded Kant's assumption that sensual perceptions were caused by an effect of an object as contradicting the proposition of the inapplicability of the categories (here causality) to the thing in itself. We remain with all our perceptions in the immanence of our awareness, he said. Consequently—he concluded—transcendent ideas had to have the same epistemological rank as sensual experience, provided they were guaranteed by an internal experience of the basis of truth, a "feeling of truth."

Such a construct could be invaluable for an apologia of religion. In fact, this possibility had been grasped back in the nineteenth century, when Arthur Schopenhauer presented an amusing account of it. In the Kantian school, practical reason had been like a Delphic temple, from whose dark shrine infallible oracular statements issued—but unfortunately not what *would* happen, but what *should* happen. The next step had been to grant theoretical reason the same privilege. When that happened, "all dabblers in philosophy and visionaries, led by the atheist denouncer Friedrich Heinrich Jacobi, stream to this unexpectedly open wicket in order to bring their little things to market or at least to save their favorite of the old heirlooms that Kant's doctrine threatened to crush."[29]

Rudolf Otto championed this philosophy of religion despite all objections. He assumed an internal experience of the basis of truth, which could not be proved but could be experienced, and this gave Marett's pre-animism a special psychological turn. "The reader is invited to direct his mind to a moment of deeply felt religious experience, as little as possible qualified by other forms of consciousness. Whoever cannot do this, whoever knows no such moments in his experience, is requested to read no further," Otto demanded in his famous book, *Das Heilige. Über das Irrationale in der Idee des Göttlichen und sein Verhältnis zum Rationalen* (The Idea of the Holy: An Inquiry into the Non-rational Factor in the Idea of the Divine and Its Relation to the Rational).[30] When this essay appeared in 1917, during the Great War, it was an immense sensation. It has been reproduced many times to this day and translated into all major languages. It was really a "broadside" against rationalism—much more than Schleiermacher's writing. Otto eliminated all rational terms from the description of the holy. A new kind of terms, unspoiled by rationalism, was to express the relation of man to the Divine: a feeling of creation, *mysterium tremendum*, the *fascinans*, monstrous, the *augustum*, the numinous, the "absolute other." Otto poured a torrent of such metaphors over the reader to make him understand the inexpressible. The organ of religious perception was not reason, but feeling. Only when a person perceives the holy as a primary affective fact of his life is it accessible to him. "This pure positive we can experience in feelings—feelings which our discussion can help to make clear to us, in so far as it arouses them actually in our hearts."[31] Georg Pfleiderer commented pertinently on this "procedure" that what Otto had in mind was a kind of topography: "The theoretician of religion, of course, is comparable to the geographer or explorer, not as an inventor, but rather only as the one who finds the phenomena."[32]

The book's inconsistency of grasping something inexpressible in words identifies Rudolf Otto as a genuine representative of "German mysticism." Over a long time, a tradition had developed in Germany that God was revealed not only in the Holy Scriptures, but also in the world and in the soul of the individual.[33] Despite its contrary claim of an inexpressible experience, this "German mysticism" was philosophical in argumentation and literary in presentation. *Pace* Schleiermacher, Otto adopted it into religious studies. As all known historical religions had risen out of the ground of a "pre-religion," so religion reemerged anew in every individual. Because this "ground" was common to all men, "the law of parallels" rules the history of religions.[34]

Otto was known for his definition of the numinous as the holy minus its moral aspects.[35] Yet that should not be understood to exclude the ethical from the category of the holy. Otto only wanted to guarantee the hierarchy. The holy can do without ethics—which, moreover, soon and correctly encountered a vigorous opposition[36]—but the ethical cannot do without the holy. Remaining in the tradition of Kant, he saw the roots of all ethics in religion. But his position really becomes clear only from a glance at his public political activities. From 1913 on, Otto was a deputy of the National Liberal Party in the Prussian State Parliament. After nationalism had led to catastrophe in World War I, he set out to establish a *Religiösen Menschheitsbund* to win over all nations for the cause of peace, in conjunction with the international association of churches and religious congregations.[37] For him, religion certainly could not dispense with ethics.

From Religious Studies to Theology: Nathan Söderblom

A similar version of the history of religions came from Nathan Söderblom (1866–1931), a scholar of religion in Leipzig and Archbishop of Uppsala after 1914. For him, too, holiness was the determining word in religion. It was not the existence of a divinity that was important for religion, but rather its power. Yet the experience of this power had been interpreted in different ways in history: either it was seen as an impersonal matter or the effect of a person. In the former case, the beginning of the world and of man was traced to an emanation from a divine substance; in the latter to the act of creation of a transcendent divinity. The major Aryan religions in India and Greece with their penchants for pantheism and mysticism started from the "emanation" model of interpretation. Creation through the will of an omnipotent person, on the other hand, was characteristic of the prophetic religions of Semitic Judaism and Aryan Zarathustrianism. Thus, two completely different types of religions, dynamism and animism, were formed. The relations of man to the divinity were different in each: in one case, an immersion in something impersonal; in the other, a recognition of the holiness of God and His Commandments.[38]

Like F. M. Müller and C. P. Tiele before him, N. Söderblom reckoned with various trends in the history of religion, yet he had to argue with racist interpretations that had become dominant in the meantime. Söderblom did acknowledge a certain elective affinity between nature mysticism and Aryans, prophetic religions and Semites. But he emphasized that he did not want to succumb to a psychology of race. History itself had made sure its problems could not be traced back to racial differences. That is, not only had the two mystical world religions of Hinduism/Buddhism and Christianity emerged from Aryanism, but so had Zarathustra's Revelatory religion. "Fortunately, both of these original Prophetic or revelatory religions are distributed between Aryans and Semites so that the idea cannot be maintained that . . . Revelatory religion or Prophecy was a Semitic inheritance in the higher sense."[39]

Söderblom's fundamental category in the history of religion was not race but experience. Moreover, like Otto, in his life, religious experiences were stages of the formation of a scholarly religious theory.[40] Ideas of God could not explain anything about such experiences. He thought that *mana* and *tabu* brought one much closer to the deepest part of the elementary religion.[41] But this did not lead Söderblom to Otto's conclusion that all rational interpretations were secondary and insufficient in comparison with this irrational experience. He was concerned instead with questions about the hierarchy of the scheme of interpretation, since he granted the prophetic ethical religiosity a higher rank than impersonal redemption through contemplation. Thus, he agreed with Weber and disagreed with Otto. Otto considered nature mysticism as the primary option for rescuing the culture of his time, while Weber saw it as an escape from responsibility. Söderblom shared Weber's (and perhaps even more, Troeltsch's) view that religion had to maintain the opposition to culture in order to prevent it from sinking into materialism.[42] Thus, he saw the major trends in the history of religions not exclusively as universal historical powers, but rather as current options of individuals.

Yet with all the agreement between Söderblom and Weber, there was one serious difference. Söderblom knew something like a positive experience of the holy. Weber—who had a religious tin ear—knew and acknowledged nothing more than an experience of a lack of meaning. Their attitude toward religion in general was correspondingly different. Söderblom was certain of an ultimate religious experience, while for Weber, religion was a means to hold one's own against the experience of meaninglessness. Behind Söderblom's option was a certainty; behind Weber's there was only the courageous decision of a sober thinker.

Van der Leeuw's Cultural Critical Repatriation
of Primitive Mentalities

Söderblom's construct met with approval in particular from the Dutch scholar of religion Gerardus van der Leeuw (1890–1950), who adopted all essential parts of Söderblom's religio-historical plot: the experience of power as the basis of all religion[43] as well as the super-fluous nature of the idea of god. "God . . . is a late comer in the history of religion. And the remarkable thing is that, if appearances are not entirely deceptive, God the son subsisted before God the fa-ther."[44] The experience of power was interpreted either as something personal or as something impersonal, as animism or dynamism. In van der Leeuw, the historical element that Söderblom still kept in mind in this connection retreated almost completely. Closer to Rudolf Otto, he wanted to trace a prehistoric structure of the human mind from the history of religions. Reminiscent of Martin Buber, he claimed programmatically, "In religion, man interprets his experience as revelation."[45]

In 1928, van der Leeuw introduced the views of the French philoso-pher Lucien Lévy-Bruhl (1857–1939) into religious studies.[46] Lévy-Bruhl had investigated ethnologists' reports about the thought of non-European peoples on epistemological categories and in the process had encountered some strange premises. Primitives assumed relations between objects that evaded rational examination and contradicted all logic. In a way we find incomprehensible, they thought objects could be both themselves *and* something else at the same time. He found this "law of participation" among the South American Bororo In-dians, in a report by the ethnologist K. von den Steinen. " 'The Bor-oros boast that they are red arara (parakeets).' This does not merely signify that after their death they become araras, not that araras are metamorphosed Bororos, and must be treated as such. It is something entirely different. 'The Bororos . . . give one rigidly to understand that they are araras *at the present time*, just as if a caterpillar declared itself to be a butterfly.' "[47] Lévy-Bruhl made the following change in this report: "It is not a name they give themselves, nor a relationship that they claim. What they desire to express by it is actual identity. That they can be both the human beings they are and the birds of scarlet plumage at the same time, Von den Steinen regards as inconceivable, but to the mentality that is governed by the law of participation there is no difficulty in the matter."[48] Lévy-Bruhl referred to other cases that supported the assumption of a mystical form of thought and which he termed *mentalité primitive*.

Van der Leeuw introduced this concept into religious studies without much ado, even though its weaknesses were not too hard to discover.[49] But in one rather important point, he parted company from
Lévy-Bruhl. Analogous phenomena found among the civilized must
not be excluded. Folk songs, dreams, and lyric poetry belong to the
class of the "primitive mentality." Thus, van der Leeuw elucidated the
primitive mentality with material from his own culture. As an illus-
tration, he quoted a German folk song:

> Down in the valley
> The water runs dull
> And I cannot tell you
> Why I love you so.

Like the primitive mentality, poetry knows no difference between
thing and meaning, reality and dream. Thus, reality itself becomes an
expression of human feeling, as in this song.

This mode of thought is potentially available to people of modern
civilization, too. In this respect, they can even learn from past and
foreign cultures. But this learning process can succeed only if it follows certain methodical rules. Like Schleiermacher, van der Leeuw
thought that understanding does not result from itself, but only
through an elimination of the misunderstandings that always threaten.
Thus he required something from the interpreters that may not make
sense logically, but which certainly suits a cultural critical hermeneutics: the scholar has to interpolate the objects of his study into his own
life in order to understand them, but at the same time he has to abstain from judging these objects (Greek *epoche*).[50] "What now?" one
might ask. Should he take its side or not? More recent studies in ethnography using the *participant observer* technique have disclosed the
same ambivalence, the same vacillation between "repulsion and attraction"—as Karl-Heinz Kohl put it.[51] Like the ethnographer, the historian of religion should be both involved and uninvolved at the
same time. He should empathize with the values of another culture
and also suspend value judgments of his own culture.

It cannot escape the careful reader of van der Leeuw's phenomenology of religion—a previous, smaller study had appeared in 1925—
that it portrays objects that had long ago lost their right to exist in the
eyes of a rationalist age. That was their fascination for van der Leeuw,
who saw primitive religions as key witnesses of a relation to the
world in which man had not (yet) risen to be ruler of his concrete
conditions of life, but rather fit into them as an organic part. In his
1933 obituary of Stefan George, "a great poet" and the most important neo-Romantic of his time, van der Leeuw expressed his satisfac-

tion that for the first time in a long time, a paganism had been put into words. "Instead of Godless positivism, instead of the Godless mechanized culture, a genuine, non-Christian religiosity appeared. 'We' Christians have waited for it, as it were. For there is genuine Christianity only where the powers of this world are acknowledged and are served. Denial is an opponent that Christianity can live and struggle with. Demonic affirmation brings the church new struggle and new hope."[52] Van der Leeuw thought that the irrationalisms of his time would justify the rejection of the Enlightenment. His statement that "what had been pushed aside as 'primitive,' 'medieval,' and 'scholastic' issues forth again as a living force" expressed not only a doubt about the rightness of the Enlightenment, but also about the possibility of its success. He agreed with the antirational tendencies of his time, but did not want to sacrifice Christianity to them. "It is certainly better to wage war against a living paganism than against the pale negation of a powerless, so-called modern rational and technical Enlightenment."[53]

Determined as few others before him, van der Leeuw converted religious history into a source of modes of consciousness that have become alien to us. If he and other historians of religion now and then presented themselves as witnesses or even prophets, this need not be ascribed to their theological origin,[54] since this kind of commitment is also encountered among nontheologians as well, like E. B. Tylor or J. E. Harrison. They were all convinced that, in foreign, primitive cultures, they had found a concept of the world and a relationship to it that had been outdated by European civilization, but that preserved a right to exist vis-à-vis modern rationalism. Van der Leeuw, too, saw his mission as repatriating the primitive mentality against the resistance of modern rationality.

CHAPTER THIRTEEN

HOW DESCRIPTIONS OF THE HISTORY OF RELIGION
REFLECT MODERNIZATION

Fact and Fiction in Historiography

IT MAY be foolhardy even to raise the question of fact and fiction at the end of this description of the development of religious studies. Does one talk about the rope in the house of the hanged man? Does not honesty demand an open admission: if no unequivocal boundaries have arisen thus far between fact and fiction, they can not be constructed afterward? The American scholar of religion Jonathan Z. Smith has more than simply played with this idea, he has also opened his significantly titled book, *Imagining Religion*, with this statement: "There is no data for religion. Religion is solely the creation of the scholar's study."[1] Although we must agree with that, honesty likewise forbids drawing hasty conclusions from it. For it cannot mean that religious studies is a total fiction and that its facts are not an independent authority. The many claims of religious studies that were tested and refuted is too long to assume that: Müller's nature mythology, Tylor's derivation of the idea of God from animism, Robertson Smith's totemism, Frazer's magic worldview, and so on and on. The development of religious studies was the same process of forming hypotheses and disproving them that is typical of other sciences. We certainly are not dealing only with fictions.

For some years, the fiction problem has been rumbling especially violently in ethnology. Simply in the investigation of the data, the social person of the scholar—his or her nationality, generation, and gender—can be sensed. If ethnographical accounts are considered as monographs, the person of the scholar is always present. As a writer, he or she relates data to discourses held in his or her own society. For example, in discussing the matriarchal system of descent of the Trobrianders, Bronislaw Malinowski raised the question of whether there is any Oedipus complex in a social order, in which the biological father is not an authority figure, unlike Malinowski's own society. There is none, was the answer. This discussion occurred because the author had his eye on his London audience in the 1920s who were raising such questions.[2] It would leave the Trobrianders cold. This example shows clearly that the anthropologist's authority is not based solely on his field research, but that his scientific prestige clearly rises when he turns his data into a contribution to discourses in his own society.[3] Literary qualities also play a role. Some time ago, Clifford Geertz analyzed classical anthropology as literary fictions. In *Works and Lives: The Anthropologist as Author* (1988), we encounter the most distinguished anthropologists of our century as imaginative writers: Claude Lévi-Strauss, Edward Evans-Pritchard, Bronislaw Malinowski, and Ruth Benedict. In their descriptions of foreign cultures, the subjective element cannot be omitted.

The so-called crisis of historicism a hundred years ago was based on a similar insight. While subjectivity was recognized in historical descriptions, there was a decline in the confidence that historical data can be conveyed objectively. What was then called the crisis of historicism is now *Postmodernism* on the intellectual market.[4] The assumption that there is a right representation as opposed to a wrong one of past and distant data has once again become dubious. There is indeed information that is right or wrong. But the description itself follows handicaps that elude such examination.

Insofar as the historian of religions is aware of this newly ignited discussion, he has shied away from its consequences. As long as the issue is the conventional criticism of sources, he feels himself to be on solid ground. But when all historical material is examined, when the implausible is excluded and the plausible is put into a probable order, another task arises: to write the history of religions. If this is really an independent step, the historian of religion also has to leave the safe area of sure facts. If his analysis can be limited to deriving reliable facts from sources, he must now willy-nilly cross the border to fictions. Therefore, scholars of religion cannot avoid this inevitable discussion. We had better take the bull by the horns and confront the question of fiction squarely. Can the kind of imagination we have encountered among the scholars of religion be described a bit more precisely? If Weber's dictum is correct that "methodology can never be anything but reflection on the means that were *proven* in practice,"[5] these means must ultimately be discussed. Is there a criterion to determine whether they have been proven or not?

Categories of Historical Meaning

"Historical narrative without analysis is trivial, historical analysis without narrative is incomplete."[6] Every scholar of religion would agree with the first part of Peter Gay's statement that analysis of sources must precede every historical narrative. The second part of the sentence, on the other hand, would make him hesitate. Back in the nineteenth century, the distinguished historian Johann Gustav Droysen recognized the description of historical research as an independent task, yet his recognition was soon confined to the dustbin. Under the heading "The Topic," Droysen told the students in his often repeated lecture, *Historik*, that what is historically researched needs representation. That is, the investigation itself was twofold: "the enrichment and deepening of the present by elucidating its past, and elucidating the pasts by finding out what of it still exists latent in the present." Such an approach necessarily leads to the conclusion that the idea the historian makes of the past could not correspond with things when they were still present.

One result of this difference is that there can be various representations of the same facts. Droysen distinguished the investigating, the narrating, the didactic, and the discussive representation.[7] In the first case, the method of investigation guides the way; in the case of narrative, it is the aesthetic reception; the didactic representation proceeds along the thought of the reader/hearer; and the discursive representation applies data to current discussions. In all cases, which are naturally not mutually exclusive, the expectation of subjective cultivation is linked with the representation, as Jörn Rüsen correctly notes.[8] But despite this common ground, note that various representations are possible for the same facts.

Ever since the 1970s, historians have once again come to understand that the form in which they present their findings is not irrelevant, but that it creates meanings itself. In the representation of history, the three tenses of past, present, and future intertwine in a special way. As a memory of the past, the representation brings up finished experiences; as an interpretation of its meaning it is directed at the future. It is worthwhile to dwell on this processing a bit longer. Is it absolutely arbitrary? I don't think so, for not everything that is subjective is also arbitrary. Not everything that is fiction is unreal. If this claim is right, the assessment of fiction turns into the search for criteria: Are there criteria for the subjective and fictive that would allow it to be distinguished from the arbitrary and the unreal? Reinhart Koselleck has given an intriguing answer: When a historian writes history, he is constrained to select some facts from the mass of historical data and to ignore others. The operating categories of knowledge are not the same as the ideas connected with the sources. From the stream of flowing events, the historian records those he considers relevant for the future. Koselleck identified two categories he called *space of experience* and *horizon of expectation*.[9] The historian reports on past events and attributes meanings to them that derive from present expectations. Koselleck's idea is productive for us since it recognizes criteria for a fiction that is not unreal or arbitrary: experiences and expectations.[10] Jörn Rüsen posed a similar approach titled "Pragmatics—the constitution of historical thought." An internal connection with the praxis of life structures historical knowledge. Rüsen also emphasizes the factor of "discontinuity." If a change of the world no longer allows the actor to act successfully in the usual way, the experience of the passing of time becomes the cause for historical reflections.[11] I consider the allusion to the experience of discontinuity especially interesting, since historical representations of past religions dealt with the break in history and is thus not arbitrary or unreal.

Meanings of "Religion" under the Conditions of Modernization

From the middle of the nineteenth century, scholars in various disciplines began turning their attention to religions. Linguists, anthropologists, Bible scholars, and archaeologists pioneered in this field, laying the foundations of the scholarly analysis of religion over a period of seventy years. Thus, in the European countries, a new type of historiography emerged that used newly discovered sources of past and foreign cultures as evidence of a history of religions. If we look through the telescope the wrong way—to use P. Leslett's image[12]— and observe the scientists of that time at work, we see that the notion of *religion* had a structure similar to the prevailing term, *nation*. In various European countries in the nineteenth century, historians reconstructed the political past as the history of a nation, expecting a national development in their countries. By dint of their historical imagination, long-ago events were also included under this rubric, since they projected onto past data a view of politics that was indebted to a contemporary perspective. Therefore, it is not surprising that historians today view the term *nation* more as an idea of European thinkers than as an objective reality of human history.[13] In this context, it is also illuminating to note that the overestimation of nation was contradicted even in the nineteenth century, as Hans Georg Schenk proved with the comments of the Frenchman Charles Nodier, who introduced Romanticism in France in the 1820s: "The rejuvenation of society has never depended on a purely political revolution as the moderns would have liked to believe. It is the religions that rejuvenate peoples; the divine spark that enlivens social man can only come from heaven, and this is the true meaning of the beautiful allegory of Prometheus."[14] The concept of *nation* was not limited to the denotation of past facts, but rather conveyed current meanings. That was also true of *religion*. Our search for a criterion for the fictive that is not arbitrary or unreal demands a closer investigation of these meanings.

Note the chronological coincidence of the study of religion and modernization. From the middle of the nineteenth century, European countries were gripped by a powerful thrust of modernization. The social change to an industrial society had considerable repercussions on the validity of customary worldviews and norms. From now on, in the area of economic behavior, market production was more important than answering traditional needs. In the area of power, the legal system was detached from common law. In the realm of science, systematic examination took the place of the self-evident nature of tradition. Because of these changes, the role of the individual in society was determined less and less by tradition and more and more by individual decisions and market opportunities. The denotation "society," as described by Friedrich H. Tenbruck, arose for the new "stateless areas" that took shape. Sociology, he wrote, "is indebted to . . . the discovery of a fundamentally unpredictable social reality. It was assigned the strange task of making predictable a society that had relinquished a long-term regulation of its order."[15] The characteristic of the new sociological quantity *society* was that, on the one hand, it was detached from the world of origin; but on the other hand, it did not sink into anomie and chaos. The context in which the historical concept of *religion* emerged and became plausible is the phenomenon of modernization. The experiences that people made of it determined the meanings *religion* assumed at that time.

The Ambivalence of Modernization: Alienation and Options

In the past decade, sociologists have paid a lot of attention to the phenomenon of modernization, and in the process, they have also focused on religion. Peter L. Berger indicated the ambivalence of modernization for all those involved. Many people experienced the modern as a liberation from the narrow boundaries of tradition. Yet they quickly noted that they had to pay a high price for it. For not only did the person now experience himself as *alone* and not attached to the strong solidarity of a group, he also became doubtful about the norms that should shape his life, and ultimately he even doubted who or what he himself was. Thus, modernity was not experienced only as liberation, but also as alienation. Religion, which had been a kind of fate, now could and must be chosen. The compulsion to choose was the sign of the modern world. The places and functions of religions in the world thus have changed fundamentally.[16]

For our interests, the "Consequences of Modernity" (1995) for the world of the individual, elaborated by the British sociologist Anthony Giddens, are illuminating. For Giddens, it is not so much the differentiation of social roles that is the fundamental characteristic of the modern as the globalization of the previously regional cultural worlds. The dynamic of modernity cut the old connection between space and time. All traditions became an object of radical examination and lost their usual embedding in space and time. This "alienation" meant that worldviews and norms that had once been valid only in certain geographical spaces and at certain times were now available beyond regions and beyond time. The global disembedding of all traditions was accompanied by a global reflection on modernization. Yet that produced no new certainty. The claim of the Enlightenment to subject all human practices to critical analysis did bring more options, but also less certainty.[17]

The seminal nature of Giddens's formulation is shown by Burkhard Gladigow's reconstruction of a "European history of religions." Gladigow has focused on the transference of religion to scholarship and vice versa. Whether it was the Renaissance, Orientalism, or the idealization of tribal societies, the European history of religions has always been characterized by shaping a scholarly fund of worldviews and norms that served a broader audience as a resource to meaning.[18] The transference of positive religions to this medium has been made permanent by modernization. The need for reliable knowledge of worldviews and norms has grown as modernization has led to a break with the traditional world. The experience of the loss of certainty and self-evident truths demanded a reflection on what was remaining of past and foreign religions. Along with the disenchantment of all ways of life grew the individual's need for meaning.

This consideration touches on a thesis that has gained a lot of attention in the last decade, which claims that the task of the humanities is to compensate for the shortcomings of the technical-industrial world. "The more modern the modern world becomes, the more inevitable do the humanities become," according to Odo Marquard.[19] Only the humanities could and should prevent the history of progress of modern civilization from becoming the only history of man. The modern sector must necessarily be emancipated from the world of origin, yet organs must also be necessarily formed to protect the memory of the past. Marquard also described the task of the humanities as a consolation function. Considering the history of religions, evidence supports comprehending it more in the sense of a complementary element.[20] Human life in modern society has remained partly dependent on continuity with religions.

The History of Religions and the Discourse on Modernization

At the very beginning, we cited Hayden White's claim that there is no historiography in the very sense of the word that is not also a history of philosophy, and derived the assumption that the same could also apply to religious studies. Now, at the end of our investigation, we can say that this assumption was correct. Long before modernization destroyed the familiar world, Enlightenment philosophers defended true religion as something independent of the self-evident traditions. The traditional positive religions could make a claim to truth, but only after critical examination. Criteria for that were ascertainable accomplishments in the fields of morality, aesthetics, and subjectivity. Scholars of religion adopted these standards of judgment and applied them to past and foreign religions in order to discover what was remaining of them. Their historiography was in line with this, and they did not refrain from pointing out that religions were ennobled by an especially old age and in any case were older than political phenomena like *nation*. Thus they gave religions outdated by progress a new place and another function in modern society.

And, vice versa, they gave the rising scientific-industrial civilization itself a place in the history of religions. They developed conceptions that related modernization to it, and undertook to determine this relationship more precisely. Initially, over decades the metaphor of *survival* dominated, as if the past were still present in traces; this metaphor was replaced by reflected concepts that determined the presence of religion in the modern age differently and more fundamentally. By giving modernization itself a place in the history of religions—as working ethos, intellectualism, individualism, rejection of tradition, and so forth—the scholars of religion restored to religions their right to exist in modern culture independent of their claims to faith. Thus, the many subjects scholars have worked on are less disparate than appears at first glance.

While their subjects ranged from nature mysticism, souls, rituals, magic, mysteries, redemption, the experience of power, social morality, rejection of the world, and ecstasy, they restored to modern society its other, officially ignored half: the power of life that does not serve progress. The means of historical representation, distinguished

by Hayden White—metaphor, metonymy, synecdoche, and irony—
also determined the representations of these scholars, who described
selected parts of the extinct and remote world of religions as a remaining index of human experiences. Thus they granted the outdated
religions authority in their own modern society, fueling and deepening the ambivalence typical of the modern age. While spokesmen of
the ascendant scientific-industrial society demanded a rejection of all
religions, historians focused on what had been superseded by mod-
ernizaton and conceived of it as remaining valid in the present world.
Like modernization itself, their approach shows a certain ambivalence. They doubted modern society, yet at the same time trusted science as the way to reliable knowledge about religion. They doubted
the claims to truth of handed-down religions, yet believed in their
lasting achievements. It was a special combination of doubt and belief
that was peculiar to them. And it was not limited to scholars of religion, but also occurred in literature.[21]

English, French, and German scholars treated the history of religions quite differently. Yet, since their positions were also accepted
abroad, these differences did not remain national. British scholars of
religions (with Hume) saw an irrational dynamic in the history of
religions, and were sensitive to the continuation of the irrational even
in the progress of civilization. Not only did they see modern civilization itself as a product of the history of religions, they also discovered
a permanent world of non-enlightened thought and feeling beneath
its surface. This also remained constitutive for modern civilization
when the concept of the soul was considered. Modern society itself
was not capable of shaping social communities either. But their view
had to do with the idea that modern civilization was only a veneer
covering unknown worlds. Writing religious history and the diagnosis of the menace of modern civilization were closely interwoven in
religious studies.

This link between the representation of religious history and the
diagnosis of the present should be kept in mind when we turn to the
distinctions between German and French scholars of religion. In
France, the fear was that a society characterized by the division of
labor would ultimately annul all social obligations. Religious history
was seen as a necessary complement to this inability of modern society, and hence both community rituals and the concept of the person
moved into the center of the reconstruction of the past. The preceding
philosophy of J.-J. Rousseau had given an important impetus in this
direction. In Germany, on the other hand, the disadvantages that
threatened to accompany modernization were assessed differently.
Here—following Romanticism and Hegel—the individual's loss of

freedom and spontaneity were considered the greater danger, and renunciation of the world was considered the genuine achievement of
religion.

Encompassing a view of modernity within a view of the history of
religions formed the pragmatic side of the new paradigm of the history of religions, and explains the modes of the descriptions. Past and
remote religions were described to counteract the claims of modern
society for a complete renunciation of religions. An explanation by
Leszek Kolakowski helps illustrate that spirit:

> There are two circumstances we should always remember: first, if the
> new generations had not revolted constantly against the inherited tradi-
> tion, we would still be living in caves; and second, if the revolt against
> the inherited tradition is ever universal, we will find ourselves back in
> the cave. The cult of tradition and resistance against tradition are equally
> indispensable for social life; a society in which the cult of tradition is
> almighty is condemned to stagnation; a society in which revolt against
> tradition is universal is condemned to annihilation. Societies always pro-
> duce both the spirit of conservatism and the spirit of revolt; both are
> necessary but can coexist always only in conflict, never in synthesis.[22]

NOTES

INTRODUCTION TO THE AMERICAN EDITION

1. Sharpe 1986.
2. Smith 1982, xi.
3. Smith 1988, 269.
4. In the 1980s anthropologists identified a similar dilemma in their field. Ethnographical "data" too have been presented by scholars in a way that allowed the subject of the scholar to enter. Cf. Clifford Geertz, *Works and Lives: The Anthropologist as Author* (Cambridge, 1988); James Clifford, *The Predicament of Culture: Twentieth-Century Ethnography, Literature and Art* (Cambridge, Mass., 1988), in particular "On Ethnographic Authority," 21–54.
5. White 1989.
6. Ricoeur 1994, 1–18.
7. Eliade 1963, xiii.
8. Segal 1989, 5–36. The entire debate can be visited in Idinopulos and Yonan 1986.
9. Cf. Strenski, "Reduction without Tears," in Idinopulos and Yonan 1986, 105.
10. Strenski 1987.
11. First published Princeton, 1954.
12. Strenski 1987, 70–103.
13. Ibid., 10.
14. Ibid., 196.
15. Ibid., 198.
16. Ibid., 2.
17. McCutcheon 1997.
18. Ibid., 24.
19. Ibid., 29
20. Benavides 1998, 186–204.
21. Lincoln 1999.
22. Wasserstrom 1999.
23. Ibid., 49.
24. Taylor 1988; Braun and McCutcheon 2000.

INTRODUCTION

1. Weber 1992, 183.

CHAPTER 1
FROM THE PHILOSOPHY OF RELIGION TO THE HISTORY OF RELIGIONS

1. White 1973, xi.
2. Hill 1972.

3. *Elements of Law Natural and Politic* (1640) was missing until F. Toennies found and published it in 1889. It was translated into German in 1926 and republished with an introduction by A. Kaufmann, Darmstadt 1983.

4. The riddle of the title was solved by Carl Schmitt (1938, 9–23). In Job 41:33–34 (King James Version), the Leviathan is one of God's conquered opponents in primeval times: "Upon earth there is not his like, who is made without fear. He beholdeth all high things." It refers to a Babylonian deity of the saga of the Flood whose opponent was Behemoth. In Hobbes, Leviathan stands for the invincible power of the state. It is a *deus moralis*. Only Leviathan can hold Behemoth, i.e., civil war in check (I. Fetscher, in Hobbes 1968 [1651], XL–XLI).

5. The connection between faith and power has been investigated historically and systematically. Natalie Zemon Davis dealt with it historically in "The Rites of Violence: Religious Riot in Sixteenth-Century France" (1973), in *Society and Culture in Early Modern France: Eight Essays* (Stanford, 1975). The "rites of violence" also occurred in France in the seventeenth century, where no class struggle existed or swelled up, which contradicted Engels's interpretation. The perpetrators wanted to remove the "defilement." Catholics reproached Protestants for desecrating churches; Protestants accused Catholics of celebrating "dirty masses." From the Catholic and Protestant point of view, the defilement was consequently something else. Accordingly, Protestants (Calvinists) exercised violence primarily against cult objects, Catholics against persons. Catholics regarded the rivers in which Protestants were drowned as a kind of holy water. Protestants considered the fire with which churches were destroyed as the proper means of purification. In both cases, massacres apparently took place without any guilt feelings. The inherent systematic link between religion and killing was analyzed by Walter Burkert, *Homo necans: The Anthology of Ancient Greek Sacrificial Ritual and Myth* (Berkeley, 1983) and by René Girard, *La Violence et le sacré* (Paris, 1972).

6. Taubes 1983, 11.

7. Hobbes 1968 [1651], 170.

8. Josephus once noted that Moses did not make religion into a civil virtue—as was usual with the heathens—but, vice versa, made civil virtue a part of belief (*Contra Apionem* II, 170ff.).

9. Hobbes 1968 [1651], 551.

10. Ibid., 183.

11. Ibid., 525

12. Ibid., 401.

13. Ibid., 415.

14. Kittsteiner 1995, 229.

15. Hobbes 1968 [1651], 527–28.

16. Ibid., 530.

17. I call it heretical because, in ancient Christianity, it was held by the Gnostics.

18. The term *depoliticization* occurs in Max Weber and was used in 1932 by Carl Schmitt for an interpretation of European cultural development.

19. Koselleck, 1959.

20. *The Philosophical Works of David Hume,* 1:307–8, 455.

21. Quoted by Röd 1984, 323.

22. Lepenies 1978.

23. Hume 1993 [1757], 134.

24. For Hume's base for separating the truth of reason from the truth of facts, the *quaestio iuris* from the *quaestio facti,* see Weber 1990, 44–50.

25. In this connection, note that this proof of God's existence stands in a certain tension with his epistemological position, according to which it is impossible to conclude a Creator with rational and compelling logic from the order of the world. Perhaps his thought that the Creator of the world had virtually imprinted men with the belief in an invisible power was to conclude this mental leap (1993 [1757], 184). In Hume, belief in God is a kind of natural belief.

26. Weber 1990, 29.

27. Hume 1993 [1757], 139.

28. Klibansky and Mossner 1954, letter no. 6, pp. 13ff.

29. Hume 1993 [1757], 158–60.

30. Ibid., 160–63. Manuel (1983, 63) talked of a "psychological domino theory": fear of the gods became a spiritual suffering from which aggression to those who believe differently emerged. Voltaire, who had similar thoughts, counted 9,468,800 victims of religious (Christian) fanatics.

31. "Si le rétablissement des Sciences & des Arts a contribué à épurer les moeurs."

32. Quoted by M. Rang in his introduction to the German translation of Rousseau's *Émile* (1963) [1776], 19ff.

33. "Sans cesse on suit des usage, jamais son propre génie" (Rousseau 1995 [1750], 10ff.)

34. Rousseau 1979 [1762], 297.

35. Ibid., 302.

36. Ibid., 308.

37. Ibid., 311.

38. Ibid., 286.

39. Ibid., 263.

40. John Locke had seen it similarly: "Those are not at all to be tolerated who deny the being of God. Promises, covenants and oaths, which are the bonds of human society, can have no hold upon an atheist. The taking away of God, though but even in thought, dissolves all." Quoted in Kleger and Müller 1985, 72. Bayle, however, thought that a society of atheists could also live morally.

41. Rousseau 1978 [1762], 129–41.

42. Ibid., 139.

43. Vorländer 1992, 144–55.

44. Kant 1956 [1781], 606.

45. Kant 1964 [1793], 142.

46. Ibid., 11.

47. Ibid., 113.

48. Ricken 1992.

49. Herder 1989 [1772], 291.

50. Berlin 1993, 72–92.

51. H. D. Irmscher in Herder 1989 [1772], 139ff. For Süssmilch, see the detailed article by F. W. Graf in *Biographisch-bibliographisch Kirchenlexikon*, 1996, 11:210–31.

52. Herder 1989 [1772], 63–64.

53. Ibid., 45.

54. Ibid., 69. Language has a powerful effect on peoples. As poetry, language is an expression of our feelings. The poet conveys nature into the soul and heart of man.

55. Herder 1967 [1784–85], 363.

56. Herder 1964 [1774], 287.

57. Herder 1967 [1784–85], 346.

58. Ibid., 352.

59. Ibid., 388.

60. Birkner 1957.

61. Hertz 1991.

62. Schleiermacher 1984, 1:2:LXXVIII.

63. Schleiermacher 1991 [1799], 168.

64. The belief that human beings were capable of improving conditions through the use of their reason gave way to profound doubt after the French Revolution. This drastic change had a long-term favorable effect on a rehabilitation of the scorned religion. It is no accident that a new belief in prophecy and a wave of reawakening movements followed in the nineteenth century.

65. Schleiermacher 1974, 82 [109–110].

66. Gadamer 1960, 173.

67. Schleiermacher 1991 [1799], 48–49.

68. Ibid., 27.

69. Schleiermacher 1958 [1799], 78–79.

70. Rohls 1985, 11.

71. Schleiermacher 1991 [1799], 129.

72. Hegel 1986, 11:58.

73. *Hegel, Hinrichs, and Schleiermacher on Feeling and Reason in Religion*, trans. and ed. Eric von der Luft, Lewiston, NY 1987, 261.

74. Hegel 1986, 16:253–55.

75. Bakker 1989; Halbfass 1988, chapter on Hegel.

76. Hegel 1986, 18:138–70.

77. Ibid., 154.

78. Ibid., 149.

79. Ibid., 140.

80. Hegel, 59.

81. Taylor 1978 [1975], 638.

82. Menne 1983, 98.

83. Schopenhauer 1969 [1818], xv. Schopenhauer referred to the translation of the *Upanishads* by Anquetil-Duperron of 1801–2 as well as a German translation of the *Bhagavad Gita* of 1802 (1960 [1818], 527 n. 1).

84. Schopenhauer 1960 [1844], 179–80.
85. Schopenhauer 1969 2:583.
86. Schopenhauer 1960 [1818], 515.
87. Ibid., 528.
88. Ibid., 536.
89. Ibid., 800.
90. Ibid., 788.
91. Ibid., 789.
92. Ibid., 571.

CHAPTER 2
DECIPHERING UNKNOWN CULTURES

1. Schwab 1934, 10.
2. Anquetil-Duperron 1771, x.
3. Schwab 1934, 6.
4. Müller 1985 [1867], 1:373.
5. Quoted by Tylor 1866, 399ff.
6. Long 1836, 350.
7. This absurdity was observed more frequently in the nineteenth and twentieth centuries. In his description of the rise of Assyriology since 1925, Wallis Budge presented a chapter with the innocent title "Miscellaneous Observations." It focuses on a compendium of dinner table stories of English scholars on the subject of "German scholars and the deciphering of cuneiform writing." Wallis Budge had several German scholars make pilgrimages to London to study the clay tablet texts in the original. Not only did the Germans always believe they knew it better, but one of them was even caught "improving" a cuneiform text on a clay tablet with his pocket knife.
8. Hardy 1901, 106 n. 1.
9. More than thirty years later it was translated into English and published with an interesting foreword by Edward W. Said, the author of the controversial *Orientalism*.
10. L. Febvre 1988.
11. Herder 1964 [1774], 286.
12. Wilhelm Halbfass presented his description of the early history of Indology in two chapters (1988): Deism, the enlightenment, and the early history of Indology and India and the romantic critique of the present.
13. Schlegel 1977 [1808], x.
14. Anquetil-Duperron 1771, vii.
15. Bitterli 1991, 327–66.
16. Gruber 1965, 388.
17. Quoted by Gruber 1965, 390.
18. Lyell 1863, 105.
19. Ibid.
20. Lepenies 1978, 45.
21. Klemt 1960.
22. Lyell 1863, 383. Lyell noted sarcastically that, if early Asian culture had

been as advanced as was assumed, railroads and telegraphs would certainly have been found (379). Tylor used this comment appreciatively in *Primitive Culture* (1958 [1871], col. 1, pp. 57ff.).

23. Darwin 1989 [1859], 676.
24. Bowler 1986, 41–58.
25. Haeckel 1891, 7.
26. Marquard 1987, 131ff.
27. Hörisch 1991.
28. Carus 1931 [1846], 8.
29. Sonntag 1991.

CHAPTER 3
WHAT LANGUAGES TELL OF THE EARLY HISTORY
OF THE RELIGIONS OF EUROPE

1. F. M. Müller 1985 [1867], 1: viii.
2. V. D. Bosch 1993, 108.
3. Tylor 1866, 435.
4. G. Müller 1902, vol. 1.
5. V. D. Bosch 1993, 108ff.
6. Emrich 1963.
7. Quoted by Chaudhuri 1974, 89.
8. Tylor 1868, 227 (discussion of Müller's *Chips from a German Workshop*).
9. Jordan 1986 [1905] collected all information about lectures addressing public issues: 386–88, 570–79.
10. Names in Jordan 1986 [1905], 568–69.
11. F. M. Müller 1878, foreword.
12. G. Müller 1902, 2:47.
13. Ibid., 48.
14. Jordan 1986 [1905], 570–72.
15. Ziolkowski 1993.
16. F. M. Müller 1901a, 254.
17. F. M. Müller 1985 [1867], 1: xxii–xxiii.
18. Humboldt 1977 [1824–26], 32.
19. Ibid., 33.
20. During Müller's time, a psychology of nations that also concentrated on language was formed in Germany. Its spokesmen, M. Lazarus (a philosopher) and H. Steinthal (a linguist), published the *Zeitschrift für Völkerpsychologie und Sprachwissenschaft* (Journal of psychology of nations and linguistics). In their "Introductory Thoughts," the authors requested all scholars who studied historical phenomena—language, religion, art, customs, law, constitution—"to explain the extant facts from the innermost reaches of the mind, and attempt to trace them to their psychological causes" (1860, 1). They reorganized Hegel's term of the objective mind into a psychological one that could be observed as a reality. Wilhelm Wundt (1832–1920) continued the tradition in the 1880s.

21. V. D. Bosch 1993, 110.
22. Knoll 1986.
23. F. M. Müller 1881.
24. F. M. Müller 1985 [1867], 2:6–8.
25. F. M. Müller, quoted by Chaudhuri 1974, 179.
26. F. M. Müller 1985 [1867], 2:1–143.
27. Turner 1981, chap. 3, "Greek Mythology and Religion."
28. Quoted by Turner 1981, 113.
29. F. M. Müller 1985 [1867], 2:10.
30. F. M. Müller in a letter to M. Arnold (G. Müller 1902, 1:424).
31. F. M. Müller 1985 [1867], 2:52.
32. F. M. Müller 1874, 375ff.
33. F. M. Müller 1985 [1867], 2:92ff.
34. Ibid., 1: ix.
35. Ibid., 2:52.
36. Ibid., 97.
37. F. M. Müller 1874, 16–18.
38. F. M. Müller 1985 [1867], 1: ix.
39. Letter of F. M. Müller of January 15, 1896, to R. Corbet (G. Müller 1902, 2:339ff.).
40. Weeks 1993, 222.
41. G. Müller 1902, 1:394.
42. Berkenkopf 1914, 68.
43. Olender 1995, 22.
44. F. M. Müller 1885b, 626.
45. F. M. Müller 1878, 154, 156.
46. Halbfass 1988, 69–83.
47. F. M. Müller 1873, 62–63.
48. F. M. Müller 1874, 9.
49. F. M. Müller 1884, 25–26.
50. F. M. Müller 1874, 151, for example.
51. Gobineau 1939–40, 2:185.
52. Ibid., 198ff.
53. F. M. Müller 1985 [1867], 1:337–74.
54. For Müller's position on nineteenth-century racism, see Mosse 1990, 67ff.
55. F. M. Müller, quoted by Chaudhuri 1974, 125.
56. Quoted by Chaudhuri 1974, 123ff.
57. Quoted by G. Beer 1990, 47.
58. L. Trilling 1963 [1939], 190.
59. Arnold 1915, 31.
60. Arnold 1887, 234.
61. Ibid., 231–34.
62. Arnold 1875 [1869], 128–49.
63. Trilling 1963 [1939], 252.
64. Quoted by Trilling 1963 [1939], 269.

65. Dorson 1971 [1955], 52.
66. Letter of November 10, 1863, to G. Cox; G. Müller 1902, 1:284.
67. Littledale 1909 [1870].
68. Dorson 1971 [1955].
69. Sharpe 1986, 46.
70. Lang 1884, 137.
71. In 1877, Tiele was appointed to the new chair for the history of religion at the University of Leiden; he died in 1902. On his life and work, see Waardenburg 1973–74, 1:96–104, 2:282–86.
72. Treiber 1992, 341.
73. Tiele 1884, 365.
74. Tiele 1897, 150–81.
75. The work of Benveniste sees *pater* as a "constant designation of the highest god of the Indoeuropeans," reconstructs an old form of invocation *dyeu pater* = Oh Father in Heaven!, and notes that *pater* does not have a physical, but rather a legal meaning (1993 [1969], 163–65). Pettazzoni has studied the findings of the history of religion. Both Zeus and Jupiter were gods of the bright sky, the highest bearers of omniscience. This omniscience was aimed especially at supervision of compacts, contracts, and oaths (1960, [1955] 35). Euler's new examination reaches similar conclusions (1987).

CHAPTER 4

THE PRESENCE OF THE ORIGINAL RELIGION IN MODERN CIVILIZATION

1. K.-H. Kohl (1981) described the view of the "noble savage." In 1987, the European views of non-European cultures was the subject of an exhibition in Stuttgart, titled *Exotische Welten/Europäische Phantasien* (Exotic worlds/European fantasies). The catalogue provides excellent documentation of the facts.
2. Kohl 1987, 92.
3. Quoted by Hodgen 1936, 29.
4. Ibid., 9–35.
5. Ibid., 31; Stocking 1968a, 78.
6. Tylor 1958 [1871], 1:38.
7. Darwin 1871, vol. 1, 183–4.
8. Kuper (1988) had described how the idea of *Primitive Society* emerged between 1860 and 1880, and took on the features of a new paradigm.
9. Tylor 1869–70, 379.
10. Tylor 1958 [1871], 1:299ff.
11. Ibid., 2:344ff.
12. Tylor 1958 [1871], 2:11.
13. Tylor 1868a.
14. Marett 1941, 167.
15. Harris 1968, 29–31.
16. Carus 1931 [1846], 2.
17. Ackerknecht 1954.
18. McLennan 1970 [1865], 6.

19. Tylor 1958 [1871], 1:16.
20. Ibid., 1:21.
21. Ibid., 1:38. Smith assumed an internal conflict in Tylor, that he withdrew his previous assumption of a diffusion of culture because of a quasi-theological interest in a universality of belief in the soul (1933, 116–83). Tylor's explanations do not justify such a claim, in my opinion, though it is quite correct that the presentation in *Primitive Culture* is oriented mainly toward sequences of development.
22. Leopold 1980, 13ff.
23. "Culture or Civilization, taken in its wide ethnographic sense, is that complex whole which includes knowledge, belief, art, morals, law, custom, and any other capabilities and habits acquired by man as a member of society" (Tylor 1958 [1871], 1:1).
24. Ibid., 1:28.
25. Ibid., 1:33.
26. Ibid., 1:28–29.
27. Stocking 1968a, 86–87.
28. See Hodgen 1936, 140.
29. Burrow 1966, 240.
30. Bowler 1986, 54.
31. Harris 1968, 144–45.
32. Tylor 1958 [1871], 1:9–10.
33. Lowie 1937, 71.
34. Tylor 1958 [1871], 1:22.
35. "He was nothing but what the German students call a Philistine, one of the most prominent features of whose special type is that the exertion and development of the mind for its own sake, where they cannot be estimated by a material equivalent in money or position or comfort, are things lying out of his own regular track, and are therefore the objects of his scarcely tolerant contempt" (Tylor 1866a, 71–72).
36. Tylor 1958 [1871], 1:29.
37. Tylor 1866a, 81.
38. Kohl 1987, 92–98.
39. Tylor 1877, 142.
40. Tylor 1958 [1871], 2:194–95.
41. Ibid., 2:333–34.
42. Lang 1898, 173–209.
43. Tylor 1866a, 72; 1866–69a, 523.
44. Tylor 1958 [1871], 2:86; and see 1866–1869a, 523.
45. Chadwick 1975 (chap. 7, "Science and Religion").
46. Turner 1974, 8–37.
47. Tylor 1958 [1871], 2:84.
48. Evans-Pritchard 1933.
49. Tylor 1866–69a, 523.
50. Tylor 1869–70, 381.
51. Tylor 1866–69a, 528.
52. Ibid., 524.

53. Stocking 1971, 100.
54. Burrow 1966, xv.
55. Stocking 1968a, 87–88.
56. Kippenberg 1984; Baeumler 1965, 332–33.
57. Müller 1884, 25–26.

CHAPTER 5
ON THE ORIGIN OF ALL SOCIAL OBLIGATIONS: THE RITUAL OF SACRIFICE

1. Jones 1984, 45; Beidelman 1974, 5.
2. A specialist in this subject, W. Speyer, has investigated their repeated appearance in pagan and Christian antiquity and has reached this conclusion; see his *Bücherfunde in der Glaubenswerbung der Antike* (Göttingen, 1970).
3. Wellhausen 1957, 295.
4. Perlitt 1965, 185–206, analyzes Wellhausen's "constructive description of history."
5. Wellhausen 1957, 412. Five years after the work was first published, in 1883, the study was expanded and republished under the new title of *Prolegomena zur Geschichte Israels*. In the foreword of the second edition, Wellhausen argued with the partly furious criticism of his book (v–vi).
6. In his letter to the minister of education of April 5, 1882, Wellhausen stated: "I became a theologian because the scientific treatment of the Bible interested me. It gradually came to me that a professor of theology also has the practical task of preparing students for service in the Protestant church, and that I did not satisfy this practical task, instead, despite all the reserve on my side, made my auditors unfit for their duty. Ever since, the theological professorship has laid heavily on my conscience" (quoted in Perlitt 1965, 153–54).
7. Beidelman 1974, 9–10.
8. Smith 1875, 637–38.
9. Smith 1880, 100.
10. Quoted by Beidelman 1974, 21.
11. Smith 1894 [1881].
12. Wellhausen 1878, 76.
13. Ibid., 77–78.
14. Ibid., 425.
15. Perlitt 1965, 228.
16. Smith 1894, 24.
17. Ibid., 215 n. 1.
18. Smith 1870, 164–65.
19. MacLennan 1970 [1865], 7.
20. MacLennan 1869, 422.
21. Kuper 1988, 82.
22. Frazer 1894, 803.
23. Smith 1894, ix.
24. Beidelman 1974, 25ff.
25. Smith 1894, 178–79.

26. Jones 1984, 36.

27. Smith 1894, 2.

28. Ibid., 19.

29. David asked forgiveness of King Saul and applied to the son of Saul: "If your father misses me at all, then say, 'David earnestly asked leave of me to run to Bethlehem his city; for there is a yearly sacrifice there for all the family'" (1 Sam. 20:6). Accordingly, Jonathan said to Saul: "'David earnestly asked leave of me to go to Bethlehem; he said, "Let me go; for our family holds a sacrifice in the city, and my brother had commanded me to be there"'" (1 Sam. 20:29).

30. MacLennan 1970 [1865], 6.

31. Smith 1894, 15–16.

32. Ibid., 320.

33. Greek text translated by Henninger 1955, 114.

34. An investigation by R. Rendtorff (1967, 241ff.) has confirmed that in ancient Israel, the community sacrifice, and the burnt offering had different antecedents, which led in the first case to the nomadic culture and in the second to the Canaanite.

35. Smith 1894, 320.

36. Kohl 1987, 97–98.

37. Steiner 1967 [1956], 27.

38. Smith 1894, 142.

39. Ibid., 143.

40. Ibid., 140.

41. Hobbes supported the view that, with the "Kingdom of God," the Holy Scriptures meant an internal worldly civil kingdom. When the Bible occasionally calls it "holy," it is to indicate its public status. No private person had a right of ownership to it (1968 [1651], 445).

42. Smith 1894, 22.

43. Ibid., 22.

44. Smith 1886, 134.

45. Smith 1894, 246.

46. Ibid., 246.

47. Newman 1993.

CHAPTER 6
UNDER CIVILIZATION: THE MENACING REALM OF MAGIC

1. Mannhardt 1876, 2: xxxvii.

2. Frazer 1890, xii.

3. Mannhardt 1876, 2: vi.

4. Ibid.

5. Ibid., viii.

6. Mannhardt 1868, vii.

7. Mannhardt 1876, 2: xx. In a letter of October 16, 1872, his academic teacher, Müllenhoff, called his attention to E. B. Tylor. He later thanked him

for this reference, which had been extremely useful (excerpts from the letters are in Scheuermann 1933, 29).

8. Mannhardt 1876, 2: xxv.

9. Ibid., viiiff.

10. Grimm 1835 [1882], 4.

11. Mannhardt 1876, 2: ix (emphasis in the original).

12. Ibid., ix.

13. Ibid., xxviii.

14. Ibid., xxiv.

15. Ibid., xiv.

16. Ibid., xxxii.

17. Ibid., xxviii, note.

18. Ibid., xxi.

19. The more detailed questionnaire with thirty-five questions can be read in Mannhardt 1868, 44–48; the shorter one with twenty-five questions is reproduced in Weber-Kellermann 1965, 41ff.

20. Weber-Kellermann 1965, 25–43.

21. Mannhardt 1865, vi, note.

22. Mannhardt 1876, 2: xxxii.

23. Mannhardt 1868, vi.

24. Ibid., viii.

25. Ibid., 45.

26. Ibid., 1–10.

27. Ibid., 35.

28. Mannhardt 1876, 2: vii.

29. Question no. 30, Mannhardt 1868, 48.

30. Letter from William James to Miss Frances R. Morse, December 25, 1900, in H. James 1969 [1920], 2:139.

31. Frazer 1885–86, 103.

32. Frazer 1890, 1: xi.

33. In 1900, Frazer visited Nemi (Ackerman 1987a, 335 n. 14).

34. Smith 1978, 214.

35. Strabo, V 3, 12, trans. Horace Leonard Jones (London, 1933), 421–23.

36. *The Aeneid*, trans. Allen Mandelbaum (Berkeley, 1981).

37. Harrison 1925, 83.

38. Frazer 1900 (2nd ed. of *The Golden Bough*), xxi.

39. Frazer 1911–15 (3rd ed. of *The Golden Bough*), ix.

40. Frazer 1968 [1913], vii. In 1922, in the preface to an abridged, one-volume edition of *The Golden Bough*, Frazer provided an explanation for the enormous expansion of the material. It was necessary to prove that the rule of the successors of Aricia were not exceptions, but rather an example of a far-reaching institution. "Whether the explanation which I have offered of the institution is correct or not must be left to the future to determine. I shall always be ready to abandon it if a better can be suggested."

41. Smith 1978, 208–39.

42. Beard 1992, 212.

43. Frazer 1900, xvi.

44. Ibid., xiv.

45. Jacobs 1890, 384.

46. Frazer 1911–15, 3:135.

47. Ibid., 146.

48. Wittgenstein 1975, 42; Wittgenstein 1979, 5e.

49. Frazer 1963 [1922], 1.

50. Ibid., 11.

51. Frazer 1900, xxv.

52. Beard 1992.

53. Frazer 1963 [1922], 13.

54. In Ackerman 1987a, 244.

55. This is Seligman's report in his scientific publication:

Although there is not the least doubt that the kings of the Shilluk were killed with due ceremony when they began to show signs of old age or ill health, it was extremely difficult to ascertain exactly what was done on these occasions, and there is no doubt that a good deal of Shilluk folklore survives in the accounts commonly given of the killing of the *ret* [king]. According to these any *niaret* [aristocrat] has the right to attempt to kill the king, and if successful, to reign in his stead. The killing could only take place at night, for during the day the king would be surrounded by his friends and his body-guard and no would-be successor would have the least chance of harming him. At night the king's position was very different. Alone in his enclosure with his favourite wives and no men in the royal village to protect him, except a few herdsmen whose huts would be at a little distance, he was represented as passing the night in constant watchfulness, prowling round his huts fully armed, peering into the shadows, or himself standing silent and watchful in some dark corner. Then, when at last his rival appeared, the fight would take place in grim silence broken only by the clash of spear and shield, for it was said to be a point of honor for the *ret* not to call the herdsmen to his assistance. (1911, 221ff.)

56. Frazer 1963 [1922], 269.

57. Evans-Pritchard 1962, 66–86.

58. Beer 1983, 106.

59. Frazer 1968 [1913], 162.

60. In the chapter "Religion and Magic" of the third edition of *The Golden Bough* (1911–15, 1:220–43), Frazer explained this assertion.

61. Frazer 1963 [1922], 455.

62. In Frazer, *The Golden Bough*, Vol. 1 (1911–15), 235ff.

63. Frazer 1968 [1913], 170.

64. Frazer 1900, xxvi.

65. Eliot 1958 [1930], 47.

66. Assmann 1991.

CHAPTER 7
THE UNFATHOMABLE DEPTHS OF LIFE IN THE MIRROR
OF HELLENIC RELIGION

1. Jauß 1974, 49.

2. Fuhrmann 1979.

3. W. Rüegg, Historisches Wörterbuch des Philosophie Vol. 4, 1971, 385ff.; A. Reckermann, *HWPh* Vol. 4, 1971, 386–89, quoted on 387.

4. Trans. by Sir Edward Bulwer Lytton (London: Frederick Warne and Co., 1887), 304.

5. Von Wiese 1956, 326.

6. The quarrel is documented in Fambach 1957, 40–73. Schiller was accused of supporting polytheism against Christianity. A comparison of the first version of 1788 with the second in 1793 shows that Schiller considered that attack fair and that he weakened it since it could be understood as a declaration of war against the monotheism of Christianity (von Wiese 1956, 325; Gerhard 1950).

7. Henrichs 1987, 7.

8. Breuer 1995, 185–91.

9. Williams 1976, 57–60 (*civilization*) and 87–93 (*culture*).

10. Elias 1977 [1936], 1:134.

11. Bäumer 1977, 134.

12. "In the soul of Sophocles, the divine intoxication of Dionysos, the profound inventiveness of Athena, and the soft-levelheadedness of Apollo were evenly blended," wrote Schlegel (quoted by Gründer 1971, 441ff.).

13. Bäumer 1965.

14. Henrichs 1984, 218.

15. After the rejection of the appointment to the philosophical professorship, Nietzsche wrote to E. Rohde: "Therefore, once again I hold the chair as a modest philologist, and all philosophical dreams, fed and watered for six weeks on your hopes, go to the level of lying and cheating. . . . Philological disgust prevails in me" (quoted by Vogel 1966, 26ff.). The students stayed away after the publication of the work. In 1869, Nietzsche had seven students; a year later that number had doubled. After the publication of the work, in the winter semester of 1872–73, they "were blown away." Only two auditors remained: a Germanist and a jurist (Vogel 1966, 31ff.). In 1879, Nietzsche resigned from the University of Basel.

16. Nietzsche 1980 [1872], 1:28.

17. This is the sign of illusion in Indian philosophy, which is how the material world appears in the Upanishads and Vedanta. It is considered real only until this false view is exalted by the higher knowledge of the All-One of Brahman.

18. Nietzsche 1980 [1872], 1:28.

19. Ibid., 29.

20. Two volumes appeared in 1890 and 1894, the second edition in 1898.

21. Crusius 1902, 189ff. Cancik has shown with extant archive material that Rohde still maintained his friendship with Nietzsche (1985).

22. This circumstance is not immediately obvious since the index does not indicate the name of any scholar for the *Psyche*. It was only Henrich's list (1984, 225) that shows that Rohde used and reworked Tylor's work.

23. "The soul, as recognized in the philosophy of the lower races, may be defined as an ethereal surviving being, conceptions of which preceded and led up to the more transcendental theory of the immaterial and immortal soul, which forms part of the theology of higher nations" (Tylor 1958 [1871], 2:110).

24. Rohde 1991 [1898], 2:2ff.

25. Crusius 1902, 183.

26. Rohde 1895, 22ff.; Rohde 1991 [1898], 2:103ff.

27. Since 1894 (Drescher 1991, 99ff.).

28. Ibid., 129–44.

29. Troeltsch 1896, 195ff.

30. "All mystics say: as long as *God* (the One) was, the *world* (the diverse) was not. As long as the world is, God is not. Thus the world wants to cease so that God is again" (Crusius 1902, 250).

31. The speech must have been read, since Rohde was ill.

32. Rohde 1895, 23.

33. Troeltsch 1895, 367.

34. Rohde 1991 [1898], 2:34.

35. Crusius 1902, 184–85.

36. Harrison 1925, 82–83.

37. Schlesier 1990.

38. Harrison 1925, 65. Goessler remarked maliciously that Miss Jane Harrison reproduced Dörpfeld's views in her lovely book, which he had presented too generously in his directions (1951, 98).

39. Payne 1978, 184.

40. Ackerman 1991c, 89ff.

41. Ackerman 1972, 227.

42. Schlesier 1990.

43. Calder 1991.

44. Ackerman 1987, 225–28.

45. Harrison 1963 [1912, 1927], 72; the seal with commentary by Harrison 1991 [1903, 1922], 496ff.

46. Peacock 1988, 185.

47. Ackerman 1991c, 104.

48. Harrison 1991 [1903, 1922], 260.

49. Ibid., 284ff.

50. She adopted Nietzsche's interpretation of a remarkable place of the Bacchi in Euripides. As the Maenads worshipped Dionysos far away on the mountain, mountain and wild animals joined their circle. Harrison saw that as a return to nature and referred to Nietzsche, who "has drawn in this respect a contrast, beautiful and profoundly true, between the religion and art of Apollo and Dionysos. Apollo, careful to remain his splendid self, projects an image, a dream, and calls it *god*. It is illusion (*Schein*), its watchword is

limitation (*Maass*), Know Thyself, Nothing too much. Dionysos breaks all bonds; his motto is the limitless Excess (*Uebermass*), Ecstasy. 'The individual, with his limits and moderations, forgot himself in the Dionysiac vortex and became oblivious to the laws of Apollo'" (Harrison 1991 [1903, 1922], 445ff. n. 4, quotes from Nietzsche's *Birth of Tragedy*). The emphasis is on the destruction of the self, not its immortality as in Rohde.

51. Ibid., 657.

52. Harrison 1915, 204; Harrison 1925, 84. Both quotations are in Schlesier 1991, 188, nn. 12 and 15.

53. Harrison 1963 [1912, 1927], xii.

54. Ibid., 43.

55. As Paul Guiraud expresses a historical self-understanding of his time in his biography of Fustel de Coulanges (1896, 45): "An Athenian of the fourth or third century B.C. is probably closer to us than a Frenchman of the Middle Ages."

56. The image of the art of classical Greece is a phantom. It overlooks the fact that the sculptures were colored and the poetry was accompanied by music. The result was to make classical Greece "boring," as Friedell put it (1929, 371–425).

57. Detienne 1985.

58. Burkert 1980, 171.

59. The reviews of the study of Greek religion done by Burkert in 1980 and Henrichs in 1987 show the described ambivalence between the explanation of the offensive and its idealization.

60. Nietzsche 1996, II, no. 218, p. 264.

CHAPTER 8
THE PRODUCTIVE FORCE OF WORLD REJECTION

1. The Gospels of Matthew and Luke are based on Mark as well as on another source that consists of the words of Jesus (saying source). The Gospel of John is not a reliable witness for the historical Jesus.

2. An excellent description of the distinction of the two models and their implications comes from Smith 1990.

3. Boas 1949 [1896].

4. See the preface in the second edition of Weiss's *Die Predigt Jesu vom Reiche Gottes*, which was republished in 1964 by F. Hahn. An appendix contained parts of the first edition of 1892 that Weiss had deleted from the second edition, as well as surveys of the relationship of the two editions. Hahn's third edition therefore makes it easier for us mainly to identify important passages of the first edition.

5. Ibid., 141.

6. Ibid., 142.

7. Ibid., 138.

8. Schweitzer 1951 [1913], 232.

9. Weiss 1971, xi.

10. Weiss 1964 [1892], 134.

11. Only the discovery of the Dead Sea Scrolls in Qumran in 1947 brought to light copies of these texts.

12. Bousset 1979 [1919], 41. In 1904, Bousset wrote in retrospect:

Anyone who personally studied in Albrecht Ritsch's school can remember how vigorously we were shown the connection of New Testament literature with the Old Testament. This indication definitely contained a great truth, but a great bias. Gradually we then learned to recognize that there was not empty space between the time and literature of the Old Testament and of the New Testament that could simply be omitted, but rather a momentous development of religion had taken place, and without knowing and understanding it, the literature of the New Testament could not be understood. In an indefatigable work, the material was compiled, sifted, processed, and many new things were added to what was already known. . . . Today, the material of the later Jewish literature has been so comfortably processed and almost completely presented by Kautzsch in the two volumes of the *Apocrypha* and the *Pseudepigrapha* that the time has now come when even those who study theology may no longer ignore these things. But what was most important is that this literature is now really grasped and understood in its historical context. And the historical significance of what previously looked like a collection of curios . . . is now appreciated and understood. Gradually the lines are extended and we now recognize the significance of the knowledge of the later literature of Judaism for the understanding of the New Testament, that it presents their contemporary milieu, from which the New Testament, especially the Gospels, arose, and with which they are bound by endless fine and coarse threads. The sensation excited by all works that advanced vigorously in this direction showed that a virgin forest was being cleared here and a decisive advance achieved in theological work. (1904, 267ff.)

13. Gunkel 1910, 171ff.

14. Bousset 1904, 273.

15. Bousset 1924 [1903, 1906], 522.

16. Ibid., 524.

17. "We Christians have absolutely no reason for the assumption that everything good and valuable in religion could come only from Israel; such Jewish chauvinism would sound very curious in our mouth" (Gunkel 1903, 14). The first part of this sentence was quoted literally by Rade in his 1913 article, "Religionsgeschichte und Religionsgeschichtliche Schule," in *Religion in Geschichte und Gegenwart*, 4:2187.

18. Bousset 1892, 43.

19. Gressmann 1914, 37ff.

20. Moore 1920–21, 243.

21. Gressmann 1914.

22. Ibid., 30ff.

23. Rollmann 1982.

24. "Religion is not purely and simply irrational power. . . . All religions contain a twofold aspect: the divine, the deity confronts man as the stranger, the almost uncanny power that is purely and simply superior to him, before which his soul quakes in fear and awe, and yet on the other hand, as the blessing power, to which he secretly feels drawn powerfully in the depths of his being. If religion were only that irrational aspect, it would be something purely and simply uncanny, destructive, fatal" (Bousset 1979 [1919], 36). With these words, Bousset took a position in the discussion that Rudolf Otto had triggered in 1917 with his *Das Heilige*.

25. Bousset 1904, 312.

26. Harnack 1908, 10.

27. Jonas 1977, 13.

28. Bousset 1904, 353.

29. Ibid., 354ff.

30. Ibid., 1904, 316.

31. Bousset 1979 [1919], 33–34.

32. Ibid., 37–38. Dialectical theologians broke radically with this view and thus systematically put an end to the Religionsgeschichtliche Schule in theology departments. Now there could be theology without religion.

33. Siebeck 1893, 1.

34. Ibid., 3.

35. Ibid., 5.

36. Ibid., 49.

37. Tiele 1897, 62, repeated on 277.

38. Siebeck 1893, 5, 78, 102ff.

39. Ibid., 264.

40. Graf 1982.

41. Troeltsch 1913 [1897], 333.

42. Ibid., 355.

43. Troeltsch 1902, iv, x, 59.

44. Troeltsch 1895, 405ff.

45. Presented excellently by Pfleiderer 1992.

46. The dictionary was published by representatives of the Religionsgeschichtliche Schule and the publisher Siebeck.

47. Troeltsch 1910, 481ff. The copy with the article "Redemption" appeared in 1907.

48. Ibid., 482ff.

49. Graf 1987, 127.

50. Overbeck 1919, 33ff.

CHAPTER 9
COMPETING MODELS OF THE RECAPITULATION
OF THE HISTORY OF RELIGIONS

1. When E. B. Tylor was a reader in anthropology at Oxford (1884–1910), the subject could be chosen only by students in other subjects and thus he had no successors. Marett was the first to change that after 1905, by insuring

that social anthropology became a subject like any other. He himself was the first reader in it (Marett 1941, 166–72).

2. In his biography, Marett gave a detailed report of the event (ibid., 156–64). This was the source of further information about the reception of pre-animism.

3. Ibid., 156–57.

4. Marett 1914 [1900], 1–28.

5. Marett 1941, 158.

6. Marett 1914 [1900], 15.

7. Ibid., 15.

8. Other terms were *pre-animism* and *dynamism*.

9. Marett 1914 [1900], 3.

10. Marett 1941, chap. 11.

11. Wundt 1900–1919, vol. 2, part 2, 171–72.

12. Preuss 1914, 20.

13. Marett 1941, 164.

14. Hewitt 1902.

15. Marett 1914 [1900], xi.

16. Marett 1941, 161.

17. Marett 1914 [1900], xxiii.

18. Ibid., xxxi.

19. Ibid., x–xi.

20. Ibid., xxvii.

21. Ibid., xxv.

22. Ibid., xxiii.

23. "The Interpretation of Survivals" (1920). Marett's criticism of the conception of *Survivals* was threefold. First, he argued on the basis of scientific logic. Not a simple lack of meaning, but a loss of meaning had to be proved before one could speak of a *Survival*. Only when a view or an act was proved to be linked organically with an outdated social organization could loss of meaning be assumed. Second, there was a psychological objection: a mere lack of meaning could have causes other than a development. A human act always precedes its explanation. Thus, there could not be an original meaning, but only rationalizations. A third and final objection was historical: the fossil hunters, as he called the supporters of this theory, ignored the fact that older traditions could assume new meanings under altered conditions.

24. Ten years later, in 1909, Marett drew the conclusions of his theory for the idea of religion: "The tabu-mana Formula as a Minimum Definition of Religion" (1909). The supernatural has positive and negative sides: either tabu or mana. The negative side, "tabu," implies holiness and impurity, the positive side, "mana," miraculous power.

25. de Vries 1967, 106–10; Sharpe 1986, 65–71.

26. From the introduction to the first volume of *Zeitschrift für geschichtliche Rechtswissenschaft* (1815), quoted by Jaeger and Rüsen 1992, 29.

27. Iggers 1971, 14–15; Kantorowicz 1937, 332.

28. Nietzsche 1998.

29. Quoted by Nowak 1987, 135.

30. The lectures were delivered in 1920 and published posthumously as a book: *Der Historismus und seine Überwindung* (Berlin, 1924). His 1922 article, "Die Krisis des Historismus," is particularly lively and concise. For these writings of Troeltsch, see Drescher 1991, 487–520, 521 n. 256. For the revolt against historical thinking during the Weimar Republic, see Graf 1988, 377–405.

31. Jaeger and Rüsen 1992, 141–60. Iggers 1971 is still indispensable for that topic.

32. For the Lamprecht quarrel and its consequences, see Jaeger and Rüsen 1992, 141–46; Iggers 1971, 256–60; Metz 1984; Raphael 1990.

33. Iggers 1984.

34. Windelband 1907 [1894], 357–8.

35. Rodi and Lessing 1984, 15.

36. Schnädelbach 1983, 78–9, 160–63.

37. Durkheim 1968 [1912], 201.

38. In his phenomenology, van der Leeuw also warned of understanding the relationship of dynamism and animism as a chronological sequence. In reality, they are simultaneous phenomena (1977 [1933], 83–84). Durkheim argued similarly when he distinguished naturalism (as an appeal to impersonal, natural things) and animism (as an appeal to a spiritual entity), and saw them as two religions existing side by side (1968 [1912], 76–77).

39. Dilthey 1981 [1910, 1927], 89–100.

40. Scheler 1972 [1913], 315.

41. A more recent description of the philosophy of life comes from Fellman 1993. As the main representatives of the philosophy of life, he mentions Henri Bergson, William James, Wilhelm Dilthey, and Georg Simmel. He classified Arthur Schopenhauer and Friedrich Nietzsche as pathbreakers.

42. Dilthey 1924 [1911], 304.

43. Droysen 1971 [1882], 329.

44. Lessing 1988.

45. The introduction to the volume by editors Braun, Holzhey, and Orth (1988, 8–9), and the essay by J. M. Krois in it (15–44) go into Cassirer's relation to the philosophy of life in parts. Strenski explains the reason for his deviant view: Cassirer "wanted to counteract irrationalist trends among his own intellectual class" (1987, 14).

CHAPTER 10
RELIGION AND THE SOCIAL BOND

1. Jones 1986–87 [1887], 177.

2. Durkheim 1887, 314–17.

3. Rudolph 1962, 67–109.

4. Ulrici 1879, 241.

5. Ibid., 244.

6. Ibid., 260n.

7. Ibid., 260.

8. Ibid., 260n.

9. Wundt 1885 [1879], 342–65.

10. Wundt 1886, 3.

11. Durkheim 1887.

12. An evaluation comes from William James that everyone who worked his way through the works of Wundt can understand. It is in a letter to Carl Stumpf (Cambridge, February 6, 1887):

> I can well understand why Wundt should make his compatriots impatient. Foreigners can afford to be indifferent for he doesn't *crowd* them so much. He aims at being a sort of Napoleon of the intellectual world. Unfortunately he will never have a Waterloo, for he is a Napoleon without genius and with no central idea which, if defeated, brings down the whole fabric in ruin. You remember what Victor Hugo says of Napoleon in the Miserables—"Il gênait Dieu"; Wundt only *gêners* [*sic!*] his *confrères*; and whilst they make mincemeat of some one of his views by their criticism, he is meanwhile writing a book on an entirely different subject. Cut him like a worm, and each fragment crawls; there is no *noeud vital* in his mental medulla oblongata, so that you can't kill him all at once. (H. James 1969 [1920], 1:263)

13. Durkheim 1986–87b, 197: "With increasing volume, societies are under pressure to make the soil more productive; the need for intensive cultivation is felt at the same time as the necessity for private property which is its condition. That is why this form of property becomes more and more of a sacred right, established by moral philosophers and sanctioned by law."

14. Ibid., 203: "Ethics is not a system of abstract rules which man finds inscribed in his conscience or which the moral theorist arrives at by deduction in the isolation of his study. It is a social function, or rather a system of functions, which forms and gradually becomes established under the pressure of collective needs."

15. Ibid., 240.

16. Ibid., 237.

17. Lepenies 1989, 80–110.

18. Clark 1981, 158ff.; Lukes 1973, 95 and chap. 5.

19. Coser 1971, 159.

20. Jones 1986–87 [1887], 177–8.

21. Durkheim 1933 [1893], 37.

22. Durkheim 1933 [1893], 221.

23. Lukes 1973, 195–99; Nisbet 1974.

24. Fustel de Coulanges n.d. [1866], 131–32.

25. Durkheim often quarreled in his work with his teacher Fustel, and hardly shared all his views (Momigliano 1994, 174–76). Fustel de Coulanges's book was also read in England, where W. Robertson Smith may have known it. In any case, Smith's views of religion as the basis of political order are generally similar to those of Fustel de Coulanges.

26. Poulat 1987, chap. 11, "L'institution des 'science religieuses.'"

27. Durkheim 1933 [1893], 118. Only with the writings of the representa-

tives of a pre-animism did this change, he wrote later (Durkheim 1968 [1912], 201–3).

28. Durkheim 1933 [1893], 122.

29. This was the *Cours de sociologie: La Religion*, of 1894–95 (Lukes 1973, 618).

30. Deploige 1923 [1911], 361–2.

31. Jones 1986, 601.

32. Durkheim 1969, 347.

33. Mauss 1968–69, 3:524.

34. Durkheim 1969, 143, 147.

35. Ibid., 163ff. Fustel de Coulanges also distinguished two religions, but different ones than Durkheim. The cult of death and the religion of nature had coexisted long and peacefully in Greek history, even if, over time, the religion of nature became more significant than the cult of death (n.d. [1866], 120–22).

36. In this context, Pickering speaks of a "riddle." No one can say for sure what Robertson Smith's significance was for Durkheim so that one can talk of a "revelation" (Pickering 1984, 62, 70).

37. Hubert and Mauss suggest the following as a "provisionally sufficient definition" of magical rite: "This is what we call every rite that is not part of an organized cult, but is rather private, secret, mysterious and tends to the forbidden rite at its extreme. . . . It is clear that we are not defining magic by the form of its rites, but rather by the conditions under which they are performed and which mark their place in the totality of social customs" (1978 [1902–3], 58).

38. Bering 1982, 32–67.

39. Adorno 1967, 14ff.

40. Durkheim 1975, 62, 65–66.

41. Ibid., 69.

42. Bellah 1973, xxxv.

43. Giddens 1971.

44. Lukes 1973, 194.

45. Quoted in Nisbet 1968 [1952], 80.

46. von Oettingen 1882, 761.

47. Durkheim 1983 [1897], 167.

48. Ibid., 170.

49. Giddens 1965.

50. Durkheim 1964 [1895], 2.

51. Durkheim 1969, 31.

52. Ibid., 138.

53. Pickering 1984, 75.

54. Durkheim 1975, 95.

55. Ibid., 27. He had previously asserted that our forms of knowledge are socially conditioned. In *De quelques formes primitives de classification* (1901–2), Durkheim and Mauss had explained this thesis. In Australia, natural phenomena like sun and moon were put in categories corresponding to categories of marriage. In China, the Yin-Yang dualism followed the assumed sys-

tem of the complementary division of labor of the sexes. The first logical categories had been social and had a high emotional affect that had only gradually given way to reflection.

56. Durkheim 1969, 211–16.

57. Ibid., 315–16.

58. In this article, for the first time, Durkheim mentions Robertson Smith, albeit *en passant* (ibid., 347).

59. Ibid., 346.

60. Spencer and Gillen 1904, 121–22.

61. Quoted by Jones 1981, 195.

62. Five components can be distinguished: an exogamous rule of marriage; the clan names; a religious relation to a plant or animal (the totem); taboos concerning eating or killing the totem; and a common origin from it (Goldenweiser 1910, 182–83). After examining the extant source materials, Goldenweiser concluded that all those elements occurred independent of one another. Totemism was a conglomerate of independent characteristics (266).

63. "A religion is a unified system of beliefs and practices relative to sacred things, that is to say, things set apart and forbidden—beliefs and practices which unite into one single moral community called a Church, all those who adhere to them" (Durkheim 1968 [1912], 44).

64. Ibid., 327–69.

65. Durkheim 1976 [1914], 369.

66. Mauss (1872–1950) was Durkheim's nephew. His parents had sent him to Bordeaux and then to Paris to study with his uncle. He studied sociology, anthropology, and the history of religion, and contributed to the establishment of *L'Année sociologique*. In 1901 he was appointed to the chair for "The History of Religions of Uncivilized Peoples" at the École Pratique des Hautes Études.

67. Clark 1981, 181.

68. Mauss 1985 [1938], 1–25.

69. Lepenies 1989, 107–8; French text in Vogt 1981 [1976], 296–97 n. 34.

70. Raulff 1989.

CHAPTER 11
THE GREAT PROCESS OF DISENCHANTMENT

1. Weber 1984 [1892], 903; Weber 1924 [1894]; Riesebrodt 1985.

2. Weber 1924 [1896]; Deininger 1988.

3. Weber 1924 [1896].

4. Weber 1924 [1909].

5. Ibid., 277–78; for the implicit contemporary meaning, see Schluchter 1980.

6. Weber 1984, 465.

7. The recent German reprint of Lichtblau and Weiss (Weber 1993 [1904–5]) gives the text of the first edition and contains in the appendix an index of the most important additions and changes of the second edition. It was an important step in research on Weber in 1975, when F. Tenbruck proved that many

Weber interpretations used texts from *The Protestant Ethic* that Weber had later inserted into the second edition in 1920. They shed more light on Weber's later works than on his earlier writings. Using Lichtblau and Weiss's index, the additions and changes of the second edition can be conveniently surveyed. A new scientific edition in the framework of the historical-critical edition of Max Weber's works is being prepared by Hartmut Lehmann.

8. Weber 1930 [1904–5, 1920], 35.

9. Gothein 1970 [1892], 674.

10. Lehmann 1988.

11. Sombart 1902, 1:380–81.

12. van Dülmen 1988, 90.

13. Weber 1930 [1904–5, 1920], 60.

14. Jellinek 1919 [1895].

15. König and Winckelmann 1985, 15.

16. Tenbruck 1975, 697 n. 19.

17. Tenbruck 1984, 118.

18. Weber 1930 [1904–5, 1920], 90.

19. Ibid., 172.

20. Lehmann 1988, 540.

21. According to this objection, Catholic, Lutheran, and Calvinist texts of devotion show no significant difference concerning virtues like diligence and frugality (Münch 1993). Yet, since Weber considered the difference of the ways and means to salvation crucial, the objection is not convincing.

22. Ay 1995.

23. Graf 1993.

24. Winckelmann 1986, 151.

25. Ibid., 168–69.

26. Weber 1989, 236.

27.   1. The undersigned enter into an association and allow the co-optation of other members. 2. The association takes the name Eranos and aspires to the research of religions and religion. 3. During the academic semester, Eranos meets once a month on a Sunday from 6 to 11 o'clock at the home of a member in regular rotation. 4. The host gives a lecture on a subject in religious studies or a report on discoveries, publications, etc., in the area of religious studies and adjacent disciplines. 5. This is followed by an orderly discussion. 6. At about 8:30, a simple meal takes place. 7. After food, the scholarly exchange takes place more freely. 8. The subjects discussed (possibly with an outline of the content and the discussion) as well as other notable information is entered in an album. 9. The members regard participation in the sessions as a duty to be dispensed with only for the soundest reasons.

The document was signed by A. Deissmann, A. Dieterich, A. von Domaszewski, von Duhn, G. Jellinek, E. Marcks, K. Rathgen, Max Weber, and W. Windelband. The names of Scholl and Thode have the note: "I still reserve the decision." Troeltsch's name is followed by the remark, "but also finds it necessary to expand the area treated by the members." Literature on "Eranos" in Honigsheim (1985) [1963], 161–271, 176; Drescher 1991, 209–10; for the broader social sphere, see Treiber and Sauerland 1995.

28. While he was writing *The Protestant Ethic* in the spring of 1905, the group met at the Webers' home. "Tomorrow, Sunday, we face the prospect of 'Eranos,' the scientific circle of ten men. Max takes care of 'Protestant asceticism,' I take care of 'ham in burgundy sauce.' For Max's sake, I wish it were over. Lately, he hasn't been well" (Marianne Weber in the beginning of Chapter 11 1988 [1926]).

29. Küenzlen 1980.

30. Although Max Weber was skeptical of and rejected the evolutionism of his day, and could even call it a "swindle" (Mommsen 1974a, 3), "in the matter of religion, he was suddenly in the camp of contemporary evolutionism" (Tenbruck 1975, 682).

31. Tiele 1897, 63.

32. Ibid., 150–81, "Directions of Development."

33. Weber 1946, 123.

34. Marianne Weber 1988, 333.

35. Tenbruck 1975, 667.

36. Weber 1930 [1904–5, 1920], 104–5.

37. Weber 1981, 179.

38. Ibid., 155.

39. Weber 1946, 139.

40. Weber 1993 [1922], 125.

41. Schluchter 1988b, 2:81.

42. Shown clearly by Mommsen 1985 and 1993, 56ff.

43. Gephart 1993, 51.

44. Bering 1982.

45. Ibid., 32–67. A similar ambivalence also characterized the somewhat older Polish and Russian *intelligentsia* (Müller 1971).

46. Bering 1982, 327.

47. Mommsen 1993, 33–61.

48. Honigsheim 1985 [1963], 161; Treiber and Sauerland 1995.

49. Karádi 1988, 682–702.

50. Löwy 1976, 44–51.

51. Weber 1930 [1904–5], 181. Weber's pessimistic vision was analyzed by Peukert 1989, chap. 3.

52. Weber 1946, 280.

53. Ibid., 275; Weber 1993 [1921–22], 144–46.

54. Weber 1946, 149.

55. Schluchter 1988b, 1:339–63 ("'The Struggle of the Gods': From Criticism of Religion to the Sociology of Religion").

56. Weber 1993 [1921–22], 117.

57. Honigsheim 1985 [1963], 240.

58. Treiber 1991, 443.

59. Weber 1946, 143, 152–3; and Hanke 1993a, 160.

60. Schluchter 1988b, 2:78ff.

61. Weber 1993 [1921–22], 177.
62. Weber 1946, 155.
63. Weber 1989, 101.
64. Weber 1993 [1921–22], 125.
65. Kippenberg 1991, 85–105.
66. Weber 1996 [1916–20], 542.

CHAPTER 12
RELIGION AS EXPERIENCE OF THE SELF

1. Vom Bruch, Graf, and Hübinger 1989, 11. Thus, for example, Hammacher wrote: "With a stretch of the usual meaning of the word, we could therefore define the social question as the relation between objective and subjective culture, which is subordinate to the contrast between capital and labor as the most obvious example" (1914, 5).
2. Perpeet 1976, 44–45.
3. Eucken 1897, 44.
4. Hammacher 1914, 10.
5. Ibid., 99.
6. Ibid., 214.
7. Hübinger 1996.
8. Diederichs 1967, 35.
9. Graf 1996.
10. Diederichs 1967, 35.
11. Hübinger 1987.
12. Buber 1993 [1909], 55.
13. Fellmann 1993, 25.
14. Hoffmann 1913, 608.
15. James 1982 [1902], 161.
16. Ibid., 62.
17. Ibid., 385–86.
18. Ibid., 380–82.
19. Ibid., 390–413.
20. Ibid., 515.
21. Isaiah 6:3, in Otto's transcription.
22. Otto 1911, 709. Other such experiences that were very significant for Otto are in Haubold 1940, 19–21.
23. Otto 1991 [1899], vii.
24. Ibid., xviii.
25. Ibid., xi.
26. Segal 1989, 5–36.
27. Windelband 1921 [1902], 299.
28. Otto 1921, 3.
29. Schopenhauer 1972 [1840], 146ff.
30. Otto 1959, 22.
31. Ibid., 27.
32. Pfleiderer 1992, 119.

33. Weeks 1993.
34. Otto 1917, 141–60.
35. Otto 1959, 6.
36. Colpe has collected important voices in the discussion of "the holy" (1977). Baetke (1942) argued strongly against the devaluation of the ethical in the category of the holy.
37. Alles 1991.
38. This construction can be studied in the encyclopedia entries "Communion with Deity" (1910) and "Holiness" (1913) as well as in his major work, *Das Werden des Gottesglaubens* (1926 [1916], esp. 149–51).
39. Söderblom 1926 [1916], 285.
40. Sharpe 1990, 44–45.
41. Ibid., 163.
42. Ibid., 74–75.
43. Van der Leeuw 1977 [1933], 9. Gladigow sought the context of van der Leeuw's concept of power in scientific models of the time (1991).
44. Van der Leeuw 1977 [1933], 103.
45. Van der Leeuw 1930, 1861.
46. Van der Leeuw 1928.
47. Cited by van Baaren 1969, 10.
48. Ibid., 10–11.
49. The equation of "Bororo equals Arara" is not direct, but is conveyed by a third concept: the idea of the soul bird. Only because a Bororo expects that his soul will become a soul bird after his death can he see himself and the Arara bird as manifestations of the same entity. It has to do with symbolism linked with the idea of the soul. It is not the forms of thought that are different, but rather the interpretations that are linked to the contents of the perception, as Evans-Pritchard described conclusively in 1934 (21).
50. Van der Leeuw 1977 [1933], 787.
51. Kohl 1987.
52. Van der Leeuw 1948, 255.
53. Van der Leeuw 1935, 230 and 235–36, in a review of Otto's book, *Dionysos* (1933), which he titled characteristically, "Die Wirklichkeit des Heidentums."
54. Flasche (1982) investigated the prophet syndrome. It was typical for an "interpretive comparative religion" that made religious experience into an object as well as a principle of knowing. Gladigow (1988, 7) notes that it was mainly theologians who represented this prophetic conception of the religious studies. The difficulty of such an assertion consists of the fact that this concept could be and was also represented without a theological link. The formulation by Kohl (1987, 130) seems to help: that in their study of past and foreign cultures, European scholars followed a twofold Eurocentrism, vacillating between partisanship for their own culture and idealizing what in other cultures appeared as a negation of their own. The idealization of otherness was expressed with missionary zeal due to a critical statement about their own culture.

CHAPTER 13
HOW DESCRIPTIONS OF THE HISTORY OF RELIGION REFLECT
MODERNIZATION

1. Smith 1982, xi.
2. Malinowski 1927.
3. See Clifford 1988.
4. Steenblock 1991.
5. Weber 1988 [1906], 217.
6. Quoted by White 1987, 16.
7. Droysen 1971 [1982], 359–66; Rüsen 1993, 248–49.
8. Rüsen 1993, 274–75.
9. Koselleck 1979, 349–75.
10. History as a "regulative term" includes "all past and future experience," wrote Koselleck (1975, 593).
11. Rüsen 1993, 48–58.
12. Laslett 1976.
13. Hobsbawm and Ranger 1983; Anderson 1991.
14. C. Nodier quoted by Schenk 1970, 254 n. 15.
15. Tenbruck 1989, 195.
16. Berger 1992 [1980], 36.
17. Giddens 1990.
18. Gladigow 1995.
19. Marquard 1986, 98.
20. Groh and Groh 1991.
21. An autobiographical comment by Thomas Mann (1983, 374), even if later than our period, explains this paradox:

Belief? Unbelief? I hardly know what is one and what is the other. In fact I could not say if I consider myself a believing or an unbelieving man. Deepest skepticism with regard to both, to so-called belief and so-called unbelief, is all I can show when I am catechized. We are so densely crowded with eternal enigmas that one had to be a beast to beat it out of your mind for only one day. On no day, since I have been aware, have I not thought about death and the enigma. But what does one demand that I believe? One 'God,' who has created the Einsteinian universe and thus demands prostration, adoration, boundless subjection? . . . The position of man in the cosmos, his beginning, his origin, his goal, that is the great mystery, and the religious problem is the human problem, man's questions about himself.

22. Kolakowski 1995 [1970], 378.

BIBLIOGRAPHY

The abbreviations of journals, series, lexicons, and sources are taken from the *Abkürzungsverzeichnis* of the *Theologische Realenzyklopädie* (TRE), compiled by S. Schwertner, Berlin, 1976.

INTRODUCTION TO THE AMERICAN EDITION

G. Benavides (1998), "Modernity." In Taylor 1998, 186–204.

W. Braun and R. McCutcheon (eds.) (2000), *Guide to the Study of Religion*. New York.

M. Eliade (1963), *Patterns in Comparative Religion*. Cleveland.

T. A. Idinopulos and E. A. Yonan (eds.) (1986), *Religion and Reductionism. Essays on Eliade, Segal, and the Challenge of the Social Sciences for the Study of Religion*. Leiden.

B. Lincoln (1999), *Theorizing Myth. Narrative, Ideology and Scholarship*. Chicago.

R. McCutcheon (1997), *Manufacturing Religion. The Discourse on Sui Generis Religion and the Politics of Nostalgia*. New York.

P. Ricoeur (1994), "Historie et rhétorique," *Diogène* 168:1–18.

R. Segal (1989) [1983], "In Defense of Reductionism." In *Religion and the Social Sciences. Essays on the Confrontation*, 5–36. Atlanta.

E. J. Sharpe (1986), *Comparative Religion. A History*. 2nd ed. London.

J. Z. Smith (1982), *Imagining Religion. From Babylon to Jonestown*. Chicago.

——— (1998), "Religion, Religions, Religious." In Taylor 1998, 269–84.

I. Strenski (1986), "Reduction without Tears." In Idinopulos and Yonan 1986, 95–107.

——— (1987), *Four Theories of Myth in the Twentieth-Century History. Cassirer, Eliade, Lévi-Strauss and Malinowski*. Iowa City.

M. C. Taylor (ed.) (1998), *Critical Terms for Religious Studies*. Chicago.

S. Wasserstrom (1999), *Religion after Religion. Gershom Scholem, Mircea Eliade and Henry Corbin at Eranos*. Princeton.

H. White (1989), "Figuring the Nature of the Times Deceased. Literary Theory and Historical Writing." In R. Cohen (ed.), *The Future of Literary History*. New York.

INTRODUCTION

M. Weber (1992), *The Protestant Ethic and the Spirit of Capitalism*, trans. Talcott Parsons. London.

CHAPTER 1
FROM THE PHILOSOPHY OF RELIGION TO THE HISTORY OF RELIGIONS

G. Alexander and J. Fritsche (1989), " 'Religion' und 'Religiosität' im 18. Jahrhundert. Eine Skizze zur Wortgeschichte." In K. Gründer and K. H. Rengstorf (eds.), *Religionskritik und Religiosität in der deutschen Aufklärung*, 11–25. Heidelberg.

H. Bakker (1989), "Die indische Herausforderung. Hegels Beitrag zu einer europäischen kulturhistorischen Diskussion." In H. Bakker, J. Schickel, B. Nagel, *Indische Philosophie und europäische Rezeption*, 33–56. Köln.

I. Berlin (1993), *The Magus of the North. J. G. Hamann and the Origins of Modern Irrationalism*. London.

S. Birkner (1957), *Die Mechanisierung des Lebens im Werk Johann Gottfried Herders*. Frankfurt/M.

H. Blumenberg (1966), *Die Legitimität der Neuzeit*. Frankfurt/M.

P. Byrne (1989), *Natural Religion and the Nature of Religion. The Legacy of Deism*. New York.

T. A. Campbell (1991), *The Religion of the Heart. A Study of European Religious Life in the Seventeenth and Eighteenth Centuries*. Columbia, S.C.

H. H. Christmann (ed.) (1977), *Sprachwissenschaft des 19. Jahrhunderts*. Darmstadt.

M. Despland (1988), *La religion en occident. Évolution des idées et du vécu*. Quebec.

E. E. Evans-Pritchard (1981) [1965], *Theorien über primitive Religionen*. Frankfurt/M.

E. Feil (1986), *Religio. Die Geschichte eines neuzeitlichen Grundbegriffs vom Frühchristentum bis zur Reformation*. Göttingen.

F. Fellmann (1993), *Lebensphilosophie. Elemente einer Theorie der Selbsterfahrung*. Reinbek.

H.-G. Gadamer (1960), *Wahrheit und Methode. Grundzüge einer philosophischen Hermeneutik*. Tübingen.

B. Gladigow (1997), "Friedrich Schleiermacher (1768–1834)." In A. Michaels (ed.), *Klassiker der Religionswissenschaft*. München.

F. W. Graf and F. Wagner (eds.) (1982), *Die Flucht in den Begriff. Materialien zu Hegels Religionsphilosophie*. Stuttgart.

R. Grimsley (1967), "Jean-Jacques Rousseau." *Encyclopedia of Philosophy*, 7:218–25.

W. Halbfass (1988), *India and Europe. An Essay in Understanding*. New York.

G. W. F. Hegel (1822), "Vorrede zu Hinrichs' Religionsphilosophie." In Hegel (1986), 11:42–67. Berliner Schriften 1818–1831. Frankfurt/M.

———— (1827), "Über die unter dem Namen Bhagavad-Gita bekannte Episode des Mahabharata. Von Wilhelm von Humboldt." In Hegel (1986), 11:131–204. Berliner Schriften 1818–1831. Frankfurt/M.

———— (1986), *Werke*. A new edition based on works of 1832–1845. 20 vols. Frankfurt/M.

———— (1995), On the Episode of the Mahābhārata Known by the name of the Bhagavad-Gītā by Wilhelm von Humboldt. Trans. and ed. Herbert Herring. New Delhi.

G. W. F. Hegel, D. Hinrichs, and Schleiermacher (1987), *On Feeling and Reason in Religion: The Texts of their 1821–22 Debate*. Edited and translated by Eric von der Luft. Lewiston, N.Y.

D. Henrich (1960), "Der Begriff der sittlichen Einsicht und Kants Lehre vom Faktum der Vernunft." *Festschrift Hans-Georg Gadamer*, 77–115. Tübingen.

J. G. Herder (1960), *Sprachphilosophische Schriften*. Selected by E. Heintel. Hamburg.

—— (1964) [1774], "Auch eine Philosophie der Geschichte zur Bildung der Menschheit." *Herders Werke in fünf Bänden*, 2:279–378. Berlin.

—— (1964) [1781], "Über die Würkung der Dichtkunst auf die Sitten der Völker in Alten und Neuen Zeiten." *Herders Werke in fünf Bänden*, 3:195–255. Berlin.

—— (1967) [1887], *Ideen zur Philosophie der Geschichte der Menschheit* (1784–85). In B. Suphan (ed.), *Sämtliche Werke*, vol. 13. Hildesheim.

—— (1989) [1772], *Abhandlung über den Ursprung der Sprache*, ed. H. D. Irmscher. Stuttgart.

D. Hertz (1991), *Die jüdischen Salons im alten Berlin*. Meisenheim.

C. Hill (1972), *The World Turned Upside Down. Radical Ideas during the English Revolution*. Harmondsworth.

T. Hobbes (1968) [1651], *Leviathan, or the Matter, Forme, & Power of a Common-Wealth Ecclesiastical and Civill*. London.

—— (1983) [1640], *Elements of Law Natural and Politic*. Darmstadt.

N. Hoerster (1986), "D. Hume. Existenz und Eigenschaften Gottes." In J. Speck (ed.), *Grundprobleme der Großen Philosophen. Philosophie der Neuzeit I*. 2nd ed., 240–275. Göttingen.

W. von Humboldt (1977), "Natur der Sprache überhaupt (1824–26)." In H. H. Christmann (ed.), *Sprachwissenschaft des 19 Jahrhunderts*, 19–46. Darmstadt.

—— (1985), *Schriften zur Sprache*, ed. M. Böhler. Stuttgart.

D. Hume (1874), *The Philosophical Works of David Hume*, ed. T. H. Green and T. T. Grose. New York.

—— (1993) [1757], *The Natural History of Religion*. Oxford.

—— (1993) [1776], *Dialogues Concerning Natural Religion*. Oxford.

W. Jaeschke (1983), *Die Religionsphilosophie Hegels*. Darmstadt.

I. Kant (1956) [1781], *Kritik der reinen Vernunft*. Hamburg.

—— (1964) [1793], *Critique of Pure Reason*. Translated by J. M. D. Meiklejohn. London, New York.

—— (1968) [1785, 1788], *Grundlegung zur Metaphysik der Sitten; Kritik der praktischen Vernunft*. Theorie-Werkausgabe, vol. 8. Frankfurt/M.

—— (1968) [1797, 1793], *Die Metaphysik der Sitten; Die Religion innerhalb der Grenzen der bloßen Vernunft*. Theorie-Werkausgabe, vol. 8. Frankfurt/M.

—— (1977) [1798], *Der Streit der Fakultäten.»* Theorie-Werkausgabe, vol. 11. Frankfurt/M.

H. D. Kittsteiner (1995), *Die Entstehung des modernen Gewissens*. Frankfurt/M.

H. Kleger and A. Müller (1985), "Bürgerreligion und politische Verpflichtung." *ABG* 29:47–98.

—— (1986), "Der politische Philosoph in der Rolle des Ziviltheologen." *StPh* 45:86–111.

R. Klibansky and E. C. Mossner (1954), *New Letters of David Hume*. Oxford.

R. Koselleck (1959), *Kritik und Krise. Eine Studie zur Pathogenese der bürgerlichen Welt*. Frankfurt/M.

W. Lepenies (1978), *Das Ende der Naturgeschichte. Wandel kultureller Selbstverständlichkeiten in der Wissenschaft des 18. und 19. Jahrhunderts*. Frankfurt/M.

F. E. Manuel (1983), *The Changing of the Gods*. Hanover, N.H., and London.

O. Marquard (1981), *Abschied vom Prinzipiellen*. Stuttgart.

—— (1987), *Transzendentaler Idealismus—Romantische Naturphilosophie—Psychoanalyse*. Köln.

A. Menne (1983), "Arthur Schopenhauer. Die Welt als Wille und Vorstellung." In Speck 1983, 98–124.

B. Morris (1987), *Anthropological Studies of Religion*. Cambridge.

K. Nowak (1986), *Schleiermacher und die Frühromantik. Eine literaturgeschichtliche Studie zum romantischen Religionsverständnis und Menschenbild am Ende des 18. Jahrhunderts in Deutschland*. Göttingen.

R. Otto (ed.) (1991) [1899], *F. Schleiermacher. Über die Religion. Reden an die Gebildeten unter ihren Verächtern*. 7th ed. Göttingen.

J. S. Preus (1787), *Explaining Religion. Criticism and Theory from Bodin to Freud*. New Haven.

F. Ricken (1992), "Kanon und Organon. Religion und Offenbarung im 'Streit der Fakultäten.'" In F. Ricken and F. Marty (eds.), *Kant über Religion*, 181–94. Stuttgart.

W. Röd (1984), *Die Philosophie der Neuzeit 2. Von Newton bis Rousseau*. Geschichte der Philosophie, vol. 8. München.

J. Rohls (1985), "Sinn und Geschmack fürs Unendliche. Aspekte romantischer Kunstreligion." *NZSystTh* 27:1–24.

J.-J. Rousseau (1962) [1762], "On the Social Contract, Considerations on the Government." In *Political Writings*, trans. C. E. Vaughan. New York.

—— (1963) [1762], *Émile*. Stuttgart.

—— (1965), *The Creed of a Priest of Savoy*, trans. with an introduction by Arthur H. Beattie. New York.

—— (1978) [1762] *On the Social Contract*. Edited by Roger D. Masters, translated by Judith R. Masters. New York.

—— (1979) [1762], *Emile: or, On Education*. Introduction, translation, and notes by Allan Bloom. New York.

—— (1984) [1755], *A Discourse on Inequality*, trans. with an introduction and notes by Maurice Cranston. New York.

—— (1992) [1750], *Discourse on the Sciences and Arts*, ed. Roger D. Masters and Christopher Kelly, trans. Judith R. Bush, Roger D. Masters, and Christopher Kelly. Hanover, N.H.

—— (1995) [1750], *Schriften zur Kulturkritik. Discourse sur les sciences et les arts*. 5th ed. Hamburg.

F. D. E. Schleiermacher (1958), *On Religion: Speeches to Its Cultured Despisers*. Translated by John Oman. New York.

—— (1974), *Hermeneutik*. ed. H. Kimmerle. 2nd ed. Heidelberg.

—— (1984), *Kritische Gesamtausgabe*. Vol. I, 2. Berlin/ New York.

—— (1984), *Kritische Gesamtausgabe*. Berlin and New York.

—— (1991) [1799], *Über die Religion. Reden an die Gebildeten unter ihren Verächtern*, ed. R. Otto (1899). Göttingen.

A. Schmidt (1986), *Die Wahrheit im Gewande der Lüge. Schopenhauers Religionsphilosophie*. München.

C. Schmitt (1938), *Der Leviathan in der Staatslehre des Thomas Hobbes*. Hamburg.

—— (1979) [1932], *Der Begriff des Politischen*. Berlin.

G. Scholtz (1984), *Die Philosophie Schleiermachers*. Darmstadt.

A. Schopenhauer (1960), *Die Welt als Wille und Vorstellung*. Band 1. (1818); Band 2. (1844). Stuttgart/Frankfurt.

—— (1969), *The World as Will and Representation*, trans. E. F. J. Payne. New York.

E. J. Sharpe (1986), *Comparative Religion. A History*. 2nd ed. London.

J. Speck (ed.) (1983), *Grundprobleme der großen Philosophen. Philosophie der Neuzeit III*. Göttingen.

J. Taubes (ed.) (1983), *Der Fürst dieser Welt. Carl Schmitt und die Folgen*. Paderborn.

C. Taylor (1978) [1975], *Hegel*. Frankfurt/M.

K. Vorländer (1992), *Immanuel Kant. Der Mann und das Werk*. 3rd ed. Hamburg.

W. Voßkamp (1990), "La 'Bildung' dans la tradition de la pensée utopique." In M. Espagne and M. Werner (eds.), *Philologiques I. Contribution à l'histoire des disciplines littéraires en France et en Allemagne au XIXe siècle*, 43–54. Paris.

J. de Vries (1967), *The Study of Religion. A Historical Approach*. New York.

J. Waardenburg (1973–74), *Classical Approaches to the Study of Religion. Aims, Methods and Theories of Research*. Vol. 1, *Introduction and Anthology*; Vol. 2, *Bibliography*. Den Haag.

M. A. Weber (1990), *David Hume und Edward Gibbon. Religionssoziologie in der Aufklärung*. Frankfurt/M.

A. Weeks (1993), *German Mysticism from Hildegard of Bingen to Ludwig Wittgenstein. A Literary and Intellectual History*. Albany.

H. White (1973), *Metahistory*. Baltimore.

J. Whitman (1984), "From Philology to Anthropology in Mid-Nineteenth-Century Germany." In G. W. Stocking, Jr. (ed.), *Functionalism Historicized*, 214–29. Madison.

W. Windelband (1924) [1902], "Das Heilige. Skizze zur Religionsphilosophie." In *Präludien. Aufsätze und Reden zur Philosophie und ihrer Geschichte*, 2:295–332, 9th ed. Tübingen. A shorter version is found in C. Colpe (ed.) (1977), *Die Diskussion um das "Heilige*," 29–56. Darmstadt.

CHAPTER 2
DECIPHERING UNKNOWN CULTURES

A. H. Anquetil-Duperron (1771), *Zend-Avesta, ouvrage de Zoroastre*, vol. 1. Paris.

G. Beer (1983), *Darwin's Plots. Evolutionary Narratives in Darwin, George Eliot and Nineteenth-Century Fiction*. London.

U. Bitterli (1991), *Die 'Wilden' und die 'Zivilisierten.' Grundzüge einer Geistes- und Kulturgeschichte der europäisch-überseeischen Begegnung*. 2nd ed. München.

P. J. Bowler (1986), *Theories of Human Evolution. A Century of Debate, 1844–1944*. Oxford.

E. A. Wallis Budge (1925), *The Rise and Progress of Assyriology*. London.

C. G. Carus (1931) [1846], *Psyche. Zur Entwicklungsgeschichte der Seele*. Leipzig.

J. Clair, C. Pichler, and W. Pirchner (eds.) (1989), *Wunderblock. Eine Geschichte der modernen Seele*. Wien.

C. Darwin (1989) [1859], *Die Entstehung der Arten durch natürliche Zuchtwahl*. Stuttgart.

—— (1992) [1874], *Die Abstammung des Menschen*. Wiesbaden.

—— (1951), *On the Origin of Species through Natural Selection*. New York.

E. Doblhofer (1993), *Die Entzifferung alter Schriften und Sprachen*. Stuttgart.

L. Febvre (1988), "Wie Michelet die Renaissance erfand." In U. Raulff (ed.), *Das Gewissen des Historikers*, 211–21. Frankfurt/M.

J. W. Gruber (1965), "Brixham Cave and the Antiquity of Man." In M. E. Spiro (ed.), *Context and Meaning in Cultural Anthropology: Festschrift for A. I. Hallowell*, 373–402. New York.

E. Haeckel (1891), *Anthropogonie oder Entwicklungsgeschichte des Menschen. Keimes- und Stammesgeschichte*, vol. 1. Leipzig.

W. Halbfass (1988), *India and Europe. An Essay in Understanding*. New York.

E. Hardy (1901), "Zur Geschichte der vergleichenden Religionsforschung." *ARW* 4:45–66, 97–135, 193–228.

J. G. Herder (1964) [1774], "Auch eine Philosophie der Geschichte zur Bildung der Menschheit." *Herders Werke in fünf Bänden*, 2:279–378. Berlin.

J. Hörisch (1991), "Die Romantische Seele." In G. Jüttemann, M. Sonntag, and C. Wulf (eds.), *Die Seele. Ihre Geschichte im Abendland*, 258–266. Weinheim.

E. Iversen (1971), "The Hieroglyphic Tradition." In J. R. Harris (ed.), *The Legacy of Egypt*. 2nd ed., 170–96. Oxford.

—— (1993) [1961], *The Myth of Egypt and Its Hieroglyphs in European Tradition*. Princeton.

G. Jüttemann, M. Sonntag, and C. Wulf (eds.) (1991), *Die Seele. Ihre Geschichte im Abendland*. Weinheim.

A. Klempt (1960), *Die Säkularisierung der universalhistorischen Auffassung*. Göttingen.

W. Lepenies (1978), *Das Ende der Naturgeschichte. Wandel kultureller Selbstverständlichkeiten in der Wissenschaft des 18. und 19. Jahrhunderts*. Frankfurt/M.

G. Long (1836), "The Rosetta Stone." In *The British Museum. Egyptian Antiquities*, 2:342–73. London.

C. Lyell (1863), *The Geological Evidences of the Antiquity of Man*. Philadelphia.

O. Marquard (1987), *Transzendentaler Idealismus—Romantische Naturphilosophie—Psychoanalyse*. Köln.

F. M. Müller (1985) [1867], *Chips from a German Workshop*. Vol. 1, *Essays on the Science of Religion*; Vol. 2, *Essays on Mythology, Traditions and Customs*. Chico, Calif.

E. Quinet (1989) [1857], *Le génie des religions. De l'origine des dieux*. Paris.

E. W. Said (1978), *Orientalism*. New York.

—— (1984), *The World, the Text and the Critic*. Cambridge.

F. Schlegel (1977) [1808], *Über die Sprache und Weisheit der Indier. Ein Beitrag zur Begründung der Alterthumskunde*. Amsterdam.

R. Schwab (1934), *Vie d'Anquetil-Duperron, suivie des usages civils et religieux des Parses par Anquetil-Duperron*. Paris.

—— (1984), *The Oriental Renaissance. Europe's Discovery of India and the East, 1680–1880*. Paris.

M. Sonntag (1991), "Die Seele und das Wissen vom Lebenden. Zur Entstehung der Biologie im 19. Jahrhundert." In G. Jüttemann, M. Sonntag, and C. Wulf (eds.), *Die Seele. Ihre Geschichte im Abendland*, 293–318. Weinheim.

M. Stausberg (1998), *Faszination Zarathushtra. Zoroaster und die Europäische Religionsgeschichte der Frühen Neuzeit.* Berlin.

E. B. Tylor (1866), "The Science of Language." Review of four books, including F. M. Müller, *Lectures on the Science of Language. Quarterly Review* 119:394–435.

——— (1958) [1871], *Primitive Culture. Researches into the Development of Mythology, Philosophy, Religion, Art, and Custom.* Reprinted as *The Origin of Culture* (Vol. 1); *Religion in Primitive Culture* (Vol. 2). New York.

F. M. Wuketits (1988), *Evolutionstheorien. Historische Voraussetzungen, Positionen, Kritik.* Darmstadt.

CHAPTER 3
WHAT LANGUAGES TELL OF THE EARLY HISTORY
OF THE RELIGIONS OF EUROPE

T. Achelis (1893), *Max Müller und die vergleichende Religionswissenschaft.* Hamburg.

M. Arnold (1875) [1869], "Hebraism and Hellenism." In *Culture and Anarchy. An Essay in Political and Social Criticism*, 128–49. London.

——— (1887, 1915), *Essays in Criticism.* 2 vols. London.

G. Beer (1990), "Speaking for the Others. Relativism and Authority in Victorian Anthropological Literature." In R. Fraser (ed.), *Sir James Frazer and the Literary Imagination. Essays in Affinity and Influence*, 38–60. London.

É. Benveniste (1973), *Indo-European Language and Society*, trans. Elizabeth Palmer. London.

——— (1993) [1969], *Indoeuropäische Institutionen. Wortschatz, Geschichte, Funktionen.* Frankfurt/M.

P. Berkenkopf (1914), *Die Voraussetzungen der Religionsphilosophie Friedrich Max Müllers.* Philosophische und pädagogische Arbeiten, no. 4. Langensalza.

L. P. van den Bosch (1993), "Friedrich Max Müller." *NTT* 47:107–18, 186–200.

E. Burnouf (1872), *La science des religions.* 2nd ed. Paris.

N. C. Chaudhuri (1974), *Scholar Extraordinary. The Life of Professor the Rt. Hon. Friedrich Max Müller, P. C.* London.

M. Detienne (1985), "Die skandalöse Mythologie (oder: Projekt einer Arbeit über das zweideutige Wesen der sogenannten Mythologie)." In R. Schlesier (ed.), *Faszination des Mythos*, 12–34. Frankfurt/M.

R. M. Dorson (1971) [1955], "The Eclipse of Solar Mythology." In T. A. Sebeok (ed.), *Myth: A Symposium*, 25–63. Bloomington.

U. Emrich (1963), "Begriff und Symbolik der 'Urgeschichte' in der romantischen Dichtung." In *Protest und Verheißung. Studien zur klassischen und modernen Dichtung*, 2nd ed., 25–47. Frankfurt/M.

W. Euler (1987), "Gab es eine indogermanische Götterfamilie?" In W. Meid (ed.), *Studien zum indogermanischen Wortschat*, 35–56. Innsbruck.

J. A. de Gobineau (1939–40), *Versuch über die Ungleichheit der Menschenrassen.* 4 vols. Stuttgart.

W. Halbfass (1988), *India and Europe. An Essay in Understanding*. New York.

W. von Humboldt (1977) [1824–26], "Natur der Sprache überhaupt." In H. H. Christmann (ed.), *Sprachwissenschaft des 19. Jahrhunderts*, 19–46. Darmstadt.

————— (1985), *Schriften zur Sprache*. Stuttgart.

M. Jastrow, Jr. (1981) [1902], *The Study of Religion*. Chico, Calif.

L. H. Jordan (1986) [1905], *Comparative Religion. Its Genesis and Growth*. Atlanta.

E. Knoll (1986), "The Science of Language and the Evolution of Mind. Max Müller's Quarrel with Darwinism." *Journal of the History of the Behavioral Sciences* 22:3–22.

A. Lang (1884), "Mythology." *Ency. Brit.*, 9th ed., 17:135–58.

————— (1898a), *The Making of Religion*. London.

————— (1898b), *Modern Mythology*. London.

M. Lazarus and H. Steinthal (1860), "Einleitende Gedanken über Völkerpsychologie als Einladung zu einer Zeitschrift für Völkerpsychologie und Sprachwissenschaft." *Zeitschrift für Völkerpsychologie und Sprachwissenschaft* 1:1–73.

R. F. Littledale (1909) [1870], "The Oxford Solar Myth. A Contribution to Comparative Mythology." In F. M. Müller, *Comparative Mythology, An Essay*, ed. A. S. Palmer, XXXI–XLVII. New York.

C. H. Long (1977), "The History of the History of Religions." In C. J. Adams (ed.), *A Reader's Guide to the Great Religions*, 2nd ed., 467–75. New York.

————— (1986), "The Study of Religion. Its Nature and Its Discourse." In *Significations. Signs, Symbols, and Images in the Interpretation of Religion*, 13–26. Philadelphia.

B. Morris (1987), *Anthropological Studies of Religion*. Cambridge.

G. L. Mosse (1978), *Toward the Final Solution. A History of European Racism*. New York.

————— (1990), *Die Geschichte des Rassismus in Europa*. Frankfurt/M.

F. M. Müller (1873), *Introduction to the Science of Religion*. London.

————— (1874), *Lectures on the Science of Language*. Second Series. New York.

————— (1878), *Lectures on the Origin and Growth of Religion as Illustrated by the Religions of India*. London.

————— (1880), *Vorlesungen über den Ursprung und die Entwicklung der Religion mit besonderer Rücksicht auf die Religionen des Alten Indiens*. Strassburg.

————— (1881), "Kant's Critique of Pure Reason." In Müller 1901b, 218–50. London.

————— (1883), *India, What Can It Teach Us*. London.

————— (1884), *Indien in seiner Weltgeschichtlichen Bedeutung*. Leipzig.

————— (1885a), *Lectures on the Science of Language*. London.

————— (1885b), "The Lesson of 'Jupiter.'" *The Nineteenth Century. A Monthly Review* 18:626–50.

————— (1891), *Anthropological Religion*. Gifford Lectures. Glasgow.

————— (1901a), *Alte Zeiten—Alte Freunde. Lebenserinnerungen*. Gotha.

————— (1901b), *Last Essays. First Series. Essays on Language, Folklore, and Other Subjects*, 218–50. London.

————— (1985) [1867], *Chips from a German Workshop*. Vol. 1, *Essays on the Science of Religion*; Vol. 2, *Essays on Mythology, Traditions and Customs*. Chico, Calif.

G. Müller (ed.) (1902), *The Life and Letters of the Right Honourable Friedrich Max Müller*. London.

M. Olender (1992), *The Languages of Paradise. Race, Religion, and Philology in the Nineteenth Century*, trans. Arthur Goldhammer. Cambridge, Mass.

—— (1995), *Die Sprachen des Paradieses. Religion, Philologie und Rassentheorie im 19. Jahrhundert*. Frankfurt/M.

R. Pettazzoni (1956), *The All-Knowing God. Researches into Early Religion and Culture*, trans. H. J. Rose. London.

—— (1960) [1955], *Der allwissende Gott. Zur Geschichte der Gottesidee*. Frankfurt/M.

E. W. Said (1978), *Orientalism*. New York.

—— (1984), *The World, the Text and the Critic*. Cambridge.

E. J. Sharpe (1986), *Comparative Religion. A History*. 2nd ed. London.

G. Steiner (1975), *After Babel. Aspects of Language and Translation*. New York.

C. P. Tiele (1882), *Histoire comparée des anciennes religions de l'Égypte et des peuples sémitiques*. Paris.

—— (1884), "Religions." *Ency. Brit.*, 9th ed., 20:358–71.

—— (1897, 1899), *Elements of the Science of Religion*. Part 1, *Morphological*; Part 2, *Ontological*. Gifford Lectures. Edinburgh and London.

H. Treiber (1992), "Wahlverwandtschaften zwischen Nietzsches Idee eines 'Klosters für Freiere Geister' und Webers Idealtypus der Puritanischen Sekte." *Nietzsche-Studien* 21:326–62.

L. Trilling (1963) [1939], *Matthew Arnold*, 4th ed. London.

F. M. Turner (1981), *The Greek Heritage in Victorian Britain*. New Haven.

E. B. Tylor (1866), "The Science of Language." Review of four books, including F. M. Müller, *Lectures on the Science of Language. Quarterly Review* 119:394–435.

—— (1868), Review of F. M. Müller, *Chips from a German Workshop. Fortnightly Review* N.S. 3:225–28.

J. de Vries (1967), *The Study of Religion. A Historical Approach*. New York.

J. Waardenburg (1973–74), *Classical Approaches to the Study of Religion. Aims, Methods and Theories of Research*. Vol. 1, *Introduction and Anthology*; Vol. 2, *Bibliography*. Den Haag.

A. Weeks (1993), *German Mysticism from Hildegard of Bingen to Ludwig Wittgenstein. A Literary and Intellectual History*. Albany.

E. J. Ziolkowski (ed.) (1993), *A Museum of Faiths. Histories and Legacies of the 1893 World's Parliament of Religions*. Atlanta.

CHAPTER 4
THE PRESENCE OF THE ORIGINAL RELIGION IN MODERN CIVILIZATION

E. H. Ackerknecht (1954), "On the Comparative Method in Anthropology." In R. F. Spencer (ed.), *Method and Perspective in Anthropology. Festschrift for W. D. Wallis*, 117–25. Minneapolis.

A. Baeumler (1965), *Das mythische Weltalter. Bachofens romantische Deutung des Altertums*. München.

U. Bitterli (1991), *Die 'Wilden' und die 'Zivilisierten.' Grundzüge einer Geistes-und Kulturgeschichte der europäisch-überseeischen Begegnung*, 2nd ed. München.

P. J. Bowler (1986), *Theories of Human Evolution. A Century of Debate, 1844–1944.* Oxford.

J. W. Burrow (1966), *Evolution and Society. A Study in Victorian Social Theory.* Cambridge.

C. G. Carus (1931) [1846], *Psyche. Zur Entwicklungsgeschichte der Seele.* Leipzig.

O. Chadwick (1975), *The Secularization of the European Mind in the Nineteenth Century.* Cambridge.

C. Darwin 1871 2 vol., *The Descent of Man.* London.

E. E. Evans-Pritchard (1933), "The Intellectualist (English) Interpretation of Magic." *Bulletin of the Faculty of Arts (Alexandria)* 1:282–311.

M. Harris (1968), *The Rise of Anthropological Theory. A History of Theories of Culture.* London.

M. T. Hodgen (1936), *The Doctrine of Survivals. A Chapter in the History of Scientific Method in the Study of Man.* London.

H. G. Kippenberg (1984), *Johann Jakob Bachofen, Mutterrecht und Urreligion.* 6th ed. Stuttgart, XX-XL.

K.-H. Kohl (1977), "Edward Burnett Tylor (1832–1917)." In A. Michaels (ed.), *Klassiker der Religionswissenschaft.* München.

——— (1981), *Entzauberter Blick. Das Bild vom Guten Wilden und die Erfahrung der Zivilisation.* Berlin.

——— (1987), *Abwehr und Verlangen. Zur Geschichte der Ethnologie.* Frankfurt/M.

A. Kuper (1988), *The Invention of Primitive Society. Transformations of an Illusion.* New York.

A. Lang (1898), *The Making of Religion.* London.

J. Leopold (1980), *Culture in Comparative and Evolutionary Perspective. E. B. Tylor and the Making of Primitive Culture.* Berlin.

R. H. Lowie (1937), *The History of Ethnological Theory.* New York.

J. F. McLennan (1869, 1870), "The Worship of Animals and Plants." *Fortnightly Review* 6:407–27; 7:194–216.

——— (1896) [1876], *Studies in Ancient History*, 2nd ed. edited by his widow and A. Platt. New York.

——— (1970) [1965], *Primitive Marriage. An Inquiry into the Origin of the Form of Capture in Marriage Ceremonies.* Chicago.

R. R. Marett (1936), *Tylor.* London.

——— (1941), *A Jerseyman at Oxford.* London.

F. M. Müller (1883), *India, What Can It Teach Us.* London.

——— (1884), *Indien in seiner Weltgeschichtlichen Bedeutung.* Leipzig.

R. A. Segal (1955), "Tylor's Anthropomorphic Theory of Religion." *Religion* 25:23–30.

J. Skorupski (1976), *Symbol and Theory. A Philosophical Study of Theories of Religion in Social Anthropology.* New York.

G. E. Smith (1933), *The Diffusion of Culture.* London.

G. W. Stocking, Jr. (1966), *After Tylor.* Madison.

—— (1968a), "Arnold, Tylor and the Uses of Invention." In *Race, Culture, and Evolution*, 69–90. New York.

—— (1968b), "Tylor, Edward Burnett." *IESS* 16:170–77. New York.

—— (1971), "Animism in Theory and Practice. E. B. Tylor's unpublished 'Notes on Spriritualism.'" *Man* 6:88–104.

—— (1987), *Victorian Anthropology*. New York.

F. M. Turner (1974), *Between Science and Religion. The Reaction to Scientific Naturalism in Late Victorian England*. New Haven.

E. B. Tylor (1863), "Wild Men and Beast-Children." *The Anthropological Review* 1:21–32.

—— (1866a), "The Religion of Savages." *Fortnightly Review* 6:71–86.

—— (1866b), "The Science of Language." Review of four books, including F. M. Müller, *Lectures on the Science of Language. Quarterly Review* 119:394–435.

—— (1866–69a), "On the Survival of Savage Thought in Modern Civilization." *Proceedings of the Royal Institution of Great Britain* 5:522–35.

—— (1866–69b), "On Traces of the Early Mental Condition of Man." *Proceedings of the Royal Institution of Great Britain* 5:83–93.

—— (1868a), Review of F. M. Müller, *Chips from a German Workshop. Fortnightly Review* N.S. 3:225–28.

—— (1868b), "Wilhelm von Humboldt." *Quarterly Review* 124:504–24.

—— (1869–70), "The Philosophy of Religion among the Lower Races of Mankind." *Journal of the Ethnological Society* N.S. 2:369–379.

—— (1877), "Mr. Spencer's 'Principles of Sociology.'" *Mind. A Quarterly Review* 6:141–56.

—— (1881), *Anthropology. An Introduction to the Study of Man and Civilization*. London.

—— (1899), "Remarks on Totemism, with Special Reference to Some Modern Theories Respecting It." *Journal of the Anthropological Institute* 28:138–48.

—— (1958) [1871], *Primitive Culture. Researches into the Development of Mythology, Philosophy, Religion, Art, and Custom*. Reprinted as *The Origins of Culture* (Vol. 1); *Religion in Primitive Culture* (Vol. 2). New York.

—— (1960) [1889], "On a Method of Investigating the Development of Institutions, Applied to Laws of Marriage and Descent." *Journal of the Anthropological Institute* 18:245–72. Reprinted in F. W. Moore (ed.), *Readings in Cross-Cultural Methodology*. New Haven.

—— (1964) [1865], *Researches into the Early History of Mankind and the Development of Civilization*, abridged ed. P. Bohannan. Chicago.

CHAPTER 5

ON THE ORIGIN OF ALL SOCIAL OBLIGATIONS: THE RITUAL OF SACRIFICE

R. Ackerman (1991), *The Myth and Ritual School. J. G. Frazer and the Cambridge Ritualists*. New York.

T. O. Beidelman (1974), *W. Robertson Smith and the Sociological Study of Religion*. Chicago.

J. S. Black and G. Chrystal (1912), *The Life of William Robertson Smith*. London.

F. Boas (1949) [1896], "The Limitations of the Comparative Method of Anthropology." In *Race, Language and Culture*, 270–80. New York.

W. M. Calder III (ed.) (1991), *The Cambridge Ritualists Reconsidered*. Atlanta.

É. Durkheim (1995), *The Elementary Forms of Religious Life*, trans. Karen E. Fields. New York.

J. G. Frazer (1894), "William Robertson Smith." *Fortnightly Review* N.S. 55:800–807.

A. A. Goldenweiser (1910), "Totemism, An Analytical Study." *Journal of American Folklore* 23:179–293.

J. Henninger (1955), "Ist der sogenannte Nilus-Bericht eine brauchbare religionsgeschichtliche Quelle?" *Anthropos* 50:81–148.

T. Hobbes (1968) [1651], *Leviathan*. New York.

G. Hubert and M. Mauss (1972) [1902–3], "Esquisse d'une théorie générale de la magie." In *A General Theory of Magic*, trans. Robert Brain. Boston.

R. A. Jones (1981), "Robertson Smith, Durkheim, and Sacrifice. An Historical Context for the Elementary Forms of the Religious Life." *Journal of the History of Behavioral Sciences* 17:184–205.

——— (1984), "Robertson Smith and James Frazer on Religion. Two Traditions in British Social Anthropology." In G. W. Stocking, Jr. (ed.), *Functionalism Historicized*, 31–58. Madison.

——— (1986), "Durkheim, Frazer, and Smith. The Role of Analogies and Exemplars in the Development of Durkheim's Sociology of Religion." *AJS* 92:596–627.

K.-H. Kohl (1987), *Abwehr und Verlangen. Zur Geschichte der Ethnologie*. Frankfurt/M.

A. Kuper (1988), *The Invention of Primitive Society. Transformations of an Illusion*. New York.

J. F. MacLennan (1869, 1870), "The Worship of Animals and Plants." *Fortnightly Review* 6:407–27; 7:194–216.

——— (1896) [1876], *Studies in Ancient History*. 2nd ed. by his widow and A. Platt. New York.

——— (1970) [1865], *Primitive Marriage. An Inquiry into the Origin of the Form of Capture in Marriage Ceremonies*, ed. P. Rivière. Chicago.

A. Newman (1993), "The Death of Judaism in German Protestant Thought from Luther to Hegel." *JAAR* 61:455–84.

L. Perlitt (1965), *Vatke und Wellhausen. Geschichtsphilosophische Voraussetzungen und historiographische Motive für die Darstellung der Religion und Geschichte Israels durch Wilhelm Vatke und Julius Wellhausen*. Berlin.

R. Rendtorff (1967), *Studien zur Geschichte des Opfers im Alten Israel*. Neukirchen-Vluyn.

R. Smend (1987), "Wellhausen in Göttingen." In B. Moeller (ed.), *Theologie in Göttingen*, 306–24. Göttingen.

W. R. Smith (1870), "The Question of Prophecy in the Critical Schools of the Continent." In Smith 1912, 163–203.

——— (1875), "Bible." *Ency. Brit.* 9th ed., 3:634–48.

——— (1880), "Animal Worship and Animal Tribes among the Arabs and in the Old Testament." *JP*, 9:75–100.

—— (1885), *Kinship and Marriage in Early Arabia*. Cambridge.

—— (1886), "Sacrifice." *Ency. Brit.* 9th ed., 21:132–38.

—— (1894) [1881], *The Old Testament in the Jewish Church. A Course of Lectures on Biblical Criticism*. 2nd ed. London.

—— (1894), *Lectures on the Religion of the Semites*. First Series. *The Fundamental Institutions*. Burnett Lectures. 2nd ed. London.

—— (1912), *Lectures and Essays of William Robertson Smith*, ed. J. S. Black and G. Chrystal. London.

—— (1995), *Lectures on the Religion of the Semites*. Second and Third Series, ed. J. Day. Sheffield.

F. Steiner (1967) [1956], *Taboo*. Harmondsworth.

G. W. Stocking, Jr. (1987), *Victorian Anthropology*. New York.

—— (1996), *After Tylor*. Madison.

J. Wellhausen (1878), *Geschichte Israels*. Berlin.

—— (1880), "Israel." *Ency. Brit.* 9th ed., 13:396–431.

—— (1884), *Abriss der Geschichte Israels und Juda's. Skizzen und Vorarbeiten*, vol. 1. Berlin.

—— (1887), *Reste arabischen Heidentums*. Berlin.

—— (1957), *Prolegomena to the History of Ancient Israel*. New York.

CHAPTER 6
UNDER CIVILIZATION: THE MENACING REALM OF MAGIC

R. Ackerman (1975), "Frazer on Myth and Ritual." *JHI* 36:115–34.

—— (1983), "From Philology to Anthropology. The Case of J. G. Frazer." In M. Bollack et al. (eds.), *Philologie und Hermeneutik im 19. Jahrhundert II*, 423–39. Göttingen.

—— (1987a), *J. G. Frazer. His Life and Work*. Cambridge.

—— (1987b), "Frazer, James G." *ER* 5:414–16.

—— (1991), *The Myth and Ritual School. J. G. Frazer and the Cambridge Ritualists*. New York.

A. Assmann (1991), "Das Gedächtnis der Moderne am Beispiel von T. S. Eliots 'The Waste Land.'" In H. G. Kippenberg and B. Luchesi (eds.), *Religionswissenschaft und Kulturkritik. Beiträge zur Konferenz 'The History of Religions and Critique of Culture in the Days of Gerardus van der Leeuw (1890–1950),'* 373–90. Marburg.

M. Beard (1992), "Frazer, Leach, and Virgil. The Popularity (and Unpopularity) of 'The Golden Bough.'" *CSSH* 34:203–24.

G. Beer (1983), *Darwin's Plots. Evolutionary Narratives in Darwin, George Eliot and Nineteenth-Century Fiction*. London.

—— (1990), "Speaking for the Others. Relativism and Authority in Victorian Anthropological Literature." In R. Fraser 1990b, 38–60.

J. P. Bishop (1948), "The Golden Bough." In *The Collected Essays*, 23–36. New York.

T. S. Eliot (1958) [1930], *The Waste Land*. New York.

E. E. Evans-Pritchard (1962), "The Divine Kingship of the Shilluk of the Nilotic Sudan." In *Essays in Social Anthropology*, 66–86. London.

—— (1965), *Theories of Primitive Religion*. Oxford.

R. Fraser (1990a), *The Making of 'The Golden Bough.' The Origins and Growth of an Argument*. London.

—— (ed.) (1990b), *Sir James Frazer and the Literary Imagination. Essays in Affinity and Influence*. London.

J. G. Frazer (1885–86), "On Certain Burial Customs as Illustrative of the Primitive Theory of the Soul." *JRAI* 15:64–101.

—— (1890), *The Golden Bough. A Study in Comparative Religion*. 2 vols. New York. 2nd ed. (1900), *The Golden Bough. A Study in Magic and Religion*. 3 vols. New York. 3rd ed. (1911–15). 12 vols. New York.

—— (1894), "William Robertson Smith." *Fortnightly Review* N.S. 55:800–807.

—— (1910), *Totemism and Exogamy. A Treatise on Certain Early Forms of Superstition and Society*. 4 vols. London.

—— (1963) [1922], *The Golden Bough. A Study in Magic and Religion*. Abridged ed. London.

—— (1968) [1913], "The Scope of Social Anthropology." In *Psyche's Task. A Discourse Concerning the Influence of Superstition on the Growth of Institutions*. 2nd ed. London.

J. Grimm (1882) [1835], *Deutsche Mythologie*, trans. James Steven Stallybrass. London.

J. E. Harrison (1925), *Reminiscences of a Student's Life*. 2nd ed. London.

S. E. Hyman (1974), *The Tangled Bank. Darwin, Marx, Frazer and Freud as Imaginative Writers*. New York.

J. Jacobs (1890), "Recent Research in Comparative Religion." *Folkl.* 1:384–97.

H. James (ed.) (1969) [1920], *The Letters of William James*. 2 vols. London.

R. A. Jones (1984), "Robertson Smith and James Frazer on Religion. Two Traditions in British Social Anthropology." In G. W. Stocking, Jr. (ed.), *Functionalism Historicized*, 31–58. Madison.

—— (1986), "Durkheim, Frazer, and Smith. The Role of Analogies and Exemplars in the Development of Durkheim's Sociology of Religion." *AJS* 92:596–627.

E. R. Leach (1965), "Frazer and Malinowski." *Encounter* 25:24–36.

S. MacCormack (1984), "Magic and the Human Mind. A Reconsideration of Frazer's Golden Bough." *Arethusa* 17:151–76.

W. Mannhardt (1865), *Roggenwolf und Roggenhund. Beitrag zur Germanischen Sittenkunde*. Danzig.

—— (1868), *Die Korndämonen. Beitrag zur Germanischen Sittenkunde*. Berlin.

—— (1875, 1876), *Wald- und Feldkulte*. Vol. 1, *Der Baumkultus der Germanen und ihrer Nachbarstämme*. Vol. 2, *Antike Wald- und Feldkulte aus nordeuropäischer Überlieferung erläutert*. Berlin.

K. Scheuermann (1933), *Wilhelm Mannhardt. Seine Bedeutung für die vergleichende Religionsforschung*. Giessen.

C. G. Seligman (1911), "The Cult of Nyakang and the Divine Kings of the Shilluk." *Report of the Wellcome Tropical Research Laboratories at the Gordon Memorial College, Khartoum* 3:216–32.

J. Z. Smith (1978), "When the Bough Breaks." In *Map Is Not Territory. Studies in the History of Religions*, 208–39. Leiden.

G. W. Stocking, Jr. (1987), *Victorian Anthropology*. New York.
—— (1996), *After Tylor*. Madison.
J. B. Vickery (1973), *The Literary Impact of the Golden Bough*. Princeton.
I. Weber-Kellermann (1965), *Erntebrauch in der ländlichen Arbeitswelt des 19. Jahrhunderts*. Marburg.
J. Whitman (1984), "From Philology to Anthropology in Mid-Nineteenth-Century Germany." In G. W. Stocking, Jr. (ed.), *Functionalism Historicized*, 214–29. Madison.
L. Wittgenstein (1975), "Bemerkungen über Frazers 'The Golden Bough.'" In R. Wiggershaus (ed.), *Sprachanalyse und Soziologie*, 37–57. Frankfurt/M. Trans. A. C. Miles (1979). Atlantic Highlands, N.J.

CHAPTER 7
THE UNFATHOMABLE DEPTHS OF LIFE IN THE MIRROR
OF HELLENIC RELIGION

R. Ackerman (1971), "Some Letters of the Cambridge Ritualists." *GRBS* 12:113–36.
—— (1972), "Jane Ellen Harrison. The Early Work." *GRBS* 13:209–30.
—— (1987), *J. G. Frazer. His Life and Work*. Cambridge.
—— (1991a), "The Cambridge Group. Origins and Composition." In W. M. Calder III (ed.), *The Cambridge Ritualists Reconsidered*, 1–19. Atlanta.
—— (1991b), "Introduction." In J. E. Harrison, *Prolegomena to the Study of Greek Religion*. Princeton.
—— (1991c), *The Myth and Ritual School. J. G. Frazer and the Cambridge Ritualists*. New York.
T. W. Africa (1991), "Aunt Glegg among the Dons or Taking Jane Harrison at Her Word." In W. M. Calder III (ed.), *The Cambridge Ritualists Reconsidered*, 21–35. Atlanta.
M. L. Bäumer (1965), "Die romantische Epiphanie des Dionysos." *Monatshefte* 57:225–36.
—— (1977), "Das moderne Phänomen des Dionysischen und seine 'Entdeckung' durch Nietzsche." *Nietzsche-Studien* 6:123–53.
E. Behler (1983), "Die Auffassung des Dionysischen durch die Brüder Schlegel und Friedrich Nietzsche." *Nietzsche-Studien* 12:335–54.
S. Breuer (1995), *Ästhetischer Fundamentalismus. Stefan George und der deutsche Antimodernismus*. Darmstadt.
W. W. Briggs and W. M. Calder III (eds.) (1990), *Classical Scholarship. A Biographical Encyclopedia*. New York.
W. Burkert (1980), "Griechische Mythologie und die Geistesgeschichte der Moderne." *Les études classiques aux XIXe et XXe siècles: leur place dans l'histoire des idées*, 159–99. Geneva.
W. M. Calder III (ed.) (1991), *The Cambridge Ritualists Reconsidered*. Atlanta.
H. Cancik (1985), "Erwin Rohde. Ein Philologe der Bismarckzeit." *Semper Apertus. Festschrift der Universität Heidelberg*, 436–505. Berlin and Heidelberg.
A. B. Cook (1914), *Zeus. A Study in Ancient Religion*. 2 vols. Cambridge.

F. M. Cornford (1912), *From Religion to Philosophy. A Study in the Origins of Western Speculation.* With a foreword by R. Ackerman. Princeton.

O. Crusius (1902), *Erwin Rohde. Ein biographischer Versuch.* Tübingen and Leipzig.

M. Detienne (1985), "Die skandalöse Mythologie (oder: Projekt einer Arbeit über das zweideutige Wesen der sogenannten Mythologie)." In R. Schlesier (ed.), *Faszination des Mythos*, 13–34. Basel and Frankfurt/M.

H.-G. Drescher (1991), *Ernst Troeltsch. Leben und Werk.* Göttingen.

N. Elias (1977) [1936], *Über den Prozeß der Zivilisation. Soziogenetische und psychogenetische Untersuchungen.* 2 vols. Frankfurt/M.

O. Fambach (1957), *Schiller und sein Kreis.* Berlin.

H. Freier (1976), *Die Rückkehr der Götter. Von der Ästhetischen Überschreitung der Wissensgrenze zur Mythologie der Moderne.* Stuttgart.

E. Friedell (1929), *Kulturgeschichte der Neuzeit.* 2 vols. München.

M. Fuhrmann (1979), "Die *Querelle des Anciens et des Modernes,* der Nationalismus und die deutsche Klassik." In R. R. Bolgar (ed.), *Classical Influences on Western Thought, A.D. 1650–1870*, 107–29. Cambridge.

A. van Gennep (1960), *The Rites of Passage.* Chicago.

M. Gerhard (1950), *Schiller.* Bern.

——— (1959), "Antike Götterwelt in Wielands und in Schillers Sicht: Zur Entstehung und Auffassung der 'Götter Griechenlands'." In J. R. Frey (ed.), *Schiller 1759/1959*, 1–11. Urbana.

P. Goessler (1951), *Wilhelm Dörpfeld. Ein Leben im Dienst der Antike.* Stuttgart.

K. Gründer (ed.) (1969), *Der Streit um Nietzsches 'Geburt der Tragödie.' Die Schriften von E. Rohde, R. Wagner, U. v. Wilamowitz-Möllendorf.* Hildesheim.

——— (1971), "Apollinisch/dionysisch," *Historisches Wörterbuch der Philosophie*, 1:441–45. Basel and Stuttgart.

P. Guiraud (1896), *Fustel de Coulanges.* Paris.

J. E. Harrison (1890), *Mythology & Monuments of Ancient Athens. Being a Translation of a Portion of the "Attica" of Pausanias by Margaret de G. Verrall.* New York.

——— (1909), "The Influence of Darwinism on the Study of Religions." In A. C. Seward (ed.), *Darwin and Modern Science*, 494–511. Cambridge.

——— (1915), *Alpha and Omega.* London.

——— (1925), *Reminiscences of a Student's Life.* London.

——— (1963) [1912, 1927], *Themis. A Study of the Social Origins of Greek Religion.* London.

——— (1991) [1903, 1922], *Prolegomena to the Study of Greek Religion.* Princeton.

H. Heine (1994), "Die Götter im Exil." *Werke in vier Bänden*, 2:835–56. Frankfurt/M.

A. Henrichs (1984), "Loss of Self, Suffering, Violence. The Modern View of Dionysos from Nietzsche to Girard." *HSCP* 88:205–40.

——— (1987), *Die Götter Griechenlands. Ihr Bild im Wandel der Religionswissenschaft.* Thyssen Vorträge 5. Bamberg.

H. R. Jauß (1974), *Literaturgeschichte als Provokation.* Frankfurt/M.

G. Murray (1975) [1912, 1925], *Four Stages of Greek Religion.* 2nd ed., *Five Stages of Greek Religion.* New York.

F. Nietzsche (1980) [1872], *Sämtliche Werke*. Kritische Studienausgabe in 15 Bänden. München.

—— (1996), *Human, All Too Human*, trans. R. J. Hollingdale. Cambridge.

H. C. Payne (1978), "Modernizing the Ancients. The Reconstruction of Ritual Drama, 1870–1920." *PAPS* 122:182–92.

S. J. Peacock (1988), *Jane Ellen Harrison. The Mask and the Self*. New Haven.

E. Rohde (1895), "Die Religion der Griechen." *Universität Heidelberg, Gelegenheitsschriften*. Heidelberg.

—— (1991) [1898], *Psyche. Seelencult und Unsterblichkeitsglaube der Griechen*. Darmstadt.

R. Schlesier (1990), "Jane Ellen Harrison." In W. W. Briggs and W. M. Calder III (eds.), *Classical Scholarship. A Biographical Encyclopedia*, 127–41. New York.

—— (1991), "Prolegomena to Jane Harrisons's Interpretation of Ancient Greek Religion." In W. M. Calder III (ed.), *The Cambridge Ritualists Reconsidered*, 185–226. Atlanta.

—— (1994), *Kulte, Mythen und Gelehrte. Anthropologie der Antike seit 1800*. Frankfurt.

E. Troeltsch (1895, 1896), "Die Selbständigkeit der Religion." *ZThK* 5:361–436; *ZThK* 6:167–218.

E. B. Tylor (1958) [1871], *Primitive Culture. Researches into the Development of Mythology, Philosophy, Religion, Art, and Custom*. Reprinted as *The Origin of Culture* (Vol. 1) and *Religion in Primitive Culture* (Vol. 2). New York.

M. Vogel (1966), *Apollinisch und Dionysisch. Geschichte eines genialen Irrtums*. Regensburg.

B. von Wiese (1956), *Die deutsche Lyrik. Form und Geschichte*. Düsseldorf.

R. Williams (1976), *Keywords. A Vocabulary of Culture and Society*. London.

CHAPTER 8
THE PRODUCTIVE FORCE OF WORLD REJECTION

F. Boas (1949) [1896], "The Limitations of the Comparative Method of Anthropology." In *Race, Language and Culture*, 270–80. New York.

W. Bodenstein (1959), *Neige des Historismus. Ernst Troeltschs Entwicklungsgang*. Gütersloh.

W. Bousset (1892), *Jesu Predigt in ihrem Gegensatz zum Judentum. Ein religionsgeschichtlicher Vergleich*. Göttingen.

—— (1904), "Die Religionsgeschichte und das neue Testament." *ThR* 7:265–77, 311–18, 353–65.

—— (1906), *Das Wesen der Religion*. Halle.

—— (1907), *Hauptprobleme der Gnosis*. Göttingen.

—— (1909), "Kantisch-Friessche Religionsphilosophie und ihre Anwendung auf die Theologie." *ThR* 12:419–36, 471–88.

—— (1924) [1903, 1906], *Die Religion des Judentums im späthellenistischen Zeitalter*, ed. H. Gressmann. Tübingen.

—— (1979) [1919], "Religion und Theologie." In A. F. Verheule (ed.), *Reli-*

gionsgeschichtliche Studien. Aufsätze zur Religionsgeschichte des Hellenistischen Zeitalters, 29–43. Leiden.

R. vom Bruch, F. W. Graf, G. Hübinger (eds.) (1989), *Kultur und Kulturwissenschaften um 1900. Krise der Moderne und Glaube an die Wissenschaft*. Stuttgart.

H.-G. Drescher (1991), *Ernst Troeltsch. Leben und Werk*. Göttingen.

F. W. Graf (1982), "Der 'Systematiker' der 'Kleinen Göttinger Fakultät.' Ernst Troeltschs Promotionsthesen und ihr Göttinger Kontext." In H. Renz and F. W. Graf (eds.), *Troeltsch-Studien*, vol. 1, *Untersuchungen zur Biographie und Werkgeschichte*, 235–90. Gütersloh.

—— (1984a), "Kulturprotestantismus. Zur Begriffsgeschichte einer theologiepolitischen Chiffre." *ABG* 28:214–68.

—— (1984b), "Religion und Individualität. Bemerkungen zu einem Grundproblem der Religionstheorie Ernst Troeltschs." In H. Renz and F. W. Graf (eds.), *Troeltsch-Studien*, vol. 3, *Protestantismus und Neuzeit*, 207–30. Gütersloh.

—— (1987), "Max Weber und die protestantische Theologie seiner Zeit." *ZRGG* 39:122–47.

—— (1988), "Ernst Troeltsch. Kulturgeschichte des Christentums." In N. Hammerstein (ed.), *Deutsche Geschichtswissenschaft um 1900*, 131–52. Stuttgart.

—— (1989), "Rettung der Persönlichkeit. Protestantische Theologie als Kulturwissenschaft des Christentums." In R. vom Bruch, F. W. Graf, and G. Hübinger (eds.), *Kultur und Kulturwissenschaften um 1900. Krise der Moderne und Glaube an die Wissenschaft*, 103–31. Stuttgart.

F. W. Graf and T. Rendtorff (eds.) (1933), *Ernst Troeltschs Soziallehren. Studien zu ihrer Interpretation*. Gütersloh.

F. W. Graf and H. Ruddies (1986), "Ernst Troeltsch. Geschichtsphilosophie in praktischer Absicht." In J. Speck (ed.), *Grundprobleme der großen Philosophen. Philosophie der Neuzeit IV*, 128–64. Göttingen.

H. Gressmann (1914), *Albert Eichhorn und die Religionsgeschichtliche Schule*. Göttingen.

—— (1923–24, 1926), "Die Umwandlung der orientalischen Religionen unter dem Einfluß hellenischen Geistes." *Vorträge der Bibliothek Warburg*, 170–95. Leipzig and Berlin.

H. Gunkel (1895), *Schöpfung und Chaos in Urzeit und Endzeit*. Göttingen.

—— (1903), *Zum religionsgeschichtlichen Verständnis des Neuen Testaments*. Göttingen.

—— (1904), "Besprechung M. Reischle, *Theologie und Religionsgeschichte*." *DLZ* 25:1100–10.

—— (1910), "Die Religionsgeschichte und die alttestamentliche Wissenschaft." *Fünfter Weltkongreß für Freies Christentum und religiösen Fortschritt*, 169–79. Berlin.

A. Harnack (1908), "Besprechung von W. Bousset, *Hauptprobleme der Gnosis*." *ThLZ* 33:10–13.

H. Jonas (1977), "A Retrospective View." In G. Widengren and D. Hellholm (eds.), *Proceedings of the International Colloquium on Gnosticism. Stockholm August 20–25, 1973*, 1–15. Stockholm.

G. Lüdemann (1987), "Die Religionsgeschichtliche Schule." In B. Moeller (ed.), *Theologie in Göttingen*, 325–61. Göttingen.

—— (1992), "Das Wissenschaftsverständnis der Religionsgeschichtlichen Schule im Rahmen des Kulturprotestantismus. Die Religionsgeschichtliche Schule und ihre Konsequenzen für die Neutestamentliche Wissenschaft." In H. M. Müller (ed.), *Kulturprotestantismus. Beiträge zu einer Gestalt des modernen Christentums*, 78–107, 311–38. Göttingen.

—— (ed.) (1996), *Die 'Religionsgeschichtliche Schule.' Facetten eines theologischen Umbruchs*. Frankfurt/M.

G. Lüdemann and M. Schröder (1988), *Die Religionsgeschichtliche Schule in Göttingen*. Göttingen.

G. F. Moore (1920–21), "Christian Writers on Judaism." *HThR* 14:197–254.

F. Overbeck (1919), *Christentum und Kultur*, ed. von C. A. Bernoulli. Basel.

W. Perpeet (1976), "Kulturphilosophie." *ABG* 20:42–99.

G. Pfleiderer (1992), *Theologie als Wirklichkeitswissenschaft. Studien zum Religionsbegriff bei Georg Wobbermin, Rudolf Otto, Heinrich Scholz und Max Scheler*. Tübingen.

H. Rollmann (1982), "Duhm, Lagarde, Ritschl und der irrationale Religionsbegriff der Religionsgeschichtlichen Schule. Die Vita hospitis Heinrich Hackmanns als geistes- und theologiegeschichtliches Dokument." *ZRGG* 34:276–79.

A. Schweitzer (1951) [1913], *Geschichte der Leben-Jesu-Forschung*. Tübingen.

H. Siebeck (1893), *Lehrbuch der Religionsphilosophie*. Freiburg and Leipzig.

J. Z. Smith (1990), *Drudgery Divine. On the Comparison of Early Christianities and the Religions of Late Antiquity*. Chicago.

C. P. Tiele (1897, 1899), *Elements of the Science of Religion*. Part 1, *Morphological*; Part 2, *Ontological*. Gifford Lectures. Edinburgh and London.

E. Troeltsch (1895, 1896), "Die Selbständigkeit der Religion." *ZThK* 5:361–436; 6:167–218.

—— (1902), *Die Absolutheit des Christentums und die Religionsgeschichte*. Tübingen and Leipzig.

—— (1910), "Erlösung II. Dogmatisch." In *Religion in Geschichte und Gegenwart*, 2:481–88. Tübingen.

—— (1912), *Die Soziallehren der christlichen Kirchen und Gruppen*. GS, vol. 1. Tübingen.

—— (1913) [1897], "Christentum und Religionsgeschichte." GS, 2:328–63. Tübingen.

J. Weiss (1964) [1892], *Die Predigt Jesu vom Reiche Gottes*, ed. F. Hahn. Göttingen.

—— (1971), *Jesus' Proclamation of the Kingdom of God*, trans. Richard Hyde Hiers and David Larrimore Holland. Philadelphia.

CHAPTER 9
COMPETING MODELS OF THE RECAPITULATION OF THE HISTORY OF RELIGION

H.-J. Braun, H. Holzhey, and W. Orth (eds.) (1988), *Über Ernst Cassirers Philosophie der symbolischen Formen*. Frankfurt/M.

E. Cassirer (1994), *Das Erkenntnisproblem in der Philosophie und Wissenschaft der neueren Zeit (1906–1950)*. Darmstadt.

———— (1994) [1923, 1925, 1929], *Philosophie der symbolischen Formen*. Part 1: *Die Sprache*; Part 2: *Das mythische Denken*; Part 3: *Phänomenologie der Erkenntnis*. Darmstadt.

W. Dilthey (1924) [1911], "Das Problem der Religion." GS, 6:288–305. Leipzig and Berlin.

———— (1957) [1907], "Die religiöse Weltanschauung und ihre Beziehungen zur philosophischen." In "Das Wesen der Philosophie," *Die Geistige Welt*. GS, 5:381–39. Stuttgart.

———— (1970) [1870], *Das Leben Schleiermachers*. GS, vol. 13. Stuttgart.

———— (1981) [1910, 1927], *Der Aufbau der geschichtlichen Welt in den Geisteswissenschaften*. Kritisch ed. von B. Groethuysen. Frankfurt/M.

H.-G. Drescher (1991), *Ernst Troeltsch. Leben und Werk*. Göttingen.

J. G. Droysen (1971) [1882], *Grundriss der Historik*. 3rd. ed. In J. G. Droysen, *Historik. Vorlesungen über Enzyklopädie und Methodologie der Geschichte*, ed. R. Hübner. 6th ed., 317–66. München.

É. Durkheim (1968) [1912], *The Elementary Forms of the Religious Life. A Study in Religious Sociology*, trans. Joseph Ward Swain. Glencoe.

F. Fellmann (1993), *Lebensphilosophie. Elemente einer Theorie der Selbsterfahrung*. Reinbek.

F. W. Graf (1988), "Die 'antihistoristische Revolution' in der protestantischen Theologie der zwanziger Jahre." In J. Rohls and G. Wenz (eds.), *Vernunft des Glaubens. Festschrift W. Pannenberg*, 377–405. Göttingen.

J. N. B. Hewitt (1902), "Orenda and a Definition of Religion." *AmA* N.S. 4:33–46.

H. Hubert (1904), "Introduction." In P.-D. Chantepie de la Saussaye (ed.), *Manuel d'Histoire des Religions*, V–XLVIII. Paris.

H. Hubert and M. Mauss (1972), *A General Theory of Magic*, trans. Robert Brain. Boston.

G. G. Iggers (1971), *Deutsche Geschichtswissenschaft*. München.

———— (1984), "The 'Methodenstreit' in International Perspective. The Reorientation of Historical Studies at the Turn from the Nineteenth to the Twentieth Century." *Storia della Storiografia* 6:21–32.

F. Jaeger and J. Rüsen (1992), *Geschichte des Historismus*. München.

H. Johach (1986), "Wilhelm Dilthey. Die Struktur der geschichtlichen Erfahrung." In J. Speck (ed.), *Grundprobleme der großen Philosophen. Philosophie der Neuzeit IV*, 52–90. Göttingen.

H. Kantorowicz (1937), "Savigny and the Historical School of Law." *LQR* 53:326–43.

G. van der Leeuw (1977) [1933], *Phänomenologie der Religion*) 4th ed. Tübingen.

H.-U. Lessing (1988), "Dilthey als Historiker. Das 'Leben Schleiermachers' als Paradigma." In N. Hammerstein (ed.), *Deutsche Geschichtswissenschaft um 1900*, 113–30. Stuttgart.

R. R. Marett (1909), "The tabu-mana Formula as a Minimum Definition of Religion." *ARW* 12:186–94.

———— (1914), *The Threshold of Religion*. 2nd ed. London.

———— (1914) [1900], "Pre-animistic Religion." In *The Threshold of Religion*, 1–28.

———— (1914) [1908], "A Sociological View of Comparative Religion." In *The Threshold of Religion*, 122–44.

———— (1920), "The Interpretation of Survivals." In *Psychology and Folklore*, 120–42. London.

———— (1936), *Tylor*. London.

———— (1941), *A Jerseyman at Oxford*. London.

F. Meinecke (1959), *Die Entstehung des Historismus*. München.

K. H. Metz (1984), " 'Der Methodenstreit in der deutschen Geschichtswissenschaft (1891–99)' ": Bemerkungen zum sozialen Kontext wissenschaftlicher Auseinandersetzungen." *Storia della Storiografia* 6:3–20.

F. Nietzsche (1998), *On the Use and Abuse of History for Life*, trans. Ian C. Johnston.

K. Nowak (1987), "Die 'antihistorische Revolution.' Symptome und Folgen der Krise historischer Weltorientierung nach dem Ersten Weltkrieg in Deutschland." In H. Renz and F. W. Graf (eds.), *Troeltsch-Studien 4. Umstrittene Moderne*, 133–71. Gütersloh.

R. Otto (1987) [1917], *Das Heilige. Über das Irrationale in der Idee des Göttlichen und sein Verhältnis zum Rationalen*. München.

K. Th. Preuss (1904, 1905), "Der Ursprung von Religion und Kunst." *Globus* 86:321–27; 87:333–37.

———— (1914), *Die geistige Kultur der Naturvölker*. Leipzig.

L. Raphael (1990), "Historikerkontroversen im Spannungsfeld zwischen Berufshabitus, Fächerkonkurrenz und sozialen Deutungsmustern. Lamprecht-Streit und französischer Methodenstreit der Jahrhundertwende in vergleichender Perspektive." *HZ* 251:325–63.

F. Rodi and H.-U. Lessing (eds.) (1984), Frankfurt/M.

M. Scheler (1954), "Probleme der Religion. Zur religiösen Erneuerung." GS, 5:101–354. *Vom Ewigen im Menschen*. 4th ed. Bern.

———— (1972) [1913], "Versuche einer Philosophie des Lebens. Nietzsche-Dilthey-Bergson." GS, 3:313–39. *Vom Umsturz der Werte*. 5th ed. Bern. Extracts reprinted in F. Rodi and H.-U. Lessing (eds.) (1984), *Materialien zur Philosophie Wilhelm Diltheys*, 88–94.

H. Schnädelbach (1983), *Philosophie in Deutschland 1831–1933*. Frankfurt/M.

E. J. Sharpe (1986), *Comparative Religion. A History*. 2nd ed. London.

W. R. Smith (1894) [1888–89], *Lectures on the Religion of the Semites. First Series. The Fundamental Institutions*. Burnett Lectures. 2nd ed. London.

N. Söderblom (1977) [1913], "Das Heilige (Allgemeines und Ursprüngliches)." In C. Colpe (ed.), *Die Diskussion um das "Heilige,"* 76–116. Darmstadt.

I. Strenski (1987), *Four Theories of Myth in the Twentieth-Century History. Cassirer, Eliade, Lévi-Strauss and Malinowski*. Iowa City.

E. Troeltsch (1922), "Die Krisis des Historismus." *Die neue Rundschau* 33:572–90.

———— (1924), *Der Historismus und seine Überwindung*. Berlin.

J. de Vries (1967), *The Study of Religion. A Historical Approach*. New York.

M. Weber (1922), *Grundriss der Sozialökonomie. III. Abteilung. Wirtschaft und Gesellschaft*. Tübingen.

———— (1988) [1904], "Die 'Objektivität' sozialwissenschaftlicher und sozialpolitischer Erkenntnis." *Gesammelte Aufsätze zur Wissenschaftslehre*, 146–214. Tübingen.

W. Windelband (1907) [1894], "Geschichte und Naturwissenschaft" (1894). *Präludien. Aufsätze und Reden zur Einleitung in die Philosophie*, 355–79. 3rd ed. Tübingen.

———— (1921) [1902], "Das Heilige. Skizze zur Religionsphilosophie." *Präludien. Aufsätze und Reden zur Philosophie und ihrer Geschichte*, 295–332. Tübingen. Abridged in C. Colpe (ed.) (1977), *Die Diskussion um das 'Heilige,'* 29–56. Darmstadt.

W. Wundt (1900–1919), *Völkerpsychologie. Eine Untersuchung der Entwicklungsgesetze von Sprache, Mythus und Sitte*. Leipzig.

CHAPTER 10
RELIGION AND THE SOCIAL BOND

W. Adorno (1967), *Introduction to E. Durkheim, Soziologie und Philosophie*. Frankfurt/M.

R. N. Bellah (1973), *Émile Durkheim on Morality and Society*. Chicago.

D. Bering (1982), *Die Intellektuellen. Geschichte eines Schimpfworts*. Berlin.

T. N. Clark (1981), "Die Durkheim-Schule und die Universität." In W. Lepenies (ed.), *Geschichte der Soziologie* 2:157–205. Frankfurt/M.

L. A. Coser (1971), *Masters of Sociological Thought. Ideas in Historical and Social Context*. New York.

S. Deploige (1923) [1911], *Le Conflit de la Morale et de la Sociologie*. 3rd ed. Paris.

E. Durkheim (1887), "La Philosophie dans les Universités allemandes." *Revue Internationale de l'Enseignement* 13:313–38, 423–40.

———— (1898), "Représentations individuelles et représentations collectives." *Revue de Metaphysique et de Morale* 6:273–302. Dt. Übers.

———— (1899), "De la définition des phénomènes religieux." *L'Année sociologique* 2:1–28.

———— (1933) [1893], *On the Division of Labor in Society*, trans. George Simpson. New York.

———— (1964) [1895], *The Rules of Sociological Method*, trans. Sarah A. Solovay and John H. Mueller. New York.

———— (1967), *Soziologie und Philosophie*, 45–83. Frankfurt/M.

———— (1968) [1912], *The Elementary Forms of the Religious Life. A Study in Religious Sociology*, trans. Joseph Ward Swain. Glencoe.

———— (1969), *Journal Sociologique*. Paris.

———— (1975), *Textes*, vol. 2, *Religion, morale, anomalie*. Paris.

———— (1976) [1914], "Der Dualismus der menschlichen Natur und seine sozialen Beziehungen." In F. Jonas (ed.), *Geschichte der Soziologie* 2:368–80. Reinbek.

———— (1983) [1897], *Suicide. A Study in Sociology*, trans. John A. Spaulding and George Simpson. Ed. with an introduction by George Simpson. New York.

———— (1985), "On Totemism." *History of Sociology* 5:91–121.

—————— (1986) [1898], "Der Individualismus und die Intellektuellen." In H. Bertram (ed.), *Gesellschaftlicher Zwang und moralische Autonomie*, 54–70. Frankfurt/M.

—————— (1986–87a), "Correspondance with Deploige." *History of Sociology* 6/7:253–66.

—————— (1986–87b), "The Positive Science of Ethics in Germany." *History of Sociology* 6/7:191–251.

E. Durkheim and M. Mauss (1901–2), "De quelques formes primitives de classification. Contribution à l'étude des représentations collectives." *L' Année sociologique* 6:1–72.

N. D. Fustel de Coulanges (n.d.) [1866], *The Ancient City*. Garden City, N.Y.

A. Giddens (1965), "The Suicide Problem in French Sociology." *BJS* 16:1–18.

—————— (1971), "The 'Individual' in the Writings of Durkheim." *European Journal of Sociology* 12:210–28.

P. Gisbert (1959), "Social Facts in Durkheim's System." *Anthropos* 54:353–69.

A. A. Goldenweiser (1910), "Totemism, an Analytical Study." *Journal of American Folkore* 23:179–293.

H. Hubert and M. Mauss (1978) [1902–3], "Esquisse d'une théorie générale de la magie."*In A General Theory of Magic*, trans. Robert Brain. Boston.

—————— (1964), *Sacrifice. Its Nature and Function*. London.

H. James (ed.) (1969) [1920], *The Letters of William James*. Reprint.

R. A. Jones (1981), "Einen soziologischen Klassiker verstehen." In W. Lepenies (ed.), *Geschichte der Soziologie* 1:137–97.

—————— (1986), "Durkheim, Frazer, and Smith. The Role of Analogies and Exemplars in the Development of Durkheim's Sociology of Religion." *AJS* 92:596–627.

—————— (1986–87) [1887], "Durkheim and the Positive Science of Ethics in Germany. Introduction to a Translation of Émile Durkheim's 'La Science Positive de la Morale en Allemagne.'" *History of Sociology* 6/7:177–89.

W. Lepenies (ed.) (1981), *Geschichte der Soziologie*. Frankfurt/M.

—————— (1989), "Gefährliche Wahlverwandtschaften." In *Gefährliche Wahlverwandtschaften. Essays zur Wissenschaftsgeschichte*, 80–110. Stuttgart.

S. Lukes (1973), *Émile Durkheim. His Life and Work. A Historical and Critical Study*. Harmondsworth.

—————— (1975), "Political Ritual and Social Integration." *Sociology* 9:289–308.

J. F. MacLennan (1869, 1870), "The Worship of Animals and Plants." *Fortnightly Review* 6:407–27; 7:194–216.

M. Mauss (1923–24), "Essai sur le don. Forme et raison de l'échange dans les sociétés archaiques." *L'Année sociologique*. N.S. 1:30–186.

—————— (1968–69), *Oeuvres*. Paris.

—————— (1978), *Soziologie und Anthropologie*. 2 vols. Frankfurt/M.

—————— (1985) [1938], "A Category of the Human Mind. The Notion of Person; the Notion of Self." In M. Carrithers, S. Collins, and S. Lukes (eds.), *The Category of the Person. Anthropology, Philosophy, History*, 1–25. Cambridge.

A. Momigliano (1994), *Studies on Modern Scholarship*, ed. G. W. Bowersock and T. J. Cornell. Berkeley.

R. Nisbet (1968) [1952], "Conservatism and Sociology." In *Tradition and Revolt. Historical and Sociological Essays*, 73–89. New York.

—— (1974), *The Sociology of Emile Durkheim*. Oxford.

A. von Oettingen (1882), *Die Moralstatistik in ihrer Bedeutung für eine christliche Socialethik*. Erlangen.

W. S. F. Pickering (ed.) (1975), *Durkheim on Religion. A Selection of Readings with Bibliographies and Introductory Remarks*. Boston.

—— (1984), *Durkheim's Sociology of Religion. Themes and Theories*. London.

E. Poulat (1987), *Liberté, Laïcité. La guerre des deux France et le principe de la modernité*. Paris.

U. Raulff (1989), "Die Geburt eines Begriffs. Reden von 'Mentalität' zur Zeit der Affäre Dreyfus." In V. Raulff (ed.), *Mentalitäten-Geschichte*, 50–68. Berlin.

K. Rudolph (1962), *Die Religionsgeschichte an der Leipziger Universität und die Entwicklung der Religionswissenschaft. Ein Beitrag zur Wissenschaftsgeschichte und zum Problem der Religion*. Berlin.

B. Spencer and F. J. Gillen (1899), *The Native Tribes of Central Australia*. London.

—— (1904), *The Northern Tribes of Central Australia*. London.

H. Treiber (1993), "Zur Genealogie einer 'Science Positive de la Morale en Allemagne.'" *Nietzsche-Studien* 22:165–221.

H. Ulrici (1879), "Der sogenannte Spiritismus. Eine wissenschaftliche Frage." *Zeitschrift für Philosophie und philosophische Kritik* 74:239–71.

W. P. Vogt (1981) [1976], "Über den Nutzen des Studiums primitiver Gesellschaften. Eine Anmerkung zur Durkheim-Schule 1890–1940." In W. Lepenies (ed.), *Geschichte der Soziologie* 3:276–97.

W. Wundt (1886), *Ethik. Eine Untersuchung der Thatsachen und Gesetze des sittlichen Lebens*. Stuttgart.

—— (1885) [1879], "Der Spiritismus." In *Essays*, 342–366. Leipzig.

CHAPTER 11
THE GREAT PROCESS OF DISENCHANTMENT

K.-L. Ay (1995), "Nachwirkungen der Konfessionalisierung in Wortkultur und Wirtschaftsethik deutscher Regionen." *SI* 33:19–47.

J. Benda (1955) [1927], *The Betrayal of the Intellectuals*, trans. Richard Aldington. Introduction by Herbert Read. Boston.

D. Bering (1982), *Die Intellektuellen. Geschichte eines Schimpfworts*. Berlin.

S. Breuer (1995), *Ästhetischer Fundamentalismus. Stefan George und der deutsche Antimodernismus*. Darmstadt.

—— (1995), "Das Syndikat der Seelen. Stefan George und sein Kreis." In H. Treiber and K. Sauerland (eds.) (1995), *Heidelberg im Schnittpunkt intellektueller Kreise*, 328–75. Opladen.

J. Deininger (1988), "'Die sozialen Gründe des Untergangs der antiken Kultur.' Bemerkungen zu Max Webers Vortrag von 1896." In P. Kneissl and V. Losemann (eds.), *Alte Geschichte und Wissenschaftsgeschichte. Festschrift für Karl Christ zum 65. Geburtstag*, 95–112. Darmstadt.

H.-G. Drescher (1991), *Ernst Troeltsch. Leben und Werk*. Göttingen.

R. van Dülmen (1988), "Protestantismus und Kapitalismus. Max Webers

These im Licht der neueren Sozialgeschichte." In C. Gneuss and J. Kocka (eds.), *Max Weber. Ein Symposion*, 88–101. München.

W. Gephart (1993), "Max Weber als Philosoph? Philosophische Grundlagen und Bezüge Max Webers im Spiegel neuerer Studien und Materialien." *PhR* 40:34–56.

E. Gothein (1970) [1892], *Wirtschaftsgeschichte des Schwarzwaldes und der angrenzenden Landschaften*. New York.

F. W. Graf (1993), "The German Theological Sources and Protestant Church Politics." In H. Lehmann and G. Roth (eds.), *Weber's Protestant Ethic. Origins, Evidence, Contexts*, 27–49. Cambridge.

E. Hanke (1993a), "Das 'spezifisch intellektualistische Erlösungsbedürfnis.' Oder: Warum Intellektuelle Tolstoi lasen." In G. Hübinger and W. J. Mommsen (eds.), *Intellektuelle im Deutschen Kaiserreich*, 158–71. Frankfurt/M.

——— (1993b), *Prophet des Unmodernen. Leo N. Tolstoi als Kulturkritiker in der deutschen Diskussion der Jahrhundertwende*. Tübingen.

P. Honigsheim (1985) [1963], "Max Weber in Heidelberg." In R. König and J. Winckelmann (eds.), *Max Weber zum Gedächtnis. Materialien und Dokumente zur Bewertung von Werk und Persönlichkeit*, 161–271. Opladen.

G. Hübinger and W. J. Mommsen (eds.) (1993), *Intellektuelle im Deutschen Kaiserreich*. Frankfurt/M.

G. Jellinek (1919) [1895], *Die Erklärung der Menschen- und Bürgerrechte*. München und Leipzig.

É. Karádi (1988), "Erst Bloch und Georg Lukács im Max Weber-Kreis." In W. J. Mommsen and W. Schwentker (eds.), *Max Weber und seine Zeitgenossen*, 682–702. Göttingen.

H. G. Kippenberg (1989), "Intellektuellen-Religion." In P. Antes and D. Pahnke (eds.), *Die Religion von Oberschichten. Religion–Profession–Intellektualismus*, 181–201. Marburg.

——— (1991), *Die vorderasiatischen Erlösungsreligionen in ihrem Zusammenhang mit der antiken Stadtherrschaft*. Frankfurt/M.

——— (1993), "Max Weber im Kreise von Religionswissenschaftlern." *ZRGG* 45:348–66.

R. König and J. Winckelmann (eds.) (1985), *Max Weber zum Gedächtnis. Materialien und Dokumente zur Bewertung von Werk und Persönlichkeit*. Opladen.

V. Krech and H. Tyrell (eds.) (1995), *Religionssoziologie um 1900*. Würzburg.

G. Küenzlen (1980), *Die Religionssoziologie Max Webers. Eine Darstellung ihrer Entwicklung*. Berlin.

H. Lehmann (1988), "Asketischer Protestantismus und ökonomischer Rationalismus. Die Weber-These nach zwei Generationen." In W. Schluchter (ed.), *Max Webers Sicht des okzidentalen Christentums Interpretation und Kritik*, 529–53.

——— (1996), *Max Webers "Protestantische Ethik."* Göttingen.

H. Lehmann and G. Roth (eds.) (1993), *Weber's Protestant Ethic. Origins, Evidence, Contexts*. Cambridge.

M. R. Lepsius and W. J. Mommsen, in cooperation with B. Rudhard and M. Schön (eds.) (1990), *Max Weber. Briefe 1906–1908*. Max-Weber-Gesamtausgabe II/5. Tübingen.

K. Lichtblau (1996), *Kulturkrise und Soziologie um die Jahrhundertwende. Zur Genealogie der Kultursoziologie in Deutschland.* Frankfurt/M.

M. Löwy (1976), *Pour une sociologie des intellectuels révolutionnaires. L'évolution politique de Lukács.* Paris.

W. J. Mommsen (1974a), *The Age of Bureaucracy. Perspectives on the Political Sociology of Max Weber.* Oxford.

—— (1974b), *Max Weber. Gesellschaft, Politik und Geschichte.* Frankfurt/M.

—— (1985), "Max Weber. Persönliche Lebensführung und gesellschaftlicher Wandel. Versuch einer Rekonstruktion des Begriffs der Geschichte bei Max Weber." In P. Alter, W. J. Mommsen, and T. Nipperdey (eds.), *Geschichte und politisches Handeln. Theodor Schieder zum Gedächtnis,* 261–81. Stuttgart.

—— (1993), "Max Weber. Ein politischer Intellektueller im Deutschen Kaiserreich." In G. Hübinger and W. J. Mommsen (eds.), *Intellektuelle im Deutschen Kaiserreich,* 33–61.

W. J. Mommsen and W. Schwentker (eds.) (1988), *Max Weber und seine Zeitgenossen.* Göttingen.

O. W. Müller (1971), *Intelligencija. Untersuchungen zur Geschichte eines politischen Schlagwortes.* Frankfurt/M.

P. Münch (1993), "The Thesis before Weber. An Archaeology." In H. Lehmann and G. Roth (eds.), *Weber's Protestant Ethic. Origins, Evidence, Contexts,* 51–71. Cambridge.

D. J. Peukert (1989), *Max Webers Diagnose der Moderne.* Göttingen.

M. Riesebrodt (1985), "Vom Patriarchalismus zum Kapitalismus. Max Webers Analyse der Transformation der ostelbischen Agrarverhältnisse im Kontrast zeitgenössischer Theorien." *KZS* 37:546–67.

W. Schluchter (1980), "Der autoritär verfaßte Kapitalismus. Max Webers Kritik am Kaiserreich." In *Rationalismus der Weltbeherrschung. Studien zu Max Weber,* 134–69. Frankfurt.

—— (ed.) (1988a), *Max Webers Sicht des okzidentalen Christentums Interpretation und Kritik.* Frankfurt/M.

—— (1988b), *Religion und Lebensführung.* Vol. 1. *Studien zu Max Webers Kultur- und Werttheorie;* Vol. 2. *Studien zu Max Webers Religions- und Herrschaftssoziologie.* Frankfurt/M.

H. Siebeck (1893), *Lehrbuch der Religionsphilosophie.* Freiburg und Leipzig.

W. Sombart (1902), *Der moderne Kapitalismus,* vol. 1, *Die Genesis des Kapitalismus.* Leipzig.

F. H. Tenbruck (1975), "Das Werk Max Webers." *KZS* 27:663–702.

—— (1984), *Die unbewältigten Sozialwissenschaften oder die Abschaffung des Menschen.* Graz.

C. P. Tiele (1897, 1899), *Elements of the Science of Religion.* Part 1, *Morphological;* Part 2, *Ontological.* Gifford Lectures. Edinburgh and London.

H. Treiber (1991), "Die Geburt der Weberschen Rationalismus-These. Webers Bekanntschaften mit der russischen Geschichtsphilosophie in Heidelberg." *Leviathan. Zeitschrift für Sozialwissenschaft* 19:435–47.

—— H. Treiber and K. Sauerland (eds.) (1995), *Heidelberg im Schnittpunkt intellektueller Kreise.* Opladen.

Marianne Weber (1988) [1926], *Max Weber, A Biography,* trans. Harry Zohn. With a new introduction by Guenther Roth. New Brunswick.

Max Weber (1920), *Gesammelte Aufsätze zur Religionssoziologie*. Tübingen.

—— (1921–22), *Grundriss der Sozialökonomie*. III. Abteilung. *Wirtschaft und Gesellschaft*. Tübingen.

—— (1924) [1894], "Entwicklungstendenzen in der Lage der ostelbischen Landarbeiter." In *Gesammelte Aufsätze zur Sozial- und Wirtschaftsgeschichte*, 470–507. Tübingen.

—— (1924) [1896], "Die sozialen Gründe des Untergangs der antiken Kultur." In *Gesammelte Aufsätze zur Sozial- und Wirtschaftsgeschichte*, 289–311. Tübingen.

—— (1924) [1909], "Agrarverhältnisse im Altertum." In *Gesammelte Aufsätze zur Sozial- und Wirtschaftsgeschichte*, 1–288. Tübingen.

—— (1930) [1904–5, 1920], *The Protestant Ethic and the Spirit of Capitalism*, trans. Talcott Parsons. London.

—— (1946), *Essays in Sociology*, trans., ed., with an introduction by H. H. Gerth and C. Wright Mills. New York.

—— (1968) [1913], "Über einige Kategorien der verstehenden Soziologie." In *Gesammelte Aufsätze zur Wissenschaftslehre*, 427–74. Tübingen.

—— (1981), "Some Categories of Interpretive Sociology." *Sociological Quarterly* 22:151–80.

—— (1984), *Zur Politik im Weltkrieg. Schriften und Reden 1914–1918*, ed. W. J. Mommsen in cooperation with G. Hübinger. Max-Weber-Gesamtausgabe I/15. Tübingen.

—— (1984) [1892], *Die Lage der Landarbeiter im ostelbischen Deutschland*, ed. M. Riesebrodt. Max-Weber-Gesamtausgabe I/3. Tübingen.

—— (1989), *Die Wirtschaftsethik der Weltreligionen. Konfuzianismus und Taoismus (1915–1920)*, ed. H. Schmidt-Glintzer in cooperation with P. Kolonko. Max-Weber-Gesamtausgabe I/19. Tübingen.

—— (1992) [1917, 1919], *Wissenschaft als Beruf; Politik als Beruf*, ed. W. J. Mommsen and W. Schluchter in cooperation with B. Morgenbrod. Max-Weber-Gesamtausgabe I/17. Tübingen.

—— (1993) [1904–5], *Die protestantische Ethik und der Geist des Kapitalismus*, ed. K. Lichtblau and J. Weiss. Bodenheim.

—— (1993) [1921–22], *The Sociology of Religion*. Boston.

—— (1996) [1916–20], *Die Wirtschaftsethik der Weltreligionen. Hinduismus und Buddhismus (1916–1920)*, ed. v. H. Schmidt-Glintzer in cooperation with K. H. Golzio. Max-Weber-Gesamtausgabe I/20. Tübingen.

J. Winckelmann (1980), "Die Herkunft von Max Webers 'Entzauberungs'-Konzeption." *KZS* 32:12–53.

—— (1986), *Max Webers hinterlassenes Hauptwerk. Die Wirtschaft und die gesellschaftlichen Ordnungen und Mächte*. Tübingen.

CHAPTER 12
RELIGION AS EXPERIENCE OF THE SELF

G. D. Alles (1991), "Rudolf Otto and the Politics of Utopia." *Religion* 21:235–56.

T. van Baaren (1969), "Are the Bororo Parrots or Are We?" *Liber Amicorum. Festschrift C. J. Bleeker*, 8–13. Leiden.

W. Baetke (1942), *Das Heilige im Germanischen*. Tübingen.

——— (1977), "Das Phänomen des Heiligen. Eine religionswissenschaftliche Grundlegung." In C. Colpe (ed.), *Die Diskussion um das 'Heilige,'* 337–79. Darmstadt.

R. vom Bruch, F. W. Graf, and G. Hübinger (eds.) (1989), *Kultur und Kulturwissenschaften um 1900. Krise der Moderne und Glaube an die Wissenschaft.* Stuttgart.

M. Buber (1993) [1909], "Ekstase und Bekenntnis." In P. Sloterdijk (ed.), *Mystische Zeugnisse aller Zeiten und Völker gesammelt von Martin Buber,* 53–67. München.

H. Cancik (ed.) (1982), *Religions- und Geistesgeschichte der Weimarer Republik.* Düsseldorf.

C. Colpe (ed.) (1977), *Die Diskussion um das 'Heilige.'* Darmstadt.

E. Diederichs (1967), *Selbstzeugnisse und Briefe von Zeitgenossen.* Düsseldorf und Köln.

R. Eucken (1897), "Der innere Mensch am Ausgang des 19. Jahrhunderts. Eine philosophische Meditation." *Deutsche Rundschau* 92:29–48.

——— (1920), *Der Wahrheitsgehalt der Religion.* Berlin.

E. E. Evans-Pritchard (1934), "Lévy-Bruhl's Theory of Primitive Mentality." *Bulletin of the Faculty of Arts* (Alexandria) 2:1–36.

F. Fellmann (1993), *Lebensphilosophie. Elemente einer Theorie der Selbsterfahrung.* Reinbek.

R. Flasche (1982), "Erkenntnismodelle und Erkenntnisprinzipien der Religionswissenschaft in der Weimarer Zeit." In H. Cancik (ed.), *Religions- und Geistesgeschichte der Weimarer Republik,* 261–76. Düsseldorf.

H. Frick (1938), "Rudolf Otto innerhalb der theologischen Situation." *ZThK* 46:3–15.

B. Gladigow (1988), "Religionsgeschichte des Gegenstandes–Gegenstände der Religionsgeschichte." In H. Zinser (ed.), *Religionswissenschaft. Eine Einführung,* 6–37. Berlin.

——— (1991), "Naturwissenschaftliche Modellvorstellungen in der Religionswissenschaft zwischen den beiden Weltkriegen." In H. G. Kippenberg and B. Luchesi (eds.), *Religionswissenschaft und Kulturkritik. Beiträge zur Konferenz 'The History of Religions and Critique of Culture in the Days of Gerardus van der Leeuw (1890–1950),'* 177–92. Marburg.

F. W. Graf (1996), "Das Laboratorium der religiösen Moderne. Zur 'Verlagsreligion' des Eugen Diederichs Verlages." In G. Hübinger (ed.), *Versammlungsort moderner Geister. Der Eugen Diederichs Verlag–Aufbruch ins Jahrhundert der Extreme,* 243–95. München.

E. Hammacher (1914), *Hauptfragen der modernen Kultur.* Leipzig und Berlin.

W. Haubold (1940), *Die Bedeutung der Religionsgeschichte für die Theologie Rudolf Ottos.* Leipzig.

W. Hoffmann (1913), "Mystik." III. "Neue Mystik." *RGG* 1st ed. vol. 4 608–12. Tübingen.

G. Hübinger (1987), "Kulturkritik und Kulturpolitik des Eugen-Diederichs-Verlags im Wilhelminismus. Auswege aus der Krise der Moderne?" In H. Renz and F. W. Graf (eds.), *Umstrittene Moderne,* 92–114. Troeltsch-Studien 4. Gütersloh.

———— (ed.) (1996), *Versammlungsort moderner Geister. Der Eugen Diederichs Verlag–Aufbruch ins Jahrhundert der Extreme.* München.

H. James (ed.) (1969) [1920], *The Letters of William James.* London.

W. James (1982) [1902], *The Varieties of Religious Experience.* London.

H. G. Kippenberg (1991), "Einleitung. Religionswissenschaft und Kulturkritik. Die Zeit des Gerardus van der Leeuw (1890–1950)." In H. G. Kippenberg and B. Luchesi (eds.), *Religionswissenschaft und Kulturkritik. Beiträge zur Konferenz 'The History of Religions and Critique of Culture in the Days of Gerardus van der Leeuw (1890–1950),'* 13–28. Marburg.

———— (1994), "Rivalität in der Religionswissenschaft. Religionsphänomenologen und Religionssoziologen als kulturkritische Konkurrenten." *Zeitschrift für Religionswissenschaft* 2:69–89.

———— (1996), *Vom Weltbildwandel zur Weltanschauungsanalyse. Krisenwahrnehmung und Krisenbewältigung um 1900,* 89–102. Berlin.

K.-H. Kohl (1987), *Abwehr und Verlangen. Zur Geschichte der Ethnologie.* Frankfurt/M.

K. Küssner (1941), *Verantwortliche Lebensgestaltung. Gespräche mit Rudolf Otto über Fragen der Ethik.* Stuttgart.

G. G. van der Leeuw (1925), *Einführung in die Phänomenologie der Religion.* München.

———— (1928), "La structure de la mentalité primitive." *RHPhR* 8:1–31.

———— (1930), "Religion." *RGG* 2nd ed. vol. 4:1860–63.

———— (1935), "Die Wirklichkeit des Heidentums." Review of Otto's *Dionysos* (1933). *Die Furche* 21:230–36.

———— (1938), "Rudolf Otto und die Religionsgeschichte." *ZThK* 46:71–81.

———— (1948), *Levensvormen.* Amsterdam.

———— (1954), "Confession Scientifique." *Numen* 1:8–15.

———— (1977) [1933], *Phänomenologie der Religion.* Tübingen.

L. Lévy-Bruhl (1910), *Les fonctions mentales dans les sociétés inférieures.* Paris.

———— (1927), *The "Soul" of the Primitive,* trans. Lilian A. Clare. London.

———— (1975), *The Notebooks on Primitive Mentality.* New York.

———— (1978) [1927], *Primitive Mentality,* trans. Lilian A. Clare. New York.

R. Otto (ed.) (1910), "Mythos und Religion in Wundts Völkerpsychologie." *ThR* 13:251–75, 293–305.

———— (1911), *Die Christliche Welt* 25:709.

———— (1917), *Vischnu-Narayana. Texte zur indischen Gottesmystik.* I. Jena.

———— (1921), *Kantisch-Fries'sche Religionsphilosophie und ihre Anwendung auf die Theologie.* Tübingen.

———— (1959), *Das Heilige. Über das Irrationale in der Idee des Göttlichen und sein Verhältnis zum Rationalen.* München.

———— (1971) [1926], *West-östliche Mystik. Vergleich und Unterscheidung zur Wesensdeutung.* München.

———— (1991) [1899], *F. Schleiermacher. Über die Religion. Reden an die Gebildeten unter ihren Verächtern.* Göttingen.

W. Perpeet (1976), "Kulturphilosophie." *ABG* 20:42–99.

G. Pfleiderer (1992), *Theologie als Wirklichkeitswissenschaft. Studien zum Religionsbegriff bei Georg Wobbermin, Rudolf Otto, Heinrich Scholz und Max Scheler.* Tübingen.

K. Rudolph (1992), *Geschichte und Probleme der Religionswissenschaft*. Leiden.

A. Schopenhauer (1972) [1840], "Preisschrift über die Grundlage der Moral." In *Sämtliche Werke*, ed. von A. Hübscher. Wiesbaden.

R. A. Segal (1989), *Religion and the Social Sciences. Essays on the Confrontation*. Atlanta.

E. J. Sharpe (1981), "Christian Mysticism in Theory and Practice. Nathan Söderblom and Sadhu Sundar Singh." *Religious Traditions* 4:19–37.

—— (1986), *Comparative Religion. A History*. London.

—— (1990), *Nathan Söderblom and the Study of Religion*. Chapel Hill.

N. Söderblom (1910), "Communion with Deity." *ERE* 3:736–40.

—— (1926) [1916], *Das Werden des Gottesglaubens*. Leipzig.

—— (1977) [1913], "Das Heilige (Allgemeines und Ursprüngliches)." In C. Colpe (ed.), *Die Diskussion um das "Heilige,"* 76–116. Darmstadt.

E. Troeltsch (1909), "Rückblick auf ein halbes Jahrhundert der theologischen Wissenschaft." *ZWTh* 51:97–135.

A. Weeks (1993), *German Mysticism from Hildegard of Bingen to Ludwig Wittgenstein. A Literary and Intellectual History*. Albany.

W. Windelband (1921) [1902], "Das Heilige. Skizze zur Religionsphilosophie" (1902). *Präludien. Aufsätze und Reden zur Philosophie und ihrer Geschichte*, 295–332. Tübingen. Abridged in C. Colpe (ed.) *Die Diskussion um das "Heilige,"* 29–56.

CHAPTER 13
HOW DESCRIPTIONS OF THE HISTORY OF RELIGION REFLECT MODERNIZATION

B. Anderson (1991), *Imagined Communities. Reflections on the Origin and Spread of Nationalism*. New York.

E. Berg and M. Fuchs (eds.) (1993), *Kultur, soziale Praxis, Text. Die Krise der ethnographischen Repräsentation*. Frankfurt/M.

P. L. Berger (1992) [1980], *Der Zwang zur Häresie. Religion in der pluralistischen Gesellschaft*. Freiburg.

J. Clifford (1988), "On Ethnographic Authority." *The Predicament of Culture. Twentieth-Century Ethnography, Literature and Art*, 21–54. Cambridge.

C. Conrad and M. Kessel (eds.) (1994), *Geschichte schreiben in der Postmoderne. Beiträge zur aktuellen Diskussion*. Stuttgart.

J. G. Droysen (1971) [1882], "Grundriss der Historik." *Historik. Vorlesungen über Enzyklopädie und Methodologie der Geschichte*, ed. R. Hübner, 317–66. München.

C. Geertz (1993) [1988], *Die künstlichen Wilden. Der Anthropologe als Schriftsteller*. Frankfurt.

A. Giddens (1990), *The Consequences of Modernity*. Stanford.

B. Gladigow (1995), "Europäische Religionsgeschichte." In H. G. Kippenberg and B. Luchesi (eds.), *Lokale Religionsgeschichte*, 21–42. Marburg.

R. Groh and D. Groh (1991), "Zur Entstehung und Funktion der Kompensationsthese." In Groh and Groh, *Weltbild und Naturaneignung. Zur Kulturgeschichte der Natur*. Frankfurt/M.

E. Hobsbawm and T. Ranger (eds.) (1983), *The Invention of Tradition*. Cambridge.

L. Kolakowski (1995) [1970], "Der Anspruch auf die selbstverschuldete Unmündigkeit." In W. Oelmüller, R. Dölle-Oelmüller, and R. Piepmeier (eds.), *Diskurs. Sittliche Lebensformen*, 378–89. Paderborn.

R. Koselleck (1975), "Geschichte, Historie." In O. Brunner, W. Conze, and R. Koselleck (eds.), *Geschichtliche Grundbegriffe. Historisches Lexikon zur politisch-sozialen Sprache in Deutschland*, 2:593–717. Stuttgart.

——— (1979), "'Erfahrungsraum' und 'Erwartungshorizont'–zwei historische Kategorien." In *Vergangene Zukunft. Zur Semantik geschichtlicher Zeiten*, 349–75. Frankfurt/M.

P. Laslett (1976), "The Wrong Way through the Telescope. A Note on Literary Evidence in Sociology and in Historical Sociology." *BJS* 27:319–42.

B. Malinowski (1927), *Sex and Repression In Savage Society*. New York.

T. Mann (1983), "Fragment über das Religiöse." *Über mich selbst. Autobiographische Schriften*. Frankfurt.

O. Marquard (1986), "Über die Unvermeidlichkeit der Geisteswissenschaften." *Apologie des Zufälligen*, 98–116. Stuttgart.

J. Rüsen (1983), *Historische Vernunft. Grundzüge einer Historik I. Die Grundlagen der Geschichtswissenschaft*. Göttingen.

——— (1993), *Konfigurationen des Historismus. Studien zur deutschen Wissenschaftskultur*. Frankfurt/M.

——— (1994), "Einige Ideen zum Thema. 'Geschichtsbewußtsein als Forschungsproblem.'" Unpublished manuscript.

H. G. Schenk (1966), The Mind of the European Romantics: An Essay in Cultural History. London.

J. Z. Smith (1982), *Imagining Religion. From Babylon to Jonestown*. Chicago.

V. Steenblock (1991), "Zur Wiederkehr des Historismus in der Gegenwartsphilosophie." *ZPhF* 45:209–23.

F. H. Tenbruck (1989), *Die kulturellen Grundlagen der Gesellschaft. Der Fall der Moderne*. Opladen.

M. Weber (1988) [1906], "Kritische Studien auf dem Gebiet der kulturwissenschaftlichen Logik." In *Gesammelte Aufsätze zur Wissenschaftslehre*, 215–90. Tübingen.

——— (1989), *Die Wirtschaftsethik der Weltreligionen. Konfuzianismus und Taoismus (1915–1920)*, ed. H. Schmidt-Glintzer in cooperation with P. Kolenko. Max-Weber-Gesamtausgabe I/19. Tübingen.

——— (1992), *The Protestant Ethic and the Spirit of Capitalism*, trans. Talcott Parsons. London.

H. White (1973), *Metahistory*. Baltimore.

——— (1987), *The Content of the Form. Narrative Discourse and Historical Representation*. Baltimore.

INDEX

Lightning Source UK Ltd.
Milton Keynes UK
UKOW06f0927070715

254726UK00012B/222/P

SOAS LIBRARY

9 780691 009094